LIBERALS AND COMMUNISM

The "Red Decade" Revisited

LIBERALS
AND COMMUNISM

The "Red Decade" Revisited

BY

FRANK A. WARREN, III

INDIANA UNIVERSITY PRESS
Bloomington & London

To my mother and father

ACKNOWLEDGMENTS

Like every historian, I have my debts. I can never hope to thank adequately Professor William McLoughlin of Brown University, whose encouragement spurred me on in my research and whose intellectual insight helped clarify my thoughts. Professor Sidney James of the University of Iowa read the first draft of the manuscript and made helpful suggestions. My friend and colleague at Queens College, Professor Michael Wreszin, also read the first draft and encouraged me to think that the endeavor was worthwhile. Miss Sarah DeLuca of the John Hay Library at Brown University was always helpful in obtaining material for me. My father gave useful suggestions drawn from his knowledge of the thirties, and my mother's typing and retyping reached sacrificial proportions. Finally, to Joyce: she was always there.

F. A. W.

CONTENTS

LIBERALS AND COMMUNISM

The "Red Decade" Revisited

1

INTRODUCTION

In 1941 Eugene Lyons wrote a book called *The Red Decade,* which purported to be an account of "the Stalinist penetration of America" in the nineteen-thirties. It was a scathing indictment, and its chief target was those liberals who had allowed themselves to believe that Russia was a "progressive" country and the Communists a "progressive" political group. Although Lyons gave credit to a few exceptional individuals who had spoken out against the Russian dictatorship and Communist tactics elsewhere, his book left the impression that American liberal thinking as a whole was dominated by Communists from the onset of the depression to the signing of the Nazi-Soviet Pact in 1939. In reply to Lyons, many liberal writers, in self-defense, attacked his position in equally sweeping terms, claiming that Communism was at most a very minor influence on liberal thinking in this period. The debate that followed was necessarily inconclusive, for none of the debaters was yet ready to engage in a careful and detailed study of the factual evidence.

The major purpose of this book is to gauge the nature and extent of Communist influence on liberal thinking in the thirties through an examination of the writings of certain liberal writers and periodicals. Other approaches to the subject are of course possible, such as biographies of leading liberals, or a study of liberal and left-wing organizations. The approach I have chosen at least delimits a field that can be subjected to intensive examination. The emphasis here is on liberal thought rather than on liberal action.

The writers selected for study do not embrace the entire gamut of "liberalism," however that somewhat ambiguous term may be defined. I have chosen to deal with what may be roughly described as the left wing of the liberal movement, on the assumption that here, if anywhere, Communist influence should be apparent. My study focuses on such figures as John Dewey, Bruce Bliven, George Soule, Freda Kirchwey, Oswald Garrison Villard, Stuart Chase, Charles Beard, Frederick L. Schuman, and Alfred Bingham, and on the periodicals *The Nation, The New Republic,* and *Common Sense.* This group can be differentiated from the somewhat more conservative liberals such as Walter Lippmann, on the one hand, and on the other, from such men as Sidney Hook, Max Eastman, V. F. Calverton, Norman Thomas, and Reinhold Niebuhr, whose philosophy was truly radical (sometimes Marxist), not reformist.

I have also discussed, in some parts of the book, the background of American liberalism as a whole. I think it will be obvious from the context when I am using the word "liberal" in its broadest sense and when I am using it in the restrictive meaning of left-wing liberals of the thirties.

My study deals with "intellectuals." By an intellectual I mean one who deals primarily in ideas and is free from the restrictions of public office. Thus I have dealt with magazine editors, political commentators, free-lance writers, and educators, and not with the "brain trusters" who had official connections with the Roosevelt administration. The writers whom I have studied were not responsible for the legislative achievements of the thirties, though they did help to create the climate of opinion that made these achievements possible.

Finally, I have felt no need to duplicate the work of other historians. Daniel Aaron's *Writers on the Left* and Ralph L. Roy's

Communism and the Churches have treated adequately the creative writers and the churchmen.

Historically, American liberalism as a whole has contained within itself many diverse and sometimes conflicting trends of opinion, and the same thing is true of that segment of liberalism which I have scrutinized in this book. Indeed, this diversity of opinion is one of the chief conclusions that emerge from this study. Broadly speaking, the left-wing liberals of the thirties fall into three groups, though these categories are by no means exact; there is much overlapping, and some writers defy classification. I have called these groups the fellow travelers, the Russian sympathizers, and the anti-Communist liberals. I am not altogether satisfied with these labels, which are used with no invidious intent and with no suggestion of any lack of intellectual integrity. But some kind of classification is necessary for purposes of analysis, and these terms are the best I have been able to come up with. For the purposes of this book, then, "fellow traveler" is defined as one who, as a rule, uncritically supported the Communist line. "Russian sympathizer" is defined as one who was more impressed by the Russian "experiment" than by Communist doctrine; who was sympathetic, though not entirely uncritical, toward the Soviet Union, without necessarily accepting the Communist line on other topics. "Anti-Communists" refers to a group of articulate liberals who were highly critical both of Russia and of Communist doctrine and tactics. While not going to the lengths sometimes denoted by "anti-Communism" today, they were in fundamental disagreement with the Communists in matters of theory, but not always averse to working with them for specific objects.

The thirties were a crucial decade in American history and one in which liberals, who during the twenties had been outside the mainstream of American life, came into their own. During this period, also, the left wing became an increasingly important segment of American liberalism as a whole. An examination of its preoccupations, its insights and errors, illuminates the history of the thirties and may help us to understand the very different liberalism of the sixties.

2

LIBERALISM RECONSIDERED: 1930-1935

The Past

In the spring of 1934, *The Nation* quoted Lillian Symes's bitter indignation at being called a liberal: "No worse insult . . . could be hurled at anyone's mentality at a time like this." The editors commented that, although they knew that liberalism had fallen into "disrepute," they did not know that it had become "such a term of reproach."[1] But indeed it had. The depression shook the intellectuals' faith in capitalism and seemed to demand radical solutions for the nation's urgent problems. Partial solutions, reform, and compromise were considered inadequate. Nurtured on nineteenth-century humanitarian and sentimental idealism with its optimistic vision of the future and its overtones of utopianism, the liberal tradition of reform had manifested itself during the Progressive period in social work and increased social services. But in the crisis atmosphere of the early thirties, "social work" and even "social welfare legislation" were not liberal badges of honor, but inadequate palliatives at best and at worst a toadying to capitalism. The term "liberalism" stood discredited, undergoing its greatest ordeal of criticism and self-criticism, even while, in the

Roosevelt administration, political liberalism reached its apogee. The liberal intellectual of the thirties challenged the economic system as liberals had never challenged it before, and, in the process, tacitly challenged the whole reform tradition of liberalism. But he never abandoned reform completely; though the roots shook, he remained within the liberal reform tradition.

When the nineteenth-century reform tradition is related to liberalism in the 1930's, one of two assumptions is usually made. On the one hand, it is sometimes said that the sentimental idealism of the nineteenth- and early twentieth-century liberal was replaced in the thirties by hard-headed Marxist analysis, that pre-World-War-I utopianism declined in the post-war years and died in the thirties. On the other hand, it has been asserted with equal certitude that liberals of the thirties remained wide-eyed sentimental idealists (continually duped by the clever and ruthless Communists) who were lost in utopian economic proposals and the self-created Utopia of Soviet Russia, and that they remained incurable optimists, firm in their belief that the future would bring peace and social justice. The evolution of liberalism is in fact more complex than these easy speculations would have it. The reality of the class struggle in the 1930's did seem to invalidate the liberal Social Gospel notions of love and human brotherhood. But the brotherhood of man was replaced by the brotherhood of all progressives; the "right-thinking men," from among the intellectuals and the masses alike, were called upon to declare their unity. The Bellamy utopian tradition—the concretization of future Utopias—was abandoned, though traces remain in the writings of Alfred Bingham. But a sense of unrealized possibilities, utopian in their essence, did manifest itself, whether in some liberals' misplaced faith in Russia, or in economic and political demands that far outstripped what even New Deal politicians considered possible. The prewar liberal optimism did disappear, though again traces remain in Alfred Bingham and the pages of *Common Sense*. The war and the Treaty of Versailles had destroyed the hopes of most liberals for an early transition to a peaceful and cooperative world. The depression, the bread lines, the rise of Fascism, the continual threats of war during the thirties—all these imbued liberals with a sense of living on the edge of disaster. Yet there was a half-buried optimism implicit in most liberal writings: if the progressives would unite and the masses would organize politically, a peaceful and just society could soon be created.

If the characteristics of earlier liberalism underwent intense modification in the thirties, the liberals, as they entered that crucial decade, did carry with them intellectual baggage constructed in the previous forty years. Lester Ward's sociocracy, Simon Patten's and Richard Ely's institutional approach to economics, Thorstein Veblen's emphasis on the engineer as catalyst for industrial reform, John Dewey's instrumental and experimental approach to social problems, and Herbert Croly's acceptance of huge industrial complexes formed a set of ideas and concepts that liberals of the 1930's drew on, even while transcending them. The thirties witnessed a type of anticapitalism among liberals that had not been present in earlier liberal reform movements; but in transcending the previous anti-big-business tradition, they carried with them the general idea of applying the principles of science and the scientific method to society through social planning. As George Soule wrote in 1931, he and Stuart Chase and others like them developed in the twenties a "hard-boiled" aproach to social problems, an approach that found the "chief fault" of capitalism in its "lack of planning and control in the general interest."[2]

While research into planning techniques was laying the groundwork for liberal thought in the 1930's, the events of the war years and the twenties were alienating liberals from the political mainstream. Disillusioned by the war, embittered by the peace treaty, scarred by Woodrow Wilson's illiberal suppression of dissent, many liberals withdrew from political action. Dewey, Charles Beard, and Veblen continued to talk about applying science to political problems; George Soule and Stuart Chase analyzed the capitalist economy. But the liberal of the twenties did not sally forth in support of progressive politicians as liberals had previously lined up behind Theodore Roosevelt and Woodrow Wilson. "No more dashes into the political jungle," wrote Herbert Croly, editor of *The New Republic.* "No more intervention without reservations, without understanding and without specific and intelligent political preparation."[3] But having withdrawn from direct political action, the liberals were still unable to protect themselves from the impact of the events of the twenties. The succession from Harding to Coolidge to Hoover, whatever their differences in personality, added up to one thing for the liberal: "normalcy." Normalcy meant laissez faire in economics, corruption in politics, and crass materialism in culture. Some fled to Greenwich Village and Europe and the bohemian life. A few became radicals. But what normalcy impressed on all their minds was the vulgarity of the capitalist culture. The Red scare and, above all, the Sacco-Vanzetti case taught them the brutality and unfairness of capitalist justice. The last also taught them their own ineffectualness.

The chief psychological effect of the twenties on the liberals, then, was to leave them with a feeling of their own impotence. They had had a sense of being in the main line of thought during the Progressive era. But during the twenties they found themselves without influence (a long time for a group whose creed entails progressive reform in society). Much of the attraction that Russia held for liberals in the thirties can be explained in terms of a typical "outgroup" seeking action after ten years of ineffectualness. They believed themselves once again in the mainstream of history and they intended to make the most of it. But power wreaks its own vengeance. In revolting against capitalism and in turning toward Russia, many liberals carried with them an image of the power they wished they had had during the twenties. Although they rejected capitalist power, power itself was attractive. They clung to certain modes of thought characteristic of capitalist society; they had the American penchant for "getting things done" regardless of the cost, and accepted the old argument that though the means involve hardship and suffering, the ends are necessary and worth while. Originally associated with the greedy exploitation of the

American frontier and the fierce competition of the robber barons, the argument was used by liberals in the thirties to rationalize the evils accompanying Russian economic activity in general and collectivization in particular. The irony of intellectual history is that the same stale argument is now being used by certain conservative historians to justify the activity of the robber barons. Thus Allan Nevins justifies the "boldness" with which John D. Rockefeller played the "hard-hitting and ruthless" game of competition by the goal he had in mind—an integrated economy.[4]

But this historical turnabout is not so unusual as it may seem. Arguments used against liberals in the twenties reappear in liberal writing in the thirties. During the First World War Richard Ely, the economist, said that Robert LaFollette, who opposed the war, was "of more help to the Kaiser than a quarter of a million troops."[5] Although most liberals had supported the war, this type of argument, with its repressive overtones, helped to convince them that the democratic slogans under which the war was fought were meaningless and hypocritical. But the same kind of argument was later to be used by liberals against the anti-Stalinist left during the Spanish civil war. The irony does not mask the horror. It indicates that at least some liberals had not learned the lessons from the one American experience within their lifetime that might have prepared them in some degree for coping intellectually with the rise of Russian totalitarianism. They had not learned that repression, even when it is couched in democratic and humanitarian terms, remains repression.

The decade of the twenties certainly did not prepare liberals for dealing with Stalinism. It furnished them with an instrumental method without buttressing democratic ends. It robbed them of old and outworn values without providing them with new values. It made them cynical about capitalism without making them cynical about all power. The twenties cannot be blamed for what befell many liberals in the thirties; however, it is important to recognize that the liberal's experience during the twenties left him ill prepared to handle the events of the thirties.

Reaffirmation

As the liberal faced the ravages of the depression, he was in no position to contemplate either the historic roots of his philosophy or the inadequacies of the past decade. In the spring of 1933 thirteen million Americans were unemployed. The average migratory worker earned a total annual income of only $110. The price of wheat had dropped from $1.03 a bushel in 1929 to a low of 38 cents in 1932. Cotton, which had sold for 35 cents in 1919 and 17 cents in 1929, was going for 6 cents a pound. These were the cold measured facts of the severest depression in American history. For the millions of Americans living through these tragic years there were immeasurable emotional consequences as well. Among the men and women cast out of work by the depression or barely managing to keep alive on meager wages and substandard diets, the prevailing feeling was one of hopelessness and helplessness. Living in fear of the future, tortured by a constant anxiety about tomorrow, the American felt himself reduced to a dependent object, a powerless pawn in a drama not of his design. For the sensitive observer of American society, certain cruel ironies were startlingly apparent: starvation in the midst of overproduction; tar paper villages in cities of great mansions; Bonus Armies, farmer strikes, and unemployment demonstrations in a land of millionaires. It was inevitable that the system under which such things were possible should be subjected to bitter attack. It was also inevitable that liberals, who traditionally had been dedicated to reforming the system, should come to ask: "Is the philosophy of liberalism still viable?"

There were plenty of voices to answer that it was not. From the right came the stale cries of retrenchment and government hands off. From the Communists came the charge that liberalism wanted to save a system that could not be saved. This Communist charge lay behind Michael Gold's accusation that George Soule was a "class collaborationist"; it moved Paul Salter and Jack Lebrome to write that liberals like John Dewey, Morris Cohen, and Bertrand

Russell had "a deep-seated fear of wide social change"; it caused the *New Masses* to ridicule *The Nation's* pretended "impartiality": "It doesn't care how the putrid corpse of capitalism . . . is perfumed and tidied up, so long as the cadaver is preserved." Behind the charge of class collaboration and capitalist support lay the Communist impatience with qualified truths, conditional opinions, and partial answers. The "open mind" of the liberal became an "empty mind" in Communist writing, and Lincoln Steffens (later a hero of the Communists for his glowing statements on the "future" in Russia) emerged from the vituperative pen of Michael Gold as the typical "BUT, *on the other hand*," liberal. Failing to recognize the class struggle, the liberals in Communist writing lined up, in the end, behind capitalism and the cops. They were "closer to the Hoovers than to the Debses."[6]

The Communists were not alone in attacking liberalism from the left. Independent radicals also found liberalism bankrupt. Reinhold Niebuhr, the Socialist theologian, argued that history had cut the ground from under liberalism; it was a "spent force." Lewis Mumford, the architectural critic and social historian, declared in 1930: "I have never been a Liberal, nor do I subscribe to the notion that justice and liberty are best achieved in homeopathic doses." C. Hartley Grattan, a social critic whose writings ranged from a biography of the James family to a revisionist history of World War I, associated liberals with "compromisers" who believed in "palliatives instead of stringent remedies" and who contributed more to the maintenance of capitalism than to the creation of a new social order. The liberal tried to "civilize capitalism," but capitalism was "incompatible with civilization." Thus, Grattan concluded, the radical had nothing to gain from cooperating with the liberals; any radical third party should refuse to "play ball" with them.[7]

The liberal who was not prepared to go this far faced a difficult problem. Attempting to defend himself against the accusation of being a mere reformer or an apologist for capitalism, he faced the additional charge that liberals had an "economic stake" in capitalism.[8] Hence the liberal found it necessary to take stock of his positions and beliefs. There were essentially two steps in this stocktaking process; the first, taken by almost all liberals except the fellow travelers, was to reaffirm liberalism and progressivism as an alternative to Communism. There were two distinct ways of differentiating liberalism from Communism: one involved a total and hostile rejection of Communism, the other merely a friendly difference of opinion. The first path was taken by a group of liberals who, starting from different positions, had by the early thirties become critical of the Russian system. It included the philosophers John Dewey, Morris Cohen, and Horace Kallen; the historians Carl Becker and Charles Beard; the journalists Oswald Garrison Villard, Elmer Davis, Alfred Bingham, and John Chamberlain; the poet Archibald MacLeish; and, to some extent, the popular economist Stuart Chase.

These liberals made a severe attack upon Communism as a philosophy. Elmer Davis saw in it the total regulation of life; Horace Kallen saw the subordination of the individual to the state; Morris Cohen noted the perpetuation of terror; and John Dewey declared that Communism in Russia had crushed all opposition, created a "cult of the infallibility of leadership," and established a dictatorship over the proletariat. The Communist doctrine of class struggle was also criticized. Dewey acknowledged that class conflict was a basic part of the social scene, but he, along with Alfred Bingham and Morris Cohen, affirmed that progress came, in Cohen's words, "through cooperation between different groups." Not only Russia and Communism as a philosophy were condemned, but the American Communist Party and its tactics were denounced. Bingham found the party to be suffering from blind dogmatism and obedience to Moscow, sectarianism, disruptive tactics, and a glorification of the industrial worker at the expense of the middle class. Dewey charged the party with falsification of facts, character assassination of opponents, a "rule or ruin" policy in "so-called united front activities," justifying the end by "*any*" means, and misrepresentation of the views of the "liberals." Elmer Davis accused Communists of an "abnegation of the intellect," and Archibald

MacLeish found them guilty of avoiding personal responsibility: they wished to return to the womb.[9]

Another tendency among these anti-Communist liberals was to link Fascism and Communism as doctrines equally opposed to liberalism. Oswald Garrison Villard granted that Stalin and Hitler might have different aims, but criticized the double standard of morality some liberals applied to Communism and Fascism. Carl Becker believed both movements had evolved from antiliberal revolutions and were establishing "ruthlessly regulated" economies opposed to a "free, competitive economy (made workable by whatever patchwork of socialist devices)." In 1930 Charles Beard criticized the elitist theory of the proletarian and Fascist dictatorships; in 1932 Archibald MacLeish condemned the stifling of intellectual freedom under both systems; and in 1934 Horace Kallen castigated Fascism and Communism for their tyrannical apotheosis of Unity. In contrast to these dual despotisms, these liberals reaffirmed democracy and democratic institutions. Alfred Bingham, though he believed in a thorough transformation of capitalism, nevertheless stressed the need for maintaining democracy in any social revolution. Charles Beard affirmed the superiority, despite its weaknesses, of representative government to the Communist system of economic representation, and Morris Cohen condemned the "verbal tricks" by which the Communists hid the "tyrannical oppression necessarily involved in all dictatorships." In 1934 Horace Kallen contrasted the coercive relations between the state and the individual under Communism and Fascism with the diminishing of fixed status under the institutions of democracy. In the same year, John Chamberlain, moving away from a farewell to reform to a renewal of acquaintance, criticized the Communists for their "strict racket" theory of government—the belief that since all government was a racket, it was legitimate for a new set of racketeers to muscle in and take control. "If "democratic dogma" had been "degraded," he said, "autocratic dogma" had been degraded long before. He urged that people be allowed to choose their own form of degradation.[10]

Finally, most of the liberals joining in this many-sided critique of Communism clearly designated their philosophy as liberal. Only Alfred Bingham called himself a radical. He criticized the liberal for believing in "petty reforms of specific abuses," and praised the radical for realizing the economy had to be "changed from the roots up." Yet his endorsement of the writings of John Dewey indicates that he, like Dewey, believed liberal ends could be achieved through radical means.[11] In 1934 Morris Cohen eloquently summed up the essential feeling of this group of liberals:

> If liberalism were dead, I should still maintain that it deserved to live, that it was not condemned in the court of human reason, but lynched outside of it by the passionate and uncompromisingly ruthless war-spirit, common to Communists and Fascists. . . . When the communists tell me that I must choose between their dictatorship and fascism I feel that I am offered the choice between being shot or being hanged. It would be suicide for liberal civilization to accept this as exhausting the field of human possibility.[12]

Thus by 1934 an articulate body of liberal opinion hostile to both Communism and Fascism had developed; but there were other liberals who did not find both systems equally inimical. They were not openly hostile to Communism, though they rejected it in the end. A bridge between the anti-Communist liberals and the nonhostile group is afforded by the writings of Stuart Chase.

In an article in *The New Republic* in February 1932, the literary critic Edmund Wilson attacked Chase as a middle-class liberal, as a critic of Russia, and as a devotee of saving capitalism by planning. Chase answered by disclaiming the typical liberal's interest in free speech and political democracy, by defending his Russian record (he had consistently defended "the Russian economic experiment"), and by pointing to his "reasonably drastic" suggestions for reforming the economic system. But he said that he had not accepted the Marxist formulas of Communism because they did not fit the development of the American economy. He was "looking for a synthesis a good way ahead of . . . orthodox communism."[13]

Chases's synthesis was the "third road." In *A New Deal* (1932)

Chase wrote that the United States was moving toward collectivism
and more social control of economic activity. The left, therefore,
was the only road open. But it had three forks: Communist revolution, Fascist commercial dictatorship,* or a change within "the
broad outlines of the law and of American tradition." Historical
necessity required the revolutionary road for Russia, he said, and
he was unconcerned about any suffering there: "A better economic
order is worth a little bloodshed." But he was apprehensive of the
technological disaster that would follow revolution in a highly
industrialized and interdependent society; the revolutionary road
was out for the United States. So was the Fascist road, not for
economic or technological reasons, but because it could not solve
the human problem; it only worsened "an ignoble way of life"
under capitalism. The third road, then, was the only one open. It
would require "drastic" changes in the economy, increased government control, possibly even a "temporary dictatorship." But unlike
the Communist and Fascist revolutions, it would not destroy all
traditions. In short, it meant national economic planning for the
public good.[14] Like the anti-Communist liberals, Chase rejected
Fascism for humane reasons; unlike them, his rejection of Communism was based chiefly on technological reasons. The effect of these
differences was to evaluate Communism more favorably than
Fascism. It is this tendency that connects Chase with the second
group of liberals, specifically the editors of *The Nation* and *The
New Republic*.

Before 1933 *The Nation* often agreed with the anti-Communist
liberals. Though there was always a large residue of sympathy for
the Communists as a result of the various persecutions they suffered, the magazine reflected Villard's own anti-Communism in
disparaging the American Communists in 1930 as "annoying and
silly." However, after 1933 its condescending attitude toward the
Communists was modified, a change perhaps connected with

---

* In placing Fascism on the left Chase was, of course, disagreeing with the
Communists. His argument was that collectivism characterized the left and
that Fascism destroyed laissez-faire economics.

Villard's departure as chief editor. It is true that *The Nation* under Freda Kirchwey made no sudden rush to eulogize the Communists. But there was a change in tone: the "silly" boys of 1930 were simply misguided and unrealistic in 1933. Commenting on *The Daily Worker*'s remark in the summer of 1933 that the Communist Party had failed to develop into "a revolutionary mass party of the proletariat," the editors of *The Nation* indicated that this result had been predicted by "sincere friends" of the Communists, but that the latter had denounced such "friendly critics." They criticized the parochialism of the Communist Party for frightening off those "eager" to work with it. And they noted the "incomprehensible jargon" and the subservience to Moscow that removed the Party from reality. But they ended on a conciliatory note: "Let them seek cooperation with other radical groups, exactly at points where they can do so without sacrificing their essential principles. Let them talk in realistic and intelligible terms. Then perhaps they will make progress."[15]

This was criticism which was not overlooked by the Communists: the next year *The New Masses* accused "*The Nation* liberals" of adhering to their "historic role" in attacking Communism. But *The Nation*'s criticism was friendly. It left the door open for possible future cooperation on terms that were to become familiar during the Popular Front, when, after 1935, the Communists gave up the unrealistic aims of revolution, began taking mawkishly in American terms, and sought cooperation with liberal groups. In 1933, then, the editors of *The Nation* regarded the Communists, not as enemies of liberalism, but as potential allies. And they consistently applauded the Communists' moves toward interradical cooperation. In 1934 they praised the Socialist Party's decision to allow a United Front with the Communists in local branches: "The suicidal tendency of the radical movement . . . to divide into minute fragments may have come to an end." In March 1935 *The Nation* was warning against forcing Communists out of the unions. Although they had made past mistakes in tactics, it said, they provided the labor movement with "much-needed vigor." Thus, often unconsciously, *The Nation* was clearing the way for the establishment of a common front with the Communists.[16]

The New Republic, even more than *The Nation*, refused to repudiate Communism for the same humanitarian reasons that led it to reject Fascism. Though the editors did reject Communism as a solution to American troubles, they obviously believed that Communism was on the side of progress. In 1933 they made clear their distinction between Fascism and Communism by insisting on their different goals. Fascism sought the preservation of capitalism and territorial conquest, Communism the elimination of capitalism and world peace.[17] This differentiation between the two determined the nature of *The New Republic*'s whole approach to the problem of liberalism. Rather than attempting to create an alternative social philosophy to both dictatorial Communism and Fascism, the editors, having rejected Fascism, set off liberalism from other "progressive" social philosophies—socialism and Communism. They spurned Communism, but not because it was antiliberal.

Since the editors of *The New Republic* placed Communism on the side of progress and often admitted the cogency of its critique of capitalism, it is not easy to see why they ultimately rejected the heart of that critique—the revolutionary way out. But they did. Yet even here they equivocated. They did not dismiss revolution as a theoretically admissible technique of social change, but they did not see any evidence for a possible revolution in America in the thirties. Writing in 1932 of an imaginary Second World War, Bruce Bliven predicted "a series of Communist revolutions," including one in the United States. But Bliven and Soule always belittled the idea of an immediate revolutionary situation. Soule wrote in 1932: "The situation is not really so revolutionary as the Communists imagine. Changes, movements and classes with which they have not reckoned must come into play if it is to become so." But immediate revolution was not the only faulty Communist diagnosis; Soule also disagreed with their contention that revolution must be violent. In a review in 1932 of William Z. Foster's *Toward Soviet America*, Soule argued against the need to "liquidate" all reformers and radicals not accepting Communist leadership. This view, he claimed, made sense only if one accepted the Communist belief in class war and violent revolution. If these were valid, then it was true that divisive reformers would impede the revolution. Here Soule stopped. It was not that the Communists were wrong, he said, but that one had no way of knowing: "Conscientious persons who want a better civilization are required to decide *a priori,* and before they decide anything else, what the nature of the revolution is going to be." Soule was not prepared to accept this a priori assumption.[18]

Though less than sanguine about the Communist emphasis on revolution, the editors of *The New Republic* showed an equal, if not greater, lack of enthusiasm for the second progressive alternative to liberalism: the Socialist Party. They did endorse Thomas in 1932, but showed their singular lack of zeal by seconding Matthew Josephson's critique of Thomas: he and his followers placed too much faith in converting people through persuasion. With "no enthusiastic loyalty to the Socialist Party" and with a belief that the Socialist proposals were "deficient in detail," the editors justified their support of Thomas: it might supply impetus to a future third party having the real backing of organized labor, the farmer, and the white collar worker. Moreover, the Socialist platform was "in the main line of social evolution."[19]

This last statement provides the key to the editors' reasoning. The main line of social evolution was "the conception of central planning." In so far as the Socialist Party advocated planning, it was to be supported. But generally Bliven and Soule found that the Socialists minimized the need for national planning and overemphasized a gradualistic, step-by-step approach to socialism. As a result, the European Social Democrats were a "liberal party of reform"; they postponed indefinitely "any drastic reorganization of the economic system" and adjusted their demands "to the going economy." Believing that little could be achieved by the Socialist reliance on political means alone and by "the stock-in-trade Socialist ideas," the editors called for a "technique and a group of ideas

. . . appropriate to the reorganization of the world of production and exchange." This technique, set forth as radically in advance of Socialist reforms, was the old dependable—the concept of planning.[20]

It is now possible to see more clearly how *The New Republic*'s rejection of Communism, as well as Socialism, differed from that of Kallen or Cohen. The editors were not really *opposed* to either, but having made central planning the *sine qua non* of liberalism, they were dissatisfied with the program of both groups. But, once they rejected Communism for its revolutionary beliefs and socialism for its evolutionary gradualism, they set about mediating a reconciliation of the Communists and the Socialists. In their role as mediator, the editors distributed the blame for disunion to both sides. However, such a "share-the-blame" plan actually favored the Communists. An editorial blaming the failure of the German Communists and Social Democrats to unite on the former's penchant for "destroying" capitalism and the latter's inclination for "preserving it till it died a natural death" might appear to be impartial.[21] But when this statement is combined with the editors' previous criticism of Socialist meliorist tactics, it is clear which side *The New Republic* felt more at fault.

This veneer of impartiality was present in all of *The New Republic*'s writings on Communist-Socialist relations. During the election campaign of 1932 the editors acknowledged that Communist lying had exceeded Socialist distortions. But their main point was that both sides should "stick to the main job": to replace capitalism with socialism. This attempt to balance censure reached its height in the editors' reaction to the Madison Square Garden riot in early 1934. The riot took place when the Communists broke up a Socialist rally to honor the Austrian workers. The editors placed major responsibility on the Communists, but said that Clarence Hathaway, a Communist leader who had pleaded for order and then been struck down by the Socialists (according to Hathaway), was the only one to emerge "with any credit." When the old-guard Socialist, Algernon Lee, wrote to correct Hathaway's version, the editors said they were "sorry" if they had been mistaken in accepting it. But instead of then criticizing the Communists more fully, they wrote: "It seems to us that the Communists tried to break up the meeting, that both sides used violence and that the leaders of both are now trying to sharpen and perpetuate the hostility thus created." The absence of severe stricture against the Communists indicates the editors' essential point: the two rival parties should end their differences, stop squabbling, and work together. Feeling that both Communists and Socialists were on the side of progress, they saw no need for partisan quarrels and a real need to concentrate on the main enemy. Hence they could only be "sorry" when the Communists lied. They, like the editors of *The Nation,* were moving toward the concept of the Popular Front in which all progressive forces were to bury their differences in a common fight.[22]

Reevaluation

By dissociating liberalism from Communism, whether for humane or for technological reasons, liberals had reasserted the uniqueness and primacy of liberalism. Yet some liberals were not content simply to reassert traditional reform liberalism; they felt the need to reevaluate it also. The reevaluation of liberalism was essentially an attempt to designate the place of liberalism in social change and to see whether it was a viable philosophy for the times. The three principal books in this reevaluation were George Soule's *The Coming American Revolution* (1934), which was a part of the larger day-by-day reevaluation going on in *The New Republic* in the early thirties; John Dewey's *Liberalism and Social Action* (1935); and Alfred Bingham's *Insurgent America* (1935).

Soule's *The Coming American Revolution* was an attempt to portray the pattern of social transformation, to discover whether America during the thirties conformed to a revolutionary pattern. He found that the Communist theory of revolution—with its rioting and mobs, driven by hunger and misery, violently and successfully revolting against a dying, but rigid, capitalism—failed to correspond to reality. In place of this revolutionary scenario of final collapse and socialist birth, Soule presented a picture of revolution dependent upon a series of previous alterations and changes in the social structure. Classes did not revolt when they were most miserable, but when they began to have some hope; revolution was not sudden, but was preceded by technological changes, sporadic revolts, the undermining of old ideas and beliefs, and attempts at reform. Indeed, reforms were a necessary part of the revolutionary process, though when history was "ripe for it," it would be impossible to avoid a revolutionary change by compromise. Only after this long prelude did a revolutionary crisis occur. Soule believed that such a crisis had two main characteristics: the ruling classes, because of their weakness, could not rule successfully, and the rising classes had attained sufficient power to supersede them. When the revolutionary crisis came, moderate leadership would generally prevail at first; later more extreme leaders would challenge it. But the moderate phase, like the long period of reform, was also a necessary part of the total revolutionary process. Since the people did not always understand how far reform had to go, it was necessary for the moderates to fail before the more extreme leaders could win popular backing. Violence, inevitable to the Communists, occurred for Soule chiefly at the end of the revolution in preserving the revolution from die-hard reactionaries seeking to recapture power.[23]

Basing his observations on this theory of revolution, Soule analyzed the existing situation in the United States: the country was "in the midst," but "nowhere near the end" of a "great social revolution." The social and intellectual ferment accompanying revolutions was present, but capitalism had not broken down for good—though capitalist breakdowns were increasing. The chief result of this ferment was the emergence of the idea of planning, "a prime example of the broad sort of idea characteristic of pre-revolutionary and early revolutionary periods." Undermining the basic intellectual rationale of the old order by challenging the automatic workings of laissez-faire economics and individualism, planning was "by nature antagonistic to the basic requirements of capitalism." Capitalism tried to plan, but was unable to do so successfully and remain capitalism. If it remained capitalism, Soule said, it would plan "badly." And this "bad" planning prepared the way for further changes by demonstrating the failure of piecemeal planning and the responsibility of the government for the failure to the public. This public demonstration of failure would lead to a "polarization of forces," a union of all those not benefiting by capitalist planning against the old order.[24]

Soule believed that the New Deal was the first attempt of capitalism to plan. It was neither a Communist plot (as the reactionaries charged) nor a capitalist plot (as the Communist charged), but "a facile reflection of the disorderly social scene" in which Roosevelt tried to reconcile irreconcilable class interests and show that "planning in the interest of private profit" would benefit the nation. This was a necessary part of the process of revolution; the New Deal was an educational lesson. It provided an indication of the dimensions necessary for true social planning. The people would eventually understand these dimensions, and with each new depression and crisis, the working class would become better organized to acquire the power to institute social planning. But Soule did not feel the current depression provided the opportunity for a shift to socialism. Of the two ingredients necessary for revolution, only one was present: the failure of the old order. In a future crisis the second ingredient, a powerful rising class, would be present. Then the final transfer of power would be made.[25]

In his theory of revolution, Soule developed *The New Republic*'s rejection of the Communist revolutionary solution and of the Socialist reform solution. Both Communism and socialism were part of the general revolutionary process, Soule said, but neither held the key to social change. Constitutionalists, antirevolutionists, and "inveterate compromisers," the socialists were fighting "a running skirmish with capitalism without ever seeking a decisive battle." Dependent on legislative majorities, they could win reforms but not their promised mission—the end of capitalism. Nevertheless, the socialists were useful by applying "pressure" to capitalism and thus contributing "to the historical development of the passing order." While the socialists, because of their vested interest in the old order, might gradually cease to fight, the Communists were fighting in a vacuum. With the "logic of history" against their theory of revolution, the Communists were not the major protagonists of the coming revolution. Currently a minority that alienated leaders and organizations seeking immediate action for the oppressed, the Communists' role—they always succeeded best in crises—would come in the "last stage" of the revolutionary process, "if at all." Meanwhile, they were chiefly instrumental in "stirring up action and opinion," but they were "impotent to achieve their announced aims."[26]

The Coming American Revolution was a synthesis of *The New Republic*'s attitudes and opinions. Soule's diagnosis of social transformation gave the editors a vantage point from which they could draw relationships between their ideas and other social movements. Thus they were able to differentiate between the Communist revolution and their own concept, and, at the same time, keep a veneer of radicalism by claiming that they were not just trying to patch up capitalism, but were working toward this real revolution. Moreover, Soule's analysis justified their mixed attitude toward the New Deal: it was inadequate, but a necessary part of revolution. His analysis also lent a radical tinge to their advocacy of planning by classifying it as part of the process of coming revolution. It made them appear to be to the left of the reformist socialists, but it prevented antagonism by granting that the socialists also had a necessary function. It gave them a basis for criticizing the sectarianism of the Communists, but placed Communism in the revolutionary stream. Finally, in shifting the burden to history (successful revolutions could not occur unless history was prepared for them), it gave them a justification for not mounting the revolutionary bandwagon.

By making planning an essential part of the process of revolution, Soule had given *The New Republic*'s brand of liberalism a vital role in social evolution. The idea of social planning became the basis of a viable social philosophy of liberalism—though the editors, in their desire to remove themselves from the odium of laissez-faire economics, dissociated themselves from the term "liberalism." They were "progressives." But the change was in terminology, not philosophy—planning was still king. There is a curious quality, however, in the use of Adam Smith as straw man in a battle that had already been won twenty years before by Herbert Croly and John Dewey. The purpose of this post-mortem critique of laissez-faire liberalism was, first of all, to dissociate their philosophy from announcements by the reactionary members of the Liberty League that only Manchester liberalism was true liberalism. More important, they wanted to prove that their economic philosophy was more radical than traditional liberal reform. In this sense the "new" liberals like Bliven and Soule were taking part in a shift within liberalism from the reformism of the Progressive era to the more drastic societal revision of the 1930's. Dewey spoke of the need for this shift in 1935 when he said that the "social legislation" of Progressive liberalism was a necessary step away from laissez-faire liberalism and had an educational value in its focus on social control. But it was necessary to go beyond "social legislation" to a socialization of "the forces of production."[27]

However, by acknowledging these ends only implicitly and by explicitly accenting the need for planning, Bliven and Soule caused some Marxist radicals, who wished to place the socialized means of production at the center of their philosophy, to believe that liberals like Bliven and Soule were still too much interested in simply reforming capitalism. In January 1931 one of these radicals, Edmund Wilson, challenged the liberals in the pages of *The New Republic*. The liberals had been "betting on capitalism," he said, and capitalism had reached a crisis. To Wilson, the liberal remedies —public ownership of utilities, nonrevolutionary labor organizations, and ineffective protests against oppression—were inadequate.

Real social planning and social control would mean socialism. He urged American progressives to "take Communism away from the Communists" and to make government ownership of the means of production and industrial representation their goals.[28]

Wilson's attack initiated a debate with the editors of *The New Republic* which provides a focal point for the reevaluation of liberalism. George Soule replied to Wilson's initial thrust by declaring that *The New Republic* had long since abandoned "political liberalism" for a "radical progressivism," a progressivism which, although it did not explicitly demand socialism, offered an alternative to capitalism. The new progressivism, he said, had studied capitalist society and had found its "chief fault" to be not the profit motive or private ownership of the means of production, but rather "the lack of planning and control in the general interest." The transformation to a planned regime in the United States would not come in a cataclysmic crisis, but through the process of evolution—the theory that he later developed in *The Coming American Revolution*. He sportingly agreed with Wilson that progressives should not "bet on capitalism." But they should not bet on violent revolution either. "What they . . . should be betting on," he asserted, "is the disappearance of traditional capitalism or its change into something radically different." This new departure was, of course, a planned economy. Four months later, in May 1931, the editors were arguing that the traditional ends of liberalism—freedom of conscience and the value of the individual personality—could be served only by planning. Traditionally liberalism had fought against a tyrant, they said, but economic liberalism had created a new tyrant in the "chaos of indeterminateness . . . the blind compulsions of a disorganized and unreasoned freedom." More than negative liberty was necessary to create "a truly humane and scientific social order"; the "power to suppress and control" was also needed to fulfill the traditional ends of liberalism.[29]

In 1932 Edmund Wilson returned to challenge the liberals for ostensibly seeking socialism while persisting in their faith in the capitalists: did not the liberal planners realize that the capitalists

—not they—would be doing the planning? Continuing to dissociate themselves from traditional laissez-faire liberalism, the editors of *The New Republic* reiterated their conception of planning as an alternative to capitalism: government agencies, backed by unions, would be the chief planners under their schemes. Those men like Wilson, who said that private ownership and planning were incompatible, could not object. If they were right, the failure of planning would prove their theory. Other steps could be taken.[30]

Soule's and *The New Republic*'s reevaluation of liberalism had led straight toward an apotheosis of planning. This is clear in a summary statement on liberalism made in 1935, a statement arguing for a "transvaluation" of liberalism. Again that transvaluation meant social planning: the liberty of the few who controlled the economy must be curbed. The curbing of liberty, however, had an anti-liberal ring and the editors had to justify this move. Seizing on one aspect of the pragmatic and environmental approach to social problems—the relativity of abstract concepts—the editors deabsolutized liberty: it was always relative and restricted and it always involved a choice between possible alternatives. From this perspective they considered the nature of democracy. They criticized the liberals who made a fetish of "superficial legal machinery." The essence of democracy was not to be confused with these devices, useful only in assuring democracy's proper functioning. True democracy, rather, corresponded to liberalism in its basic belief that social organization should be adapted to the needs of the masses at any particular time. The real test of such a device as electoral machinery was its ability to guarantee the masses their rights. Unfortunately, the editors were typically vague concerning the solution of the current impasse: "What the propertyless citizen faces in reality is a choice between being ruled by capitalists or their agents and . . . delegating the functions of economic management to more genuine and competent representatives under a system where pains are taken to consult his welfare and his wishes, as a matter of fundamental right." Though they had spoken in the past of a "powerful political movement devoted to social planning," they generally refused to consider the political problems involved in such statements of general aims. It was as if the masses were to adopt a system of social planning by osmosis.[31]

The reevaluation of liberalism had ended in the editors' de-absolutizing liberty and democracy. The effect of this process was to extend the application of the relativity of abstract concepts to other areas: while liberalism could not sanction autocratic governments cherishing "ends hostile to the basic tenets . . . of liberalism and democracy," violence and revolution were relative matters. Circumstances might make them necessary; it was not an abstract choice between "elections and force." If, for instance, an ousted ruling class attempted by violence to destroy a revolution, the alternative would be to resist or to forfeit the revolution. The choice between force and elections would no longer exist; the liberal decision would have to rest upon "approval of the aims of the revolution." This relativism still left the basic tenets of liberalism —"reason, persuasion, objective search of truth, free speech, education"—superficially intact. To forfeit these prerogatives meant to take the road of "unreasoning dogma and blind prejudice." At the end of the road lay Hitler (but not Stalin). In fact, the editors used similar tenets—"a belief in the brotherhood and inherent value of man, a belief in equality, a belief in objective reason and science, a belief in material welfare"—as reasons for preferring a socialist or Communist regime to a Fascist regime. It was necessary to preserve these basic values in a revolutionary period, as well as in a transitional period, like the one the United States was going through. Their loss was "tragically apparent" in Fascist Germany and Italy. But the editors made no mention of Russia.[32]

The same tenets were also used to defend their lack of a "detailed program." Admitting preference for some social movements, they refused to become advocates of any one movement. "We would rather present the varied points of view of those who are in the same large procession," the editors wrote; ". . . we prefer to mediate, as well as possible, among the many schools of radical thought and between them and people who have not yet made up their minds." They promised to take sides when necessary (in strikes, elections, large social crises), to endorse or oppose specific ideas and projects, to "hold the door open" to all views seeking to move from capitalism to "a collectivist society," and to tolerate those who dissented.[33]

It would be easy to point to examples of the editors' failure to live up to their proclamations; that, however, is not the important point here. More vital to an understanding of this "transvaluated" liberalism are two assumptions. It was assumed, first of all, that all of the social reform movements were on the side of progressivism, were all part of "the same large procession." Second, it was assumed that it was possible to "mediate" among the various radical and reform groups. These assumptions clearly foreshadow the later Popular Front. If the Socialists, the Communists, the Roosevelt Democrats, the Progressive Republicans, the Farmer-Labor Political Federation were all moving in the same general collectivist direction, what could be better than a united front among them? And since they were all headed in the same direction, there were no irreconcilable differences among them. Thus it was possible to mediate among them, to compromise differences in a common front. The role of the editors was clear.

At the same time that Soule and *The New Republic* were developing their "radical progressivism" which apotheosized planning and muted the immediate Communist message, but included Communism in the forward march of progress, Alfred Bingham and John Dewey were working out a new philosophy which, among other things, ruled out Communism. Bingham called himself a radical, but he endorsed Dewey's synthesis of radicalism and liberalism. The two men worked closely together; Dewey was a contributor to Bingham's magazine, *Common Sense*, and Bingham was a member of the League for Independent Political Action, of which Dewey was the most prominent member.[34] Moreover, their programs complement each other. Dewey was trying to develop a philosophy combining liberalism and radicalism; Bingham was attempting to develop a radical method of social change without forfeiting the benefits of liberal democracy. Dewey supplied the theory, Bingham the program, for social change.

Like the editors of *The New Republic*, Dewey was revolting against nineteenth-century laissez-faire liberalism. In *Liberalism and Social Action* Dewey wrote that laissez-faire liberalism had become the "intellectual justification of the *status quo*." Resembling Bliven and Soule also in wishing to preserve "enduring values" of liberalism—individual development and free inquiry—Dewey sought to disengage the concept of liberty from the absolutism of the Liberty Leaguers. To make "relevant" these basic values it was necessary to remember the "conception of historical relativity." Liberty was always defined as a "release from the impact of oppressive forces," but the social forces changed from century to century, from serfdom, to chattel slavery, to oppression by concentrated wealth in 1930. Sharing *The New Republic*'s faith in planning, Dewey made social planning *the* prerequisite for a viable liberalism, a liberalism that refused to surrender its own basic values. To achieve social planning and a cooperatively run social organization, Dewey believed liberalism must become radical: "thorough-going changes" in capitalist institutions were necessary, though he specifically rejected the Communist version of the proletariat revolution. Admitting the gradualism of this change, he insisted that radical "re-formation" of society differed from piecemeal reform in having a "social goal based upon an inclusive plan." Where Dewey diverged sharply from *The New Republic*'s reinterpretation of liberalism was in his attitude toward violence. He believed that the liberal was "committed to the organization of intelligent action." The method of force was merely a carbon copy of the methods of the present social system; the method of intelligence was the application of the experimental scientific method to social problems. And where the editors of *The New Republic* justified, by its ultimate aims, the use of violence to preserve the revolution, Dewey stressed the inability of freedom to develop out of forceful restraint: "It requires an unusually credulous faith in the Hegelian dialectic of opposites to think that all of a sudden the use of force by a class will be transmuted into a democratic classless society. Force breeds counterforce. . . . It is possible to look with considerable suspicion upon those who assert that suppression of democracy is the road to an adequate establishment of genuine democracy." Clearly, Dewey's liberalism had no place in it for Communism, even as part of a wide progressive movement.[35]

While Dewey provided the theory justifying socialism as a goal for liberalism, Alfred Bingham provided a method by which liberals and radicals might reach that goal. The technique was essentially political action through a third party devoted to a socialized economy. Unlike the Communists, however, Bingham rested his analysis on the middle class as well as on the laboring class. He believed that the middle class was predominant in the United States: its values and attitudes permeated all strata of society. In contrast, the working class was declining, becoming "bourgeoisified," having its stakes in the present order. Therefore, the working class was unable to lead in any social transformation. Moreover, relying on labor alone would antagonize the middle classes; fears of violent revolution and of job losses would turn them to Fascism. Thus any social movement required a union of the middle class and the working class. Against those who pointed to the conservatism of the middle class, Bingham argued that the middle class had a stake in its jobs and in the status quo—not in capitalism. In fact, because of its craving for security, it was possibly even more attracted to the ideal of a classless society than the workers. A classless society would replace "the anarchy of capitalism" with "an intelligent planned economy" ensuring security. The trick of social change, therefore, was to maintain the smaller individual occupations of the middle class, and thus protect their capitalist jobs, while socializing the "basic industries and services." This transition depended on the victory of a radical third party, a victory dependent on not alienating the middle class. Like the New Deal, a new party, Bingham believed, would have to refrain from emphasizing class distinctions. But unlike the New Deal, it must be seriously devoted to changing the economic system. The new movement should not violate the middle-class devotion to security and personal property, but should respect the traditional American middle-class characteristics: optimism, sentimentality, patriotism, and Puritanism. It should rely on political activity: the ballot, not the bullet, was Bingham's key to social change. Here, as in his whole program, Bingham was consciously refuting the Communists and their emphasis on the working class and violent revolution.[36]

Despite differences in their views, especially in regard to Communism, when Bliven, Soule, Bingham, and Dewey had finished reinterpreting liberalism, one central fact stood out: the need for collective planning. This consensus should not be interpreted as a sharp break with the past. In many ways it was simply an extension of the Progressive concept of governmental action on a national scale and a culmination of pragmatism's accent on the application of science to the problems of society, of "social engineering" for humane ends. But one should not minimize the significance of this reinterpretation of liberalism. Clearly left behind were the moral absolutes of the Progressive age; absent too was any longing for the premonopolistic days of capitalism. Liberalism in the 1930's clearly accepted historical relativity, the industrial complex, and was clearly associated with collectivism. If this had been all, though, liberalism would still have been only an extension of the New Nationalism. But it was not simply collectivism that Dewey and his fellow liberals were requesting: it was socialized collectivism. It is true that this was not always set forth as the warp and woof of the program. Bingham, in fact, argued that public ownership was important only in so far as it promoted "the substitution of a planned and ordered mechanism of distribution in place of anarchy of the free 'market.' "[37] And, in their emphasis on planning, Bliven and Soule were anxious to set themselves apart from the socialists, who argued that public ownership was a necessary prerequisite of proper planning. But implicit within the writings of Bingham, Bliven, Soule, and Dewey was the belief that public ownership of the major industries was both desirable and necessary. No matter how much these four men differed on means, they all agreed the goal was a socialized economy.

Thus the belief in economic planning for communal ends became a basic touchstone of liberalism. Even liberals like Carl Becker or Morris Cohen, who remained largely "civil libertarian" liberals, were not averse to planning and increased social control. If the quasi-socialist ends are of most historical significance, it was the means—planning—that were most loudly proclaimed.

3

CRISIS OF CAPITALISM

Crisis

As the country floundered hopelessly in its third year of depression, George S. Counts, liberal educator and disciple of John Dewey, surveyed capitalist culture and concluded that capitalism had failed to meet the pragmatic test: it no longer worked.[1] For a generation of liberals who had learned their social philosophy under the humanistic influence of Dewey, this meant not only a failure economically, but a failure in human terms—capitalism did not permit the fullest human development. Yet Counts's apparently obvious statement left many questions unanswered. Among them was whether the capitalist system was permanently disabled or whether it would respond to corrective measures.

The Communist answer was clearly established by the official Party line. For the Communists, the years between 1929 and 1935 constituted the "third period" in history dating from the Bolshevik Revolution. This was the period of new imperialist wars, "gigantic class struggles," and "the further shattering of capitalist stabilization." In 1932 William Z. Foster, the leading American Communist, pronounced the death sentence: "Capitalism is doomed. The capitalist system . . . is reaching the end of its course. It has outlived its historic mission." And part of the report of the Central Committee of the Communist Party in April of 1934 read: "The capitalist world is now passing from the end of capitalist stabilization to a revolutionary crisis." The irreparable breakdown of American capitalism was thus at hand; a Communist-led working class would soon do battle with a Fascistic bourgeoisie.[2]

According to some accounts, the liberals agreed with the Communists about the nature of the capitalist crisis. For some fellow travelers this may be true; but once beyond the sphere of the fellow traveler, the differences between liberals and Communists, as well as between liberals and liberals, become apparent. Here one finds two diverging tendencies: an interpretation paralleling the Communists', but arrived at by anti-Communist liberals, and an interpretation postponing the death notice of capitalism. Principal spokesman for the first of these interpretations was Alfred Bingham, son of the conservative Connecticut Senator, Hiram Bingham. Bingham had graduated from Yale in 1927 and during 1930 and 1931 had traveled throughout Europe, Asia, and the Soviet Union, returning to the United States convinced of the death-throes of capitalism and the expectant birth of a socialist nation. But Bingham was suspicious of what he considered the European dogma of the Marxist parties, and in late 1932 he, along with the poet and fellow Yale graduate, Selden Rodman, began editing *Common Sense,* a periodical devoted to "spontaneous native revolts—Populist, Progressive, Farmer-Labor."[3] In editorial after editorial, Bingham subjected capitalism to a blistering attack, loudly proclaimed the need for a new economic system, and vehemently criticized the liberal reformers for wanting to patch up capitalism. The crisis had come; it was time to abandon halfway measures. But Bingham's analysis of capitalism was concomitant with, rather than derived from, the Communist line, a fact demonstrated by the rest of his program: he minimized the class struggle, he was optimistic about possible middle-class revolt and skeptical about violent revolution.

While Bingham trumpeted the end of capitalism, liberals like

Bruce Bliven, George Soule, Charles Beard, and Oswald Garrison Villard were not so certain. When challenged by Norman Thomas to state where he stood on the future of capitalism, Villard answered that he believed in planning, but not in the abolition of capitalism. And Beard, at that time considered by many conservatives a dangerous radical (had not he undermined the schoolboy's faith in the Constitution?), predicted the passing of the crisis. Crises would occur until science supplanted "rule of thumb" methods and the "untrammeled acquisitive instinct." But he suggested no displacement of the capitalist system itself. In contrast to this relative complacency, Bliven and Soule were appalled by the havoc wrought under the capitalist system and occasionally spoke as if capitalism had reached the end of the road. But they allowed for the possibility of economic recovery under capitalism. Whereas the Communists saw the depression as representing *the* crisis of capitalism, Bliven and Soule were inclined to regard it as *a* crisis. It is true that the Communists were willing to admit the possibility of a kind of recovery. William Z. Foster wrote in 1932: "Any recovery . . . that may be registered . . . can, at most, be only very partial and temporary in character. It must soon be followed by another crash still more far-reaching and devastating to the capitalist system." At first glance this might not seem too different from the outlook of Bliven and Soule, who talked about future recoveries and future depressions. But there was an important (important because it shaped their approach to reform), if technical, distinction between the two conceptions of the crisis of capitalism, a distinction understandable in terms of the difference between a chronically ill person and a man suffering from incurable cancer. The Communists believed that capitalism was suffering from economic cancer. It might rally weakly, but it would soon die. But if capitalism were only chronically ill, as Bliven and Soule believed, the periods of sickness and respite, the ups and downs, could go on indefinitely, unless, of course, a cure were found. No one period of sickness necessarily marked the definite approach of death.[4]

Rejecting the possibility of any remedy for capitalism's disease, the Communists rejected any partial reform: nothing could be done; the only way out was violent revolution, revolution that would install a Communist system modeled on Russia's. But the liberals, even those like Bingham, were not quite so dogmatic in their approach: something could be done. The question was: was what was being done enough? And if not, what then? What should be done?

New Deal or Reshuffle?

The New Deal was, in the briefest and simplest terms, capitalism's attempt to reform itself. "Above all, try something," Roosevelt told the American people, and the New Deal zigzagged its way through the thirties, seeking here and then there a solution to the staggering problems plaguing the United States. If it had a dominant and consistent theme, it was a mood, not a program—a mood of experimentation.

Because of its experimental character, the New Deal was opposed by the Communists, who maintained a rigid, a priori attitude toward social events. Although they later supported it, the shift was not the result of a conversion (on either side), but of the temporary demands of Russian foreign policy. But before 1935 the Communist line was clear in its opposition: "The policies of the government in Washington have one purpose, to make the workers and farmers and middle classes pay the cost of the crisis, to preserve the profits of the big capitalists at all costs, to establish fascism at home and to wage imperialism abroad." The charges contained in this 1934 Party manifesto were constantly reiterated. The N.R.A. was created by big business; the C.C.C. was "forced labor camps"; the Wagner Act was an attempt to put labor in "strong chains." Roosevelt was attacking "more brutally" than Hoover the "living standards of the masses"; there was "less food, less clothing, less shelter" than under Hoover. Although the Communists did not consider the New Deal "developed" Fascism, the programs of Roosevelt and Hitler were, "in political essence and direction . . . the same." Roosevelt was doing Fascism's work by seeking to preserve capitalism and crush labor; when the time came, he, along with Huey Long, Father Coughlin, and Hugh Johnson, would be "waving the U.S. swastika." As a form of incipient Fascism, the New Deal, unable to solve the contradictions of capitalism, was increasing the arms race and leading the country toward imperialist war. Its foreign policy was "the sharpest national chauvinism," and even its domestic policy was part of the war effort: the N.R.A. was "from beginning to end a part of the program of war," and Muscle Shoals, a fertilizer plant by "after thought," was primarily a *monster munitions plant, to provide explosives for war.*" In short, Roosevelt, like Hitler, an "executive of finance capital," had created "the unmasked dictatorship of capital" and with it had, in the questionable arithmetic of William F. Dunne, a leading Communist, "multiplied exploitation of the working class and quadrupled oppression of the masses."[5]

In February 1935 the Communist Party manifesto announced its opposition to the " 'New Deal' of Hunger, Fascism and War!" Three months later, however, Earl Browder wrote that the New Deal was turning leftward and carrying the masses with it. The Communist about-face—brought on by the change in the Communist line to support of a Popular Front—had begun. But it took time; in April of 1936 Alex Bittelman, a Party theoretician, was still urging the formation of a farmer-labor party to wean the masses from the old capitalist parties. Failure to do so, he said, would mean "helping Roosevelt, helping the Republicans, helping reaction." But by the summer of 1936 a definite shift had developed. The Communists continued to pay lip service to a farmer-labor party and to the old criticisms of Roosevelt and to defend posthumously their 1933 line: the New Deal, A. B. Magil said, had been "a step toward fascism." But, he went on, the situation had "materially changed"; Wall Street was no longer unanimously behind Roosevelt. According to Earl Browder (and in line with the new Popular Front position), the issue was no longer socialism or capitalism, but "progress or reaction, democracy or fascism." The Republicans were on the side of reaction, the mass organizations of the people were on the side of progress, and Roosevelt was endeavoring to take an impossible middle-of-the-road course. But the "impossibility" of Roosevelt's straddling was simply face-saving; the Communists tacitly supported him by designating Landon as their chief enemy. Browder freely admitted that the Communists' aim was to win votes away from Landon even though those votes were given to Roosevelt. Since Fascism, and not capitalism, was the main enemy according to the Popular Front line, Roosevelt's support of capitalism was dismissed as irrelevant and his supporters could be included in a united front. Thus the evils of Roosevelt and the New Deal slid silently into the background as the Communists centered their double-barreled attack on Landon. By 1937, except for criticism of reduced relief appropriations and of the arms embargo on Loyalist Spain, the Communists viewed Roosevelt as a progressive. In that year, Browder called Roosevelt's program "progressive, liberal and democratic in character," and the next year A. B. Magil designated Roosevelt as "a major statesman" and the "champion of democracy." In the same year, Browder announced the existence of only two parties: the New Deal Party and the Anti-New Deal Party. In this division, Browder said, the Communists stood unhesitatingly behind Roosevelt in his fight against those who would lead the country back to Hoover and Hoovervilles—once considered better than the New Deal. There the Party remained until August 24, 1939.[6]

While the fellow travelers followed the Communist line on the New Deal (Harry F. Ward accused it in 1935 of establishing "the political form of American fascism"), the reactions of most free-lance liberal intellectuals, as distinguished from the "New Dealers" directly engaged in governmental work, were more complex. There were liberals like Stuart Chase who gave critical support to Roosevelt's domestic policies throughout the thirties. Chase disagreed with some specific measures (e.g., the plowing under of cotton) and regretted the absence of a "long-swing program." But he believed the New Deal was negotiating the American phase of the

shift to collectivism and had made an "impressive beginning."
After the election of 1936 he was particularly impressed with
Roosevelt's pragmatic pursuit of collectivism: "Short of revolution,
he has brought about reforms and breaches in the old order so
colossal as to stagger the imagination." In its efforts, Chase believed, the New Deal deserved the support of the radical and
progressive intellectuals, whose place was on the left urging Roosevelt forward.[7]

Other liberals, like Oswald Garrison Villard and Charles Beard,
began with a position similar to Chase's: critical support. Villard
believed Roosevelt temporized too much with business and that
the N.R.A. had too little labor and consumer participation. But
in 1934 he felt the American people were under "a deep obligation"
to Roosevelt and in the spring of 1935 he still expressed satisfaction
even though Roosevelt was not the "whole loaf." Beard, too, welcomed the New Deal's break with past ideas of laissez faire, though
he thought its measures were inadequate to cope with the demands
of a technological civilization. By 1935, however, both men, always
critical of Roosevelt's foreign policy, were becoming increasingly
disillusioned with the domestic scene. Beard, surveying the New
Deal in February 1935, found little significant economic change
since 1933: the privileged economic stratum had not been destroyed and the "little fellow" had been "frozen out as usual." And
in December of 1935, focusing on the encouragement to reaction
resulting from Roosevelt's attempt to please everyone, Villard
concluded: Roosevelt was responsible for "the rout of liberal forces"
and "the rise of Fascism." During Roosevelt's second term, both
men became increasingly obsessed with Roosevelt's foreign—or as
they called it "war"—policy. Beard, though he acknowledged in
1939 that Roosevelt was a democratic humanist, increasingly demonstrated the bitterness toward Roosevelt that later spilled over into
his revisionist histories of World War II. Villard was preparing to
enter the Willkie camp in 1940, convinced of the Fascist dangers
in a Roosevelt third term. In 1938 he publicly bade good-bye to

the New Deal: "The disrupter of the liberal forces in America answers to the name of Franklin D. Roosevelt."[8]

Most liberals, however, followed neither Chase's consistent path of critical support nor the growing disillusionment and disenchantment of Beard and Villard with the New Deal. The typical pattern was, in fact, the opposite of Beard's and Villard's. The editors of *The New Republic, The Nation,* and *Common Sense* all found more to criticize than to praise in the early New Deal and came out in support of Roosevelt only in 1936. Neither *The New Republic* nor *The Nation,* often thought of as pro-New-Deal magazines, supported Roosevelt for the presidency in 1932. Bruce Bliven found Roosevelt "notably progressive for one of his background," but condescending toward the poor. He concluded that Roosevelt would do nothing detrimental to the wealthy and this made him inadequate: "The rich must be seriously hurt before our economic maladjustment is cured." *The Nation,* at that time still edited by Villard, asserted that the choice between Roosevelt and Hoover was a case of "Tweedledum and Tweedledee." Neither would propose fundamental reform, it said, and described Roosevelt as a man who did not "advance the cause of reform one whit." Though Villard was soon to express partial satisfaction with Roosevelt, *The Nation,* after his departure as chief editor in 1933, continued to accent the need for more than half-way measures.[9]

Throughout his first term in office, Roosevelt was constantly criticized by all three magazines. He was accused of being a glad hander and a friend to everyone, of trying to be "all things to all people." He was constantly portrayed as trying to "serve both big business and the people," of moving left and then right and getting nowhere, and of following "the path of least resistance"—the path of private business—with his "misplaced" faith that private industry could plan for the public good. Behind these charges of swerving and backsliding lay the basic charge that all Roosevelt wanted was to patch up, not fundamentally change, the capitalist system. All three weeklies wished to push beyond piecemeal reform. *The*

Nation did place Roosevelt on its January 1934 Honor Roll for his attempt to organize industry and end the depression, and it did urge support of "the left-ward impulses" of the New Deal. But it also urged Roosevelt to take over the basic industries of the country; only then could a "balanced economy" be achieved. Immediately after the election of 1932, the editors of *The New Republic* declared that Roosevelt's program failed to reach "the heart of the existing system." Although they did not agree with the Communists on the indistinguishability of Roosevelt and Hoover, they felt that the programs of both lacked essential changes: "They constitute a belated application of liberalistic meliorism to a civilization which we ought to be remodeling." *The New Republic,* like *The Nation,* did praise the most progressive aspects of the New Deal (and consequently was criticized by the Communists as a supporter of the New Deal). But more often it contrasted Roosevelt's "cooperation" with business with true national planning: Roosevelt was "occupied . . . with the trimmings of planning rather than with a socially efficient operation of industry itself." The editors of *Common Sense* were prepared to go even farther than Bliven or Freda Kirchwey in demanding "production for use." But, as a "liberal," Roosevelt was "essentially a conservative," engaged in "a blundering attempt to make the old system better,"—an attempt both blundering and impossible. In September of 1934 the editors wrote: "When an egg is rotten, painting it pretty colors won't improve it."[10]

Since the demands of all three periodicals outstripped the performance of the New Deal, it is not surprising that the editors were particularly critical of the very heart of the early New Deal program, the National Industrial Recovery Act. *Common Sense* asserted that the N.R.A. was "only a step away from the Nazi policy of deliberately abandoning machines as public enemies," and, along with the A.A.A., it was in line with the policy of "artificial scarcity." Unlike the Communists' similar statements, this was not connected with a picture of Roosevelt as a "brutal agent of the capitalist class." Bingham and Rodman saw Roosevelt as "well-intentioned and humane," though his program tried to preserve a dying capitalist system by not always "well-intentioned ... increasing dictatorship." While *Common Sense* spoke harshly of the N.R.A. from the beginning, the early reaction of *The New Republic* and *The Nation* was sympathetic, though critical of the N.R.A.'s ignorance of the class struggle and its hesitation in the face of business recalcitrance. But they both praised General Johnson and Roosevelt for their early N.R.A. performance and Bliven and Soule saw it as a laboratory test for capitalism: "The question of whether it [capitalism] will live or die is being submitted to the scientific test of social action." But by the fall of 1933 both periodicals were disillusioned with the N.R.A. From then until the 1935 Supreme Court decision declaring the N.R.A. unconstitutional, the editors barraged the N.R.A. with charges of business domination, bias toward radical labor, and opposition to consumer controls, and called for General Johnson's resignation. The editors of *The Nation* wrote sympathetically of the report on the N.R.A. by W. O. Thompson, who stressed its trend toward Fascism, and in August of 1934 the editors of *The New Republic* accused the N.R.A. of creating a "super government by business" and Johnson of using the "tactics of Hitler" against labor. When the decision in the Schechter case was announced, the weeklies reacted in slightly different ways. *The Nation*, still believing the N.R.A. was a highly imperfect instrument, was concerned with whether its elimination would lead to plutocracy. *The New Republic*, while regretting the undemocratic process of judicial review, rejoiced at the N.R.A.'s demise: "The slate is wiped clean ... we can begin anew."[11]

Despite this difference in emphasis, neither *The Nation* nor *The New Republic* had supported the N.R.A. Bruce Bliven, George Soule, and Freda Kirchwey had regarded it initially as a promising move, but they soon became discouraged with its workings. As a failure, the N.R.A. paralleled the whole New Deal in the mind of these liberals. In April of 1934 Bruce Bliven summed up their common attitude by refuting the usual image of Roosevelt as Kerensky. Instead he noted the resemblance to Lloyd George:

"Kerensky, after all, promised little and accomplished nothing. The greater tragedy is that of a Lloyd George who promises everything, has the power to do much and leaves behind him a page so nearly blank in history's book."[12]

Since the Communists and liberals like Bruce Bliven, George Soule, Freda Kirchwey, and Alfred Bingham shared a critical attitude toward the core of the early New Deal program, it becomes necessary to examine how far the liberal criticism was a result of any adherence to the Communist line or to any direct Communist influence. It is obvious that Bingham was not influenced by the Communist line. He made a radical critique of the New Deal in the pages of *Common Sense*, but his conclusions had little reference to the Communist position: he rejected both revolution and a proletarian dictatorship. The question of Communist influence on *The Nation* and *The New Republic* is more complex. Given the editors' general sympathy for Russia and their not unsympathetic attitude toward the Communist Party, it would be senseless to deny that either magazine's attitude toward the New Deal from 1933 to 1935 was free from all Communist influence. Parallel criticisms of New Deal planning and Fascistic tendencies in the N.R.A. abound. But it is important to remember that many anti-Communists were voicing similar criticisms. Norman Thomas, for example, condemned the Fascist-like activities of General Johnson and the N.R.A.; Reinhold Niebuhr, friendly toward Russia but no devotee of the Communist line, saw parallels between Roosevelt's and Hitler's economic program.[13] Moreover, the criticism in *The New Republic* and *The Nation* differed from the Communist diatribes. The Communists spoke of the N.R.A. as a Fascist scheme; the editors saw only certain Fascist tendencies. To the Communists, Roosevelt and Mussolini and even Hitler were blood brothers; to Bruce Bliven and Freda Kirchwey, Mussolini and Hitler were Fascists, whereas Roosevelt was a well-meaning but vacillating reformer who hoped to work recovery and save capitalism by moral persuasion and sheer magic. No matter how inadequate

Roosevelt was as a President, they believed him an improvement over Hoover—a view denied by the Communists. Whereas the Communists viewed the New Deal as the servant of finance capital, Bliven and Miss Kirchwey felt that it straddled the capitalist-progressive fence with no great success. The Communists called the Wagner Act an "anti-strike" measure; the editors called it a much-needed reform measure.

Underlying all these specific differences was the Communist diagnosis of the New Deal according to a preestablished formula: its measures were only symbols in the dream world of Fascist finance-capital they had created. On the other hand, though operating under certain preconceived notions of the degree of necessary reform and the ability of capitalism to plan, Bliven and Freda Kirchwey were responding to events as they occurred. *The New Republic* attempted to develop this point in January of 1935:

> The Communists have from the beginning persistently misrepresented *The New Republic's* attitude toward the New Deal. . . . During the presidential campaign we did not support Roosevelt. . . . As Roosevelt's program developed, we praised those parts of it that seemed to tend in the right direction, attacked the others, pointed out the inconsistencies, and continually expressed unbelief that his ambitious announced aims could be achieved by the means he was using. Our underlying belief was that social-economic planning for the benefit of the masses could not be successful under capitalism, and our method of education was to test this thesis by candid examination of an experiment avowedly aimed at that result, in detail and while it was developing. . . . The Communists, on the other hand, adopted the line of declaring in advance that Roosevelt was not trying to do anything for the masses, and that everything he did, without exception, was wrong. This line had the primary disadvantage of being . . . obviously untrue.[14]

One must be cautious in accepting the editors' own analysis of the situation, but this does seem a fair statement of the differences between the two approaches to the New Deal: the editors sought to interpret New Deal measures; the Communists had already pre-interpreted them. The editors of *The New Republic* and *The*

Nation may have responded favorably to particular Communist analyses, but to see any great Communist influence in their reaction to the New Deal before 1935, as distinct from other influences, would be gross exaggeration.

That *The Nation, The New Republic, Common Sense,* and the Communist Party all shifted from criticism to support of the New Deal at the same time presents another problem in the question of possible Communist influence. In October of 1935 *The New Republic* specifically rejected Roosevelt's plea for liberal union behind the New Deal. A year later it supported his presidential candidacy. In 1935 Max Lerner wrote in *The New Republic* that the "logic of the New Deal" was becoming increasingly "the naked fist of a capitalist state." The next year he supported Roosevelt. In June of 1936 the editors of *Common Sense* were warning radicals and progressives against identifying themselves with the New Deal and the "inevitable collapse of the next four years." That fall they supported Roosevelt.[15]

Since it had been the most clearly anti-New Deal of these journals before 1936, the *volte-face* of *Common Sense* was the most dramatic. Alfred Bingham and Selden Rodman had, in April 1933, endorsed the steps taken by the Dewey-led League for Independent Political Action to form a third party. And they had specifically criticized the post-1935 Communist demand for a farmer-labor party as being labor-dominated, appealing to narrow class interests, and designed to split the workers and middle class and thus pave the way for Fascism. Instead, they pushed for a non-Communist third party including both middle class and workers. By June of 1936 Bingham and Rodman had conceded the impossibility of running a third party nationally; in October they gave their tentative support to Roosevelt, support that progressives were advised to withdraw after election day. Again this support was completely unrelated to the Communists' view of the 1936 election with its picture of Landon and the Republican Party as black reactionaries and Fascists. To Bingham and Rodman, the whole country was moving leftward, and even Landon was part of this leftward trend. He and his party were still too conservative for them, but the issue was not democracy and reaction as the Communists pretended.[16]

What had begun as temporary support, however, soon became total support (domestically); by 1937 Bingham and Rodman were praising the New Deal's democratic planning techniques and the pragmatic, experimental way it was using to move America from one economic system to another. In September they warned that a break with the New Deal would be "tragic"; all those who believed in "a new social order of economic democracy" should "cement their ties to the New Deal." Embracing the New Deal with a vengeance, they continually gibed at the Communists and Marxist liberals who talked of a future labor-oriented Farmer-Labor Party. *The Nation* was taken to task for this suggestion and for noting Roosevelt's new surrender to business; it did not realize, the editors declared, that the New Deal was in "many respects all," and in some respects more than, such a party could be. It had not attacked the profit system directly, but its "actual accomplishments and potentials" were "no less radical."[17]

The question of Communist influence on *The Nation* and *The New Republic* again is more complicated. Clear areas of difference still remained after 1935. The Communists regarded Landon as a Fascist stooge; Bruce Bliven and Freda Kirchwey attributed Fascist influence only to certain groups supporting him. After 1937, except for a few objections to the Spanish embargo, Communist criticism of the New Deal practically stopped. But *The Nation* and *The New Republic,* though now supporting Roosevelt, periodically noted the timidity of his domestic program and his retreats before business pressure. However, the range of criticism had changed. Whereas neither magazine had supported the N.R.A., both lined up behind Roosevelt's major second-term program—the attack on the Supreme Court and his government reorganization bill. They no longer regarded Roosevelt as a vacillator. In fact, the editors of *The Nation* believed his policy to be one of "unflinching firmness" and thought Roosevelt himself not simply a reform President who "flashed a brief instant and then flickered out." When the two journals did criticize, their tone was different: the aims of the New Deal were no longer in question; after 1936, when Roosevelt was criticized, it was only for straying from the progressive path.[18]

This gentle second-term criticism of Roosevelt as the occasionally errant progressive points out another difference from the Communist shift. The change in the Communist line was a complete about-face. In a little more than a year, Roosevelt changed from an ally of Fascists to the leader of the progressive anti-Fascist forces. On the other hand, the eventual move toward support was inherent within *The Nation's* and *The New Republic's* early analysis of Roosevelt, even when their criticism of his program was most scorching. In an interesting passage at the height of their criticism of Roosevelt in late 1935, the editors of *The Nation* wrote: "He is true neither to the best that is in himself nor to his program."[19] The implication of this statement was that at heart Roosevelt was a progressive and that his program was also progressive. Through weakness of character, from not sticking to his guns, or from trying to please everybody, he allowed his good tendencies to be obstructed. Thus when they proclaimed Roosevelt as a progressive after 1936, liberals like Freda Kirchwey and Bruce Bliven were proclaiming something they had always felt to be true of him "at heart." This leads to another difference from the Communists. Concrete realities, not the needs of Russian foreign policy, entered into the switch by *The Nation* and *The New Republic*. After 1935 came the passage of much of the progressive legislation of the New Deal, chiefly the Wagner Act. The year 1936 saw the growth of the C.I.O., an industrial union fulfilling a traditional liberal demand. The C.I.O. was clearly behind Roosevelt. After 1936 came Roosevelt's attempt at Court and party reforms, reforms long demanded by these periodicals Thus the post-1935 progressive tinge of the New Deal had some correspondence to real events. Since they had always regarded Roosevelt as a misled progressive, it is easy to see why these liberals should see him as a full-fledged progressive after 1935. He was being true to the best that was in himself.

The growth of Fascism must also be considered as a factor in the liberal switch to support of the New Deal. The Communists were afraid of Fascism, but their support of the New Deal as a defense against it was ordered from above. However, it is entirely likely that, spurred by the growth of Fascism abroad and reaction at home, liberals like Bruce Bliven and Freda Kirchwey would have supported Roosevelt even without the shift in the Communist line. They were haunted by a fear of the reactionary forces, and the national surveys at the time of the election of 1936 failed to reveal the overwhelming popularity of Roosevelt. Unwilling to chance the loss of everything in a conservative victory, many liberals felt the times called for the preservation of half gains, an attitude they carried over in their second term support. A protest vote, or severe post-election protest, seemed too risky.

It is apparent that pressures other than the weight of the new Communist line led liberals like Bliven and Miss Kirchwey to line up behind Roosevelt. The shift in the Communist line may have helped, but it would have had little force if it had not corresponded to popular feeling. Yet there are important facts pointing to increased Communist influence. The demand for a labor party by *The Nation* and *The New Republic*, though it predated the Communist demand, intensified throughout 1935 when the Communist demand began, and subsided after the election, when the Communist demand also faded. There is also the almost simultaneous shift to support of Roosevelt, and, during Roosevelt's second term, the seizure by the Communists and editors of *The New Republic* and *The Nation* alike of the Supreme Court issue as a focus for the progressive-reactionary fight out of all proportion to its actual significance. After 1936 there is an increasing similarity of rhetoric and terminology: Fascist and Tory for opponents of the New Deal, democratic-progressive for supporters. Before 1935 this indiscriminate lumping of all shades of opinion into mere symbols of reaction and progressivism had been principally a Communistic device; in the late thirties the terms were applied almost as loosely by *The Nation* and *The New Republic*. Thus, although it would be incorrect to say that the shift in the Communist position on the New Deal determined the shift in the positions of liberals like Bliven and Freda Kirchwey, it is true that, given the context of the Popular Front, it played a significant role.

Before 1936, however, most liberals were not ready to take part in any uncritical support of the New Deal. They were critical of its attempts to save the capitalist economic system. Out of the deluge of the depression, the liberals asked for something more stringent than reformed capitalism.

Planning the Way Out

What should be done? From the multitude of particular reforms, one central concept emerged as the economic scalpel to operate on the sick capitalist system: national economic planning. Whatever the consequences of this concept in terms of public ownership or a "mixed" economy, liberals like Stuart Chase, Charles Beard, Alfred Bingham, and George Soule believed that only large-scale national planning could create order out of the chaos and anarchy of capitalism. John Dewey, in *Individualism Old and New* (1930), had envisaged an Economic Council which would coordinate the industrial development of the United States and take her "constructively and voluntarily" on the path Russia was traveling by force and with such destructive consequences. Buttressed by Dewey's ideas and the Veblen tradition of the "engineering mind" and spurred on by the contrast between the American depression and the Russian Five-Year Plan, liberals more and more made planning the key to recovery and reform. Thus the editors of *The Nation* wrote in 1931 that "rational planning or inescapable decay" were the two alternatives between which capitalism had to choose.[20]

From the Communist left, however, the liberals were told that there could be no such thing as rational planning under capitalism.

According to Earl Browder, general secretary of the American Communist Party from 1929 to 1945, the two-class division of society made equitable planning under capitalism impossible; attempts at planning would simply aid the capitalist class and thereby intensify the depression. True planning required the abolition of capitalism: "The abolition of private property is the precondition for the beginnings of the development of planned economy. Here we have . . . the dispute between liberalism . . . and Marxism-Leninism." The only solution was revolution. "Violence and destruction" were "unavoidable": the only thing open to choice was the side of the struggle. Communist literary lights like Michael Gold and Granville Hicks and prominent fellow travelers like Louis Fischer, *The Nation's* Russian correspondent, seconded the Party's attack on planning and its defenders. Gold labeled supporters of planning like George Soule "class collaborationists" and criticized Chase and *The New Republic* for preparing the way for Fascism under the slogan of a "planned economy." Writing in an article in the *New Masses* in 1932, "How I Came to Communism," Hicks designated as "preposterous" the ideas of Soule and Chase; there was only "one way out"—Communism. In a debate with George Soule in 1932, Fischer argued that the success of Russian planning had required the nationalized and collectively-owned economic system. Therefore, he concluded: "Capitalism and planning are incompatible. . . . Planning and capitalism belong to two unrelated species. They cannot mingle."[21]

While the Communists dwelt on the inherent conflicts under capitalism that made planning impossible, Beard, Soule, Chase, and even Bingham believed that some kind of planning could be started before the elimination of capitalism. The more extreme Bingham expressed the most doubt, worrying that planning under the profit system might crush small business and benefit monopolistic corporations. He had less faith than Soule in "the inevitability of gradualness," and was skeptical of Soule's belief that "profit planning" would evolve into "social planning."[22] Nevertheless, when Bingham presented his economic plans for the United States, they were not dependent on a prior revolution or even a prior nationwide adoption of socialism. Immediately all four liberal planners challenged the central Communist assumption and, instead, shifted their concern to what seemed to them much more basic: the aims of planning. Should planning simply reform capitalism or should it transform it into a new system?

Beard, less drastic in his demands than the other three, stressed the nonutopian aspects of planning; it was simply a method for ironing out the worst problems in the system. The system itself should remain intact. In 1932 he saw only small differences between his plans for industrial reform and those of the conservative Chamber of Commerce and the industrial leader, Gerard Swope. Beard had praise for the limited aims of the 1931 Chamber of Commerce plan; it held out hope, not for the end of all depressions, but for the reduction of "the depth of the valleys of the depressions."[23] That Beard could find good qualities in these conservative plans indicates the wide gulf separating him from the Communists, who found Fascist overtones in them. In contrast to Beard's restricted aims for planning, Alfred Bingham spoke constantly of the displacement of capitalism by a "planned system of use." Clearly socialistic in intent, if not in phraseology, Bingham's plans were still evolutionary in approach.

If Bingham's aim was clear, the aims of Stuart Chase and George Soule were not always evident. Victims of their own rhetoric, they often portrayed their ideas as more radical and drastic than they really were. This was especially true of Chase. In 1931 he spoke as if the depression might be just another business cycle, but by 1934 he was declaring, "Capitalism . . . has walked out on us." His remedies, however, were not in line with this radical statement: his planning proposals would have instituted only a mixed economy. At one point he listed eighteen reforms necessary for abundance, but none reached the heart of capitalism—the profit system. Chase rejected mere regulation, except in temporary situations, yet he preferred control without ownership to outright ownership by the state or collective group. The latter was only a last resort.

When the British Communist, John Strachey, charged Chase with inconsistency in diagnosing the end of capitalism without prescribing socialism, Chase answered: "In a distributive age it is not of cardinal importance who owns what, except as a matter of administrative efficiency." Such an admission indicated Chase's unwillingness to venture beyond a mixed economy.[24]

George Soule journeyed farther along the road to socialism, but he showed the same ambiguous attitude toward capitalism and socialism and their relation to planning. In 1932 *The New Republic* presented an economic plan drawn up by Soule and three other economists. In its introduction the magazine stated that the aim of the plan was to demonstrate how industry and government, "without a drastic change to collective ownership," might learn how to plan. It set "the minimum conditions of possible success in creating economic order, without a definite transfer of ownership and power." Soule's and *The New Republic*'s hope was apparently for a reformed capitalism or at most a mixed economy. But the next month's issue declared: "The planning we have recommended is not designed to preserve the capitalist system. It is designed to hasten the alteration of capitalism in the direction of an economy efficiently serving social purposes. . . . Every step toward regulating, checking or eliminating private enterprise . . . is a step away from capitalism. . . . The agitation for national planning is . . . not an agitation for the preservation of capitalism, but an eventually socialized society, no matter what terminology may be used in describing it." Soule repeated this reasoning in his own *Planned Society* (1932). He refused to advocate socialism explicitly, but made planning necessarily—not just possibly—a transitional stage in the direction of socialism. He effected this questionable maneuver in logic by focusing on a particular, if somewhat familiar, attribute of capitalism. "Capitalism is fundamentally unsystematic," he wrote. "That is its chief characteristic." Hence, "anything which introduces an element of conscious system into it changes it, not merely in degree but in kind." In an article in *Common Sense* and in his debate with Louis Fischer, Soule defended this essentially evolutionary approach to socialism, from planning for private profit to public planning and the disappearance of capitalism. In the debate he admitted doubts about the success of planning unless speculative profits were eliminated. However, he defended himself against the Communist assertion that a revolution was necessary prior to planning. Revolution, he said, occurred only after all reform had failed; if reformers took the necessary steps, revolution might be avoided and society transformed by planning.[25]

But the Communists refused to grant this possibility. Planning under capitalism, they said, would simply serve to oppress the masses because it would be conducted in the interests of big business. Again the liberal advocates of planning were unanimous in rejecting this proposition. Planning would aid the masses, they thought; the question was not whether to plan, but what type of planning should be undertaken and what position the businessman should have in a planned economy. Beard's answer was a National Economic Council consisting of representatives from economic agencies of the basic industries. Although Beard allowed for labor participation in planning and for more governmental supervision than the more conservative Chamber of Commerce and Swope plans, he made central use of the business corporation. As he recognized, his plan, like the more conservative plans, implied a honeymoon between government and business: "The initiative must come from both sides: from industry and government. . . . There must be a reasonable meeting of minds."[26]

This mutual cooperation was designed by Beard for the preservation and reform of capitalism. Far to the left of Beard, Alfred Bingham offered a plan for the transformation of capitalism. Proposed in 1935, it would neither " 'take over' private industry in one sweeping overturn," as the Communists suggested, nor would it "fall into the trap of 'gradualism,' " as the liberal reformers like Chase and Soule did. Endorsed by the liberal philosopher of planning, John Dewey, the plan called for the establishment of a cooperative organization known as the "Cooperative Commonwealth." Voluntary in nature and open to all producers and consumers, this organization was to acquire part of the industrial plant and put the unemployed to work in it. Within the organization, the system would be run for use and not for profit. A Central Planning Board was to be established to "coordinate private industry and the Cooperative Commonwealth." During the transition period to socialism, private enterprise would continue to function, but the cooperative system would prove so much superior and effective in providing for the people's welfare that it would eventually be extended to take the place of private enterprise throughout the nation.[27]

Bingham believed that the plan would excite the least possible opposition. Rather than making a direct attack on capitalism, it sought to outflank it by demonstrating its own superiority. It entailed no confiscation, only a "minimum of compulsion," and, in the end, would even permit private enterprise in certain specialty and luxury businesses.[28] It is easy to see how this plan differed from the Communists' prior revolution theory. But though it also differed from the proposals of Chase and Soule, the dissimilarities should not be overstated. Chase would have stopped short at a mixed economy, yet Bingham also granted a limited area of free enterprise. Soule and Chase would have initiated their planning within the mainstream of capitalism, while Bingham would have utilized a flank attack. Yet the latter's plan betrays the same faith in "the inevitability of gradualism," with capitalism giving way slowly but surely. Soule and Chase would beat capitalism over the head with government planning; Bingham would try to outskirt it by example. While one cannot discount completely Bingham"s more radical verbiage, neither should that verbiage blind one to the similarities between Bingham's methods and those of other liberal planners.

The more direct method of Chase involved Central Planning. This would be—history indicated it—the state's function. But, unlike the Communists and fellow travelers, he was not averse to business cooperation. He dismissed the orthodox socialist's charges against the businessmen. Rather, he said, the businessmen had more ability and energy than any other group in the United States. The enlightened businessman was no longer committed to usurious profits or perpetuating mass misery. "For the first time in history," Chase wrote in 1931, "businessmen have a genuine stake in the abolition of poverty. This hardly converts them into angels, but their horns and tails have visibly receded." Even occasional excessive profits could be permitted, if the "main objective" of planning were achieved. "We do not care who controls the wild horses," he wrote, "so long as they are controlled." Thus, the state would plan, business would cooperate, and only "embittered Marxists" would object. The embittered Marxists did object, of course. Michael Gold scoffed at Chase's Utopianism, Robert Evans criticized his "superficial reforms," and David Ramsey and Alan Calmer referred to the liberal Fascism of Stuart Chase. Largely unperturbed, Chase suggested the creation of a Central Planning Board modeled on the War Industries Board and having mandatory powers in administering plans, but nondictatorial powers overall: he was not an advocate of total planning. Yet he admitted openly what many liberals were coming to feel in the depression-ridden thirties: faced with a choice between economic security and the ballot, he would "exchange all the political democracy ever heard of . . . for the real democracy of the universal right to be born clean, to grow strong, and not to be crawling on one's belly to a petty tyrant for a job." He would even submit to "an economic dictatorship to secure this happy state." Sweden indicated that economic democracy and parliamentary methods could be combined; given time the United States could follow her. But in 1935—"at this particular juncture in history"—Chase wondered if time had not run out on America.[29]

Apparently it had not, for he never advocated total planning; actually it was George Soule who came closest to this concept. In a review of John Maynard Keynes's *A Treatise on Money*, in 1931, Soule declared: "It is really much more difficult to attempt to control a laissez-faire economy than it would be to attempt to plan an economy in all its important phases." Soule's own planning scheme, as it appeared in *The Planned Society* in 1932, called for "a central administrative organ" for each industry, with overall control by a presidentially appointed National Economic Council representing the "nation as a whole" and not, as in Beard's scheme, made up of "representatives of various interests." The Board would call on labor and management in each industry to draw up a plan for their industry. If the industry failed to present an acceptable plan, the Board would be empowered either to establish one or to recommend to Congress the needed legislation. The enforcing power of the Board would be voluntary at first; if that proved too weak, Congress would be requested to grant it more power. Although organization of industry would be its central work, there was a great deal of fence-straddling as to its long-range aims: reform capitalism or transform it into a new system. Soule stated that the Board should operate with no preconceived bias toward private enterprise, regulation, or socialization; it was an application of the "scientific, experimental method." But Soule's argument was misleading; he also criticized the "habit of trying to graft control into a fundamentally individualistic chaos" and saw the aims of a planned society as "akin to the broad ambitions of socialism." He wanted more than regulation, more even than a mixed economy. But either *might* have resulted from an "impartial" Board. He wanted more, but he was willing to settle for "partial measures" lacking the opportunity for "a clean sweep." His whole position can be understood only if one remembers his belief that every advance of planning—partial or not—was a step away from capitalism and toward some form of socialism. His position also illustrates his and *The New Republic*'s whole ambiguous and evasive attitude toward socialism and planning. By refusing to make an outright commitment to socialism and, at the same time, arguing for the inherent radicalism of the idea of planning, they kept their feet in the reform camp and their heads in the radical camp.[30]

In searching for patterns of planning beyond capitalism, the liberal planners inevitably were faced with the example of Russia.

For the Communists, Russia provided the only model for a planned society. To follow it was their aim. But Beard, Bingham, Chase, and Soule all repudiated this aim. Beard was typically farthest from the Communists, viewing his ideas as alternatives to Communist planning and sarcastically noting that the Russians had replaced Marx with Frederick Winslow Taylor and "borrowed foreign technology to save their political skins." His comments on planning were filled with specific comments on the terror and tyranny of the Russian system. Her agricultural experiments violated "every human decency cherished by the American people" and her dictatorial planning was a "bureaucratic despotism" trying to manipulate people as if they were "inanimate engines." The American people, he insisted, could not "be moved like pawns on a chessboard by bureaucrats, no matter how wise or despotic." In presenting his own plan in 1932 he offered "a purely native product" and "no foreign concoction or importation."[31] Although he was inspired by Russian economic achievements, Alfred Bingham joined Beard in rejecting the Russian example. One of the aims of his transition plan was, like Beard's more conservative plans, to avoid the coercive and compulsive elements associated with Russian ventures into a planned economy.

Stuart Chase and George Soule were more directly influenced by Russia than either Beard or Bingham. In *The Planned Society* Soule told how Russia's endeavor to build an industrial civilization by a national economic plan had increased "a hundredfold" the interest of American planners in the Soviet Union. "We could not assimilate the hard dogmas and terminology of Marxism. . . ," Soule wrote, "but we were irresistibly attracted by the idea of planned use of modern industrial technique." Their achievements in increasing consumer purchasing power, correlating consumption and production, and eliminating crises caused by over-production indicated that Russian and American planning would have the same long-range goal—"the enhancement of the general well-being." Although particular aims and methods might differ, he said, the United States could adapt "the economic technique" being used in Russia. Like Soule, Chase, who had visited Russia to study her planning endeavors in 1927, was attracted by Russian planning activity. For Chase, this attraction was not simply that Russia was in the forefront in social legislation, that the profit motive was being displaced, or that her industry was growing at an unprecedented rate. The important thing was that Russia, by planning, was *doing* something, while the United States was drifting. This was especially discouraging for America because Russians were traditionally technically incompetent: "If the Russians can plan, one is almost moved to say, so can cows." But there she was, and he was induced to pay high tribute to her administrators who, through hard work and devotion to the community, had "died at their desks and . . . in the field."[32]

Behind this eulogy to the dead was a considerable amount of administrative jealousy—jealousy of the useful planning expert in Russia. "Why," Chase burst out, "should Russians have all the fun in remaking a world?"[33] In his soberer moments, however, Chase realized that the problems of Russia and the United States differed, and, therefore, that the methods used would differ. Realizing this, he did not want to remake America in the Russian image, nor according to the Communist design. Nor was this simply a difference in method; there was also a difference in theory. Both Soule and Chase minimized the importance of the class struggle, the doctrine dominating Communist thought on capitalist America. Soule admitted its existence, but put his faith in the concept of planning as a substitute for it. Planning and the idea of "organization" would have greater appeal than the revolutionary class struggle. Whereas Soule minimized the class struggle for tactical reasons—his theories would be more effective in winning social change—Chase believed class war was rapidly vanishing in America. Marxism, he said, was a scarcity philosophy, and material abundance in the United States had made it and the class struggle outmoded and inapplicable.[34]

It was the material abundance of the United States that ultimately convinced both men of the incompatibility of Russian and

American planning methods. The contrast between preindustrial Russia and industrialized America, Soule argued, made the two countries' planning objectives different. In their great rush to industrialize, Russians were making "great sacrifices" unnecessary for the United States. And Chase pointed out: "Russia is still carrying on in scarcity and will continue to do so for several decades more." In short, imitation of the Five-Year Plan was irrelevant to the American situation. This did not mean, however, that America could not profit from the Russian lesson. If the United States did not absorb the Russian lesson of planning "scientifically," Chase said, she would soon be propelled, after intense "suffering and bloodshed, to the Russian formula." In the last analysis, then, Soule and Chase wanted to "meet the challenge of Russia," rather than to emulate her. Unlike the Communists and fellow travelers, who were interested in imitating the Russian system, Soule and Chase regarded Russian planning as a challenge to the United States to devise alternative plans. America might learn from the Russians —they were an inspiration, a lesson, and a challenge; she need not duplicate their method.[35]

Yet, unlike the present-day world, which speaks of the dangerous challenge of Russia, these men foresaw peaceful rivalry. In *Out of the Depression—and After* (1931), Chase wrote of the possible error in both the American emphasis on private property and individual ownership and the Russian rejection of them. The efficient individual industrial unit in the United States was offset by the uncoordinated whole; the less efficient Russian individual unit was partially compensated for by central planning, which had solved the worst evils—overproduction and unemployment— of the capitalist system. The American economy resulted in business cycles of booms and busts, while the "terrific centralization" in Russia created the danger of "bureaucratic red tape." Neither had ended poverty, though that was the goal of both—a goal that Russia kept "more steadily in mind." Chase predicted the fusion of these two imperfect systems: the United States might authorize more government activity and planning; Russia might grant private business greater scope and reduce her Marxian dogmatism. The result might be "keen, fair competition" and mutual respect—with fusion the long-term end. A new economic system would thus be "hammered out in the two great laboratories," and, retaining the best features of both systems, it would one day replace capitalism as capitalism had replaced feudalism.[36] Chase's prediction of a future mixed economy for Russia and the United States, while not directly anti-Communist, like Beard's views, was decidedly different from the future America of the Communists and fellow travelers. An American society patterned after the Russian one—the dream of Foster and Browder—was rejected by all of the liberal planners. In its place they substituted a planned society. Though their aims and techniques differed, they all repudiated the Communist answer to the depression: a Communist society created out of a Communist revolution.

Since the concept of national planning was so central to liberal thought in the early thirties, the inevitable question occurs: why did the liberal furor over planning die down? In one sense, the idea of planning did not disappear; it became a cornerstone of liberal thought and remains so among many liberals today. In the late thirties it continued as an important part of the writings of Max Lerner, Bruce Bliven, and Freda Kirchwey, as well as in the work of Soule, Chase, and Bingham. All of these people continued to criticize the anarchy of capitalism and to offer planning to bring order. But in another sense, the idea of planning faded, or at least the emphasis shifted. Symbolic of this change in emphasis was Alfred Bingham's transition after 1936 from an advocate of socialist planning to an adherent of limited planning within the basic capitalist framework. But before 1936 planning had had a more urgent note. While Stuart Chase denied in 1932 that he belonged to the "plan or perish" school,[37] his and Soule's and Bingham's writings in the early thirties revealed a definite belief that unless the United States undertook some kind of planning, chaos would be her immediate fate. When it became clear that chaos had been temporarily avoided, the emphasis shifted from "plan or perish" to "plan or muddle along in this unsatisfactory arrangement." With the urgency of its message muffled, planning became more of a tacit assumption, a guidepost in criticizing particular measures, than the basic goal for which to strive. In short, it no longer served as a substitute for ideology.

That the New Deal was responsible for by-passing the road to chaos is probably true. But it was not merely the New Deal and its appropriation of certain planning techniques that stole the thunder from the concept of planning. A combination of events tended to take planning out of the foreground. The first Russian Five-Year Plan had created heights of exhilaration for planning among liberals. But enthusiasm for planning as a liberal synthesis began to wane with the growth of Fascism in Europe and the United States. In the later thirties, although many liberals continued to talk of domestic planning as the means of eliminating the conditions breeding Fascism, planning alone seemed more and more inadequate to the task of combating Fascism. With the rise of Fascism, there also came a reorientation in the Communist line. A "defense of democracy"—capitalist or otherwise—became the order of the day. The liberals who were caught up in the Popular Front had their hands full defending democracy without thinking about large concepts like central planning, which might alter drastically the status quo.

Thus a series of events focusing on the rise of Fascism forced the idea of national planning into the background. But during the early thirties, when liberals were first facing the economic and psychological shock of the depression, planning was a central concern. To many of these liberals, Russia constituted an example of a country developing a planned economy. However, the liberal fascination with Russia involved more than an admiration for her planning techniques: the American liberal of the 1930's felt the impact of all aspects of Soviet life.

4

SOVIET RUSSIA: LODESTONE OF THE AMERICAN LIBERAL

The Late Twenties: Two Views

In 1928 and 1929 two small, but important, books about the Soviet Union appeared in the United States. They were written by two leading American liberals returning from visits to Russia. The author of the first book, *Liberty under the Soviets,* was Roger Baldwin, Director of the Civil Liberties Union and a veteran defender of civil liberties in the United States. The other book, *Impressions of Soviet Russia,* was by the elder statesman of American liberalism, John Dewey. The importance of the two books lies in their anticipation of ideas that were to become commonplace in certain liberal circles after 1930. Of particular significance was Baldwin's assumption that liberty could be legitimately separated into two distinct parts: although there was no *political* liberty in the Soviet Union, *economic* liberty was being rapidly achieved. Economic liberty (the abolition of privileged classes based on wealth and the economic freedom of the workers and peasants) was more important to Baldwin, despite his ardent defense of civil liberties in the United States. Equally significant was Dewey's conception of Russian society as an economic and cultural experiment—"the most interesting one going on upon our globe."[1]

These ideas of the divisibility of liberty and the experimental nature of Russia were to become the tacit assumption of a great many liberals in the thirties. Also important with respect to later attitudes toward Russia was the total picture. Baldwin and Dewey projected a "forward-moving" image of Russia in contrast to a "stationary" United States. An economic democracy was being molded, Baldwin said, that would usher in an unknown degree of civil liberty. A new type of human nature was being created, Dewey said, cooperative instead of individualistic and selfish. A "collective mentality" was replacing "the individualistic psychology." The intellectuals had "constructive tasks" and had become "organic members of an organic movement." The Russian experiment, he said, sought to provide economic security without the "competitive struggle for personal profit," and aimed at the full participation of the people in a "cultivated life." It had released a wave of energy and spirit; a new purpose was being infused into life. Neither Dewey nor Baldwin was wholly uncritical, but both tended to minimize the significance of the unfavorable aspects of Russian life. Baldwin recognized the danger of the perpetuation of "rigid controls," yet he justified Russia's repressions in terms of her revolutionary aims. Whereas violations of liberty would have been intolerable in the Western democracies, they were "weapons of struggle" in the transition to socialism in the Soviet Union. Freedom could grow out of repression. Baldwin also distinguished between the anti-majority, one-man, dictatorship of Fascist Italy and the party dictatorship opposed by only a small minority in Russia. Dewey was less tolerant of the repressions than Baldwin, yet he believed they did not affect the great masses of people. He did not like the "rigid dogmas" of orthodox Marxism, but thought that the creative spirit being unleashed was more important. Both men agreed on the post-Czarist improvement of the Russian people and both assumed that Russia's fanatical practices would diminish as she felt more secure.[2]

Baldwin's and Dewey's views might have been historically arrested, might have remained isolated statements, if it had not been

for the major event of the thirties—the depression. Most liberals
had been vaguely sympathetic to Russia during the twenties, but
they had not felt its impact directly. Significantly, the Five-Year
Plan did not generate intense excitement until 1930—two years
after it had begun. What happened to cause this excitement was
1929 and the depression, the real impetus in turning liberals eastward toward Russia. What they saw was the Five-Year Plan. Without the depression, and the economic and emotional upheavals
following in its wake, there would have been no general gravita-
tion toward Russia among liberals. Even with the depression, the
impact of Russia on the liberal imagination would not have been
so great if anything less than the Five-Year Plan had been going on
in Russia. It was the confrontation of the Five-Year Plan with the
depression that served as the catalyst. If the depression had struck
during the NEP period or during the Moscow trials, the influence of
Russia on liberalism would have been decidedly reduced. The circumstances were propitious in terms of deepening that influence;
nothing could have made so startling the contrast between the
United States and Russia. And, once established in the liberal mind,
the contrast proved difficult to purge.

The Spectrum

Writing in *The New Republic* in the winter of 1930, George
Soule articulated the multiple reasons for the tremendous impact
of the Five-Year Plan on the United States. Defenders of capitalism, he said, had justified any attendant evils on the grounds that,
despite everything, it worked. They had argued for the necessity
of the profit motive in industrial civilization. By conducting a concrete experiment in the theory of Communism, Russia was testing
the truth of these ancient, and perhaps antiquated, propositions.
Soule noted the audacity of the Plan, the "arresting . . . spectacle"
of a nation feverishly working to create a modern industrial civilization "overnight and by fiat." He cited its sacrificial aspects—the
Russian people, "mustered as if for war," were undergoing "great

temporary sacrifices to conquer poverty, ignorance and confusion."
Here was a great challenge to the United States, Soule felt;
whether it took four or ten years, it would prove that socialism
"worked." While this proof need not convert Americans, Soule said
(there were other important values besides the "maximum industrial development in the shortest possible time"), and while the
problems of industrialized America and agricultural Russia differed, the "daring" of the Soviet plan could stimulate America
to initiate her own system of planning. Thus, in this article in
1930, a pattern of thought was established: planless, chaotic, inert,
purposeless United States stood opposed to planned, daring, sacrificial, purposeful Russia. Freda Kirchwey, Alfred Bingham, and
Sherwood Eddy all contrasted in the early thirties the Russian
advances with American drift. "Poverty which accompanies progress," *The Nation* wrote in 1933, "is less disheartening than poverty
in the midst of plenty." And Stuart Chase asserted that the Five-
Year Plan had made the Russian world "exciting, stimulating, challenging," while for Americans the world was "dull and uninspired,
wracked with frightful economic insecurity." The Five-Year Plan
hammered this message home to liberals in America.[3]

With the contrast established, sympathy for Russia vividly increased among liberals, but the total capitulation of liberalism to
Russia never occurred. This theory is historically fallacious. There
were always differences and tensions within the liberal camp. The
fellow travelers, who, except for an occasional mild reservation,
were entirely uncritical of the whole Russian regime, stood in
opposition to a group of anti-Communist liberals, who either took,
or were moving toward, a critical position on Russia in the early
thirties. Between these groups were the Russian sympathizers,
men with general sympathy for the overall aims of the Soviet
Union, but who either cautiously disapproved of certain aspects
of Russian life or set forth serious reservations about them.

The critical liberal group included John Dewey, Charles Beard,
the historian Carl Becker, the philosopher Horace Kallen, the
popular journalist Elmer Davis, and the man who was the *Christian*

Science Monitor's Russian correspondent until 1934, William Henry Chamberlin. Of these men, Beard, Becker, and Elmer Davis had never been sympathetic to the Russian regime. Beard believed representative government superior to dictatorship; Becker condemned "cutting off heads" and the "horrors" under Communism; and Davis preferred depression-ridden America to the absence of freedom in Russia and to the Siberian outlet for criticism. The other liberals in this group were in the process of freeing themselves from misconceptions about Russia in the early thirties. In 1931 Dewey was still sympathetic to Russia, although he was concerned about the "ruthlessness of means" to achieve "humanitarian ends." By 1932 he was worrying more about the "excess of dogma and indoctrination" and the ruthless political and intellectual measures in Russia. But he was still sympathetic to the overall aims of the Soviet Union. By 1934, however, the unfavorable aspects of the Russian regime had become uppermost in Dewey's mind; in "Why I Am Not a Communist" Dewey placed the Communist and Fascist systems in the same dictatorial, oppressive category.[4]

Dewey's progress from a degree of sympathy for Russia to outright criticism was paralleled by Horace Kallen, William Henry Chamberlin, and Oswald Garrison Villard. Though Kallen had always dissociated his ideas from those of the Russian bureaucracy, he had believed in 1928 that the individual was being freed in Russia. But by 1935 Communist and Czarist "mass exploitation" had come to seem alike. Chamberlin, like Kallen, had never been overly sympathetic to Russia, but by 1935, through cataloguing the multifarious repressions under Stalin in *Russia's Iron Age*, he moved into a position of open hostility. Villard, too, had never been willing to abandon democracy or his liberal principles. But when he visited Russia in 1929, he had pronounced it "the greatest human experiment ever undertaken," and, like Dewey, wished it well. As an old Progressive, Villard admired what he took to be Russia's aim: a society based on "social service." Although he disliked the dictatorial practices of the Russian rulers, he believed that, in contrast to Mussolini, they were selflessly working for the

good of the masses. Hence, the "progressive" and the "humanitarian" should prefer the Russian experiment, despite "its cruelties
and intolerance," to the Italian autocracy. Like Roger Baldwin
earlier, Villard saw the coming victory of economic liberty. If
Russia ever achieved political liberty, he said, then she would be
"the freest of all countries." Yet when he faced the problem of
the correct liberal attitude toward Russia, Villard, even in 1929,
urged the liberal to reject it forthrightly. The government was "a
bloody despotism" and the leaders retained power by "violence,
terrorism, and murder." Their rationalization that the ends justified
the means was the eternal "language of despots." The means would
corrupt their ideals and aims, for they were the means of "a Caesar"
or "a Mussolini." He still recognized the "fine idealism" of the
leaders and their "genuine desire to uplift humanity and to mod-
ernize Russia"—an aspect existing next to their "bloody and bad
side." But he was not prepared to give them his liberal endorsement, and by 1934 he was more uncompromisingly critical. Villard found "indefensible" the purges and executions following the
assassination of Sergei Kirov. The Soviet leaders had been reduced to the level of Hitler, terror had been perpetuated, and the
Russian system was "a blood-cemented edifice erected upon . . .
dead bodies of vast multitudes." A liberal should not adopt a
double standard in judging the Russian and German purges:
"wrong never yet made right, nor ever will."[5]

All of these liberals who were critical of Russia in the early
thirties shared a strong belief in civil liberties, though those like
Becker and Elmer Davis, who valued civil liberty above "social
service," tended to be critical sooner than liberals like Dewey and
Villard, who balanced the two. Some of these men, principally
Dewey and Villard, like others more sympathetic, viewed Russia
as an experiment which should be left free to serve as a kind of
social laboratory. However, unlike liberals who continued to hold
this view throughout the thirties, Dewey and Villard believed that
a true experiment would soon begin to show worthwhile results.
When the results became more oppressive and the means more

repressive, they ceased thinking of Russia as a genuine experiment and began to think of her as they would any other autocratic country. All of these men shared a strong belief in democratic ends and a conviction that the means used should be proportionate to the ends involved. When the means became unrelated to the stated ends, or to any ends for that matter, when they became ends in themselves, then they knew that the time had come to reject the notion that the ends justified the means or that one could judge Russia differently from any other country.

In contrast to this critical body of liberals stood others who were indulgent with Russia: the fellow travelers and Russian sympathizers. The fellow travelers included Harry F. Ward, the Methodist theologian; Jerome Davis, a Yale professor who had traveled extensively in Russia during the twenties; Corliss Lamont, chairman of the Friends of the Soviet Union; the Moscow correspondents, Louis Fischer of *The Nation* and Walter Duranty of the *New York Times;* and Anna Louise Strong, who worked in the progressive movement in the United States before she journeyed to Russia, there to find a new home and new loyalties. Frederick L. Schuman, under the guise of "objective" scholarship and a passion for *Realpolitik,* maintained positions similar to those of the fellow travelers. Men like Roger Baldwin and George S. Counts, although they disagreed with the Communists on important points, also shared views similar to the fellow travelers' on certain aspects of Russian life. Among the Russian sympathizers were Stuart Chase, Bruce Bliven, George Soule, Freda Kirchwey, Maurice Hindus, a popular author on Russia, and Sherwood Eddy, a Y.M.C.A. leader and frequent conductor of Russian tours. Other liberals, such as Alfred Bingham and Selden Rodman—anti-Communist on most issues—shared certain of the attitudes of the Russian sympathizers on the Russian economy.

The first area that impressed all degrees of sympathizers was, of course, the Russian economic effort, the Five-Year Plan in general, and the collectivization of agriculture in particular. It was the audacity, the boldness, the enormity of Russian planning that riveted the attention of sympathizers. When Sherwood Eddy called the Five-Year Plan the "boldest experiment in history," and when Bruce Bliven extolled Russian industrialization as "one of the most desperate ventures" of all times, they were recording the dazzled feeling shared by the admirers of Russian planning. Yet amazement at Russia's gigantic undertaking was not the exclusive property of liberals. Even the conservative *New York Times,* usually unimpressed by Russian achievements, was awed by the boldness of the Five-Year Plan—the "most extraordinary enterprise in the economic history of the world." Still the displacement of critical judgment by pure astonishment was more characteristic of the liberal. In a review of M. Ilin's book for Russian children on the Five-Year Plan, Stuart Chase let his imagination follow the Plan's forward march: "Fifty years," he marveled; "Ten Five-Year Plans, one arching into the next. Will the great span break? Who knows, and for the moment, who cares? It is enough for little children and philosopher-engineers to rear them towering into the blue sky."[6]

This uncritical wonder was combined with a more pedestrian appreciation of Russia's actual economic achievements. Surveying Russian economic growth in 1935, Louis Fischer announced the absence of "fundamental weakness" in the Russian methods of production and distribution, and elsewhere he spoke of the "uninterrupted achievements" in every aspect of life. Here the line between the uncritical fellow traveler and the Russian sympathizer is clear. Sherwood Eddy, like Fischer, reported Russia's economic and social progress, but acknowledged the coexistence of "the most unfeeling infliction of pain, privation, punishment or persecution upon inividuals." Though the good outweighed the evil in Eddy's ledger, statements like this brought down the wrath of the Communists and fellow travelers. In 1931 Anna Rochester wrote in the *New Masses* that Eddy was a "voluble enthusiast, emotional, illogical, dangerous," and three years later, in a review of Eddy's *Russia Today,* Corliss Lamont criticized him for failing to see the connection between the "so-called evils" (denial of liberty, the use of violence and compulsion, the antireligious campaign) and the "many and far-reaching benefits." The same year, Liston Oak (later to feel the Communists' wrath himself) declared Eddy's "futile, ineffectual 'religious liberalism' " helped bring Fascism rather than socialism.[7]

Collectivization also revealed an underlying current of dispute beneath the ocean of mutual praise. Although Bliven and Soule in *The New Republic* were ecstatic over collectivization and often reflected the Communist interpretation (as when they blamed the Ukrainian famine of 1933 on counterrevolutionaries), they occasionally admitted difficulties in collectivization and made minor criticisms of Stalin's policy. But for Anna Louise Strong Stalin was always right—whether he was moving swiftly against the kulaks or ordering a slow-down. In her writings, collectivization became a great Soviet morality play of good triumphing over evil. This difference was not a difference in kind, but in degree—and often a small degree. A clearer line existed between Maurice Hindus, who interpreted collectivization in his books and lectures for thousands of Americans, and Michael Gold, the Communist novelist and critic. Hindus had been so overwhelmed by the amazing feat of collectivization that, while he innately sympathized with the suffering of its victims, he was convinced of the long-run good of what was happening. Yet Hindus' picture of collectivization was hardly satisfactory to Gold and the Communists. Reviewing Hindus' *Red Bread*, Gold noted that Hindus' report of the suffering of the kulaks revealed "a rather mawkish and 'artistic' nostalgia for the past." An old economic system was dying, Gold said, and Hindus did not "love the raw, bold, exciting new." Like the Southern agrarians, he belonged to the "anti-machine school of literature."[8]

Despite the differences in their evaluation of Russian industrialization and collectivization, the fellow traveler and Russian sympathizer both evinced a quality not generally associated with the liberal mind: hardness in the face of human suffering. Maurice

Hindus criticized the early Communist attempts at collectivization as "too rapid and too reckless," but it was the historic sweep of events that caught his imagination. The suffering was lost in the tidal wave of history: "The *kolhoz* with all its turmoil, all its agony, all its romance and all its promise rolls on and on." Force had been used, he admitted, and famine had occurred. But peaceful and voluntary methods would have delayed development for more than a decade. "In Revolution as in war," he calculated, "it is the objective that counts, and not the price, whether in gold or in blood." Elsewhere he said blandly: "It was a cruel thing, this liquidation of the kulak, but cruelty is one of the chief weapons of the Revolution."[9]

Hindus' failure to recoil in the face of suffering was carried farther by the two Moscow correspondents: Louis Fischer, with his cold, hard acceptance of power, "historical necessity," and the *fait accompli,* and Walter Duranty, who justified every maneuver by the "time-table of the revolution." Fischer admitted the brutality of collectivization, but there was always the other side—the end in view. That end justified the means: "Let no one minimize the sadness of the phenomenon. But from the larger point of view the effect was the final entrenchment of collectivization." Writing on collectivization and socialization in 1935, Duranty carried the same argument to its terrifying extremes: "Their cost in blood and tears and other terms of human suffering has been prodigious, but I am not prepared to say that it is unjustified. In a world where there is so much waste and muddle it may perhaps be true that any plan, however rigid, is better than no plan at all and that any altruistic end, however remote, may justify any means however cruel." In this type of reasoning, reminiscent of nineteenth-century Social Darwinism, the means were justified by the ends. As Harry F. Ward wrote: the "repressive aspect of dictatorship" was "only instrumental" to the "constructive" end. Or as Corliss Lamont admonished Sherwood Eddy: new societies "cost something." And Duranty, sounding every bit like a Social Darwinist justifying a robber baron, explained why Stalin triumphed: "Stalin deserved his victory because he was the strongest."[10]

This "hardness" and "toughness" of many liberals is ironic when one considers that one of the things liberals looked for in Russia was the development of the "new man," a man who would be cooperative and peaceful, rather than acquisitive, selfish, and "hard." George S. Counts described the "new man" as "sturdy, confident, class-conscious, socially-sensitive and practical-minded." Maurice Hindus' picture of him ironically joined the individualistic American rebel of the twenties with the new collective, socially-conscious man. On the one hand, the "new man" had lost all fear of God, of sex, of family, and of insecurity. On the other hand, the Five-Year Plan had displaced man's "I" as "the center of things." The concept of the "new man" was closely related to the belief that Russia had created new motives for individuals. In 1934 Sherwood Eddy reported the replacement of the old selfish profit motive by cooperative, creative, and humanitarian motives and incentives. Maxwell S. Stewart returned from a visit to Russia to tell the readers of *The Christian Century* that Russians worked hard for the "joy and satisfaction" of work "done for a definite social purpose . . . done collectively." In 1933 Harry F. Ward combined the picture of the "new man" with the new "creative purposes." Communism had supplied a "moving goal," an ideal that was being "diffused" to all Russians by education, by example, and by "contagion." Out of this process came a transformation of human nature —the "socialized individual." The atomized Western individual was giving way to the integrated Russian man. "The significance of the Plan," Ward wrote, "is that it gives the masses that which our liberals are so afraid of, that which life has not had since the breakup of the Middle Ages—a central purpose."[11]

Whether the Russian economic system was the model and guide or a challenge and inspiration, whether it provided "higher reasons" of creative purpose and transformed human nature or simply focused "American criticism upon the weaknesses in our system," initially it was the key factor in creating liberal sympathy for Russia. But as the thirties progressed, and war seemed imminent, Russian foreign policy came to have greater importance. Sympathy for Russian foreign policy dated from fears of capitalist attack on Russia after World War I, when Russia appeared to be an innocent nation menaced by aggressive imperialists. This view continued into the thirties and was voiced continually in *Soviet Russia Today* and by such writers as Corliss Lamont and Frederick L. Schuman. "Unceasing vigilance and preparedness," wrote Schuman in 1932, ". . . is the price of the preservation of the proletarian revolution." The effect of this image of Russia as a victimized innocent was to build a legacy of sympathy for Russia and continual distrust of the capitalist nations, that later found vent in the suspicion of Neville Chamberlain's foreign policy.[12]

There was another tradition of Russian foreign affairs, also dating from the immediate postwar world: the threat of world revolution. In 1932 Frederick L. Schuman analyzed Russian foreign policy and placidly foresaw the eventual overthrow of world capitalism. But for the Russian sympathizer, world revolution was not such a palatable thought. Sherwood Eddy criticized it and Maurice Hindus predicted the collapse of the idea as Russia concentrated on socialism in one country. It was not the thought of a transported revolution (the consuming fear of conservatives) that created the large reservoir of liberal sympathy for Russia. What created this sympathy was Russia's apparent stand for peace in a world threatened by war, a stand made to appear all the more noble because the war threats were aimed at Russia herself. The argument for Russia's peaceful intentions was set forth by fellow travelers like Louis Fischer and Corliss Lamont, by Russian sympathizers like Bruce Bliven, and by supposedly "neutral" commentators like Frederick L. Schuman. They all cited her apparently peaceful activities. Schuman pointed to her disarmament proposals and her nonaggression agreements. The editors of *The New Republic* said that Soviet diplomacy, because it was "direct and honest," was "the best in the world." "I don't see how anyone can come to Russia," Bruce Bliven wrote in 1931, "and still believe that the Russians want war." This belief was buttressed by a "tactical" argument: they all agreed that war would mean the interruption of the Five-Year Plan. Therefore the world could be assured of the peaceful desires of the Soviet Union.[13]

However, it is also important to remember that this was not solely a Communist belief. In 1931 the *New York Times* wrote: "peace with every foreign power is a prime necessity for the Communist Government . . . that STALIN's Russia cherishes no aggressive aims may be taken for granted. . . . STALIN . . . needs peace in order to 'build' socialism." But there was an important difference between the *New York Times*'s position and that of the fellow travelers and Russian sympathizers: the *New York Times* did not assume the permanence of Russia's peaceful intentions. The fellow travelers assumed these intentions were inherent within a Communist state, and, in this tendency to absolutize the relative, the Russian sympathizer generally followed suit. Corliss Lamont asserted that peace was a "fundamental principle" of the founding philosophy of the Soviet Union. Discussing the Italian-Turkish dispute at the beginning of the 1930's, Louis Fischer found it unthinkable that Russia would side with Italy, even if it might be materially advantageous to do so. "A Soviet state," he said, "could not possibly barter the life interests of a foreign revolutionary regime for a consideration from a capitalist power." Behind *The New Republic*'s argument for the self-interested nature of the Soviet Union's peaceful policy lay the basic belief that a workers' state was nonimperialist and nonaggressive because it had eliminated the principal cause of war under capitalism—the profit motive. Russia, the editors said, was "no longer an imperialist power," but the "world's first communist state." And in speaking of a possible Japanese-Russian alliance, they wrote in 1932: "A workers' government could hardly make an alliance, explicit or implicit, with such a band of Fascist adventurers as rules Japan today." But what would happen to liberal sympathy if a workers' state did make an alliance with a band of Fascist adventurers? In 1932 this seemed inconceivable.[14]

If the Russian economic system and Russian foreign policy were the positive factors contributing to the liberal sympathy for Russia, the Russian political system was the fly in the Soviet ointment. The political system presented two clearly illiberal positions—the political dictatorship and the absence of civil liberties. The fellow traveler faced these issues rather easily (at least publicly), but even he occasionally betrayed some uneasiness. Louis Fischer admitted there was excess government "repression" in Russia and acknowledged that free speech would be an asset "as a check on government error." But the incidental and mild criticisms of the fellow travelers were generally buried beneath a deluge of praise. The Russian sympathizers were more disturbed by the presence of the dictatorship and the lack of civil liberties, and some faced the issue squarely. Sherwood Eddy was unequivocal in his criticism of the tyranny and terror of the Russian political system, and Alfred Bingham, who shared the sympathizers' enthusiasm for Russian planning, was open in his opposition to Russian political methods. But too often the criticism of the Russian sympathizers was couched in rationalizations. Maurice Hindus recognized the repressions under the dictatorship, but lost sight of them as he chronicled the growth of the industrial matrix, the force of the audacious scheme of collectivization, and the mighty sweep of the Revolution. The editors of *The Nation* and *The New Republic* were also less straightforward than either Eddy or Bingham. *The Nation* admitted Stalin was a dictator, but made no extended critique of the fact. Although Bruce Bliven and George Soule were never as uncritical as the fellow travelers, they were often apologetic. In 1930 they wrote of the "pyramid of power" in Russia, the "dictatorship of an infinitesimal minority," and compared Stalin to an "eastern despot" with "no principles of conduct." "Nobody," they wrote, "least of all the Communists themselves has seriously maintained that Russia is a democratic republic." Yet elsewhere they backed off; they qualified the picture so greatly that their overall enthusiasm for Russia was not jeopardized by a few unhappy qualms about the dictatorship.[15]

In rationalizing the existence of the dictatorship, the fellow travelers and Russian sympathizers used a number of "indirect" arguments. Instead of focusing directly upon the dictatorship, they sought to justify it in terms of historical origins, the possible alternatives to it, its differences from other dictatorships, and its future aims. Declaring it "impossible to appraise the Soviet system by the standards of Western democracies," Jerome Davis, along with Louis Fischer and Bruce Bliven, argued the necessity of understanding it in terms of Russia's Czarist past. Closely aligned with this diversionary technique was the argument that the present regime was better than Czarism or any of the alternatives to it. Thus Davis and Corliss Lamont claimed that if there was not a Communist dictatorship in Russia, there would be something infinitely worse—a dictatorship of capitalists, reactionaries, or counterrevolutionaries. And Louis Fischer claimed there were more "privileges and liberties" than in prerevolutionary Russia. Furthermore, the Russian dictatorship was said to differ from other dictatorships. Jerome Davis described Russia, in contrast to the Fascist nations, as "a step toward democracy." The editors of *The New Republic* wrote: "Stalin is not and never has been a dictator in Russia, in the same sense in which a Mussolini . . . or a Primo de Rivera is a dictator." The reason for the difference was, as Baldwin had said earlier, the absence of a one-man dictatorship. Instead, there was a dictatorship of the Communist Party; Stalin, according to Davis and Bruce Bliven, could be deposed any time the Party was dissatisfied. As the educator George S. Counts said, this party was not a "mere mechanism in the hands of an autocrat," but "an organism throbbing with life in every one of its thousands of separate cells." The Party line emerged from "little groups of Communists scattered throughout the country"; Stalin might "affect" it, but he did not "fashion" it. As the "product of the collective mind," it might change at any time: "To its man-

dates even Stalin must yield, if he would not be destroyed."
Finally, the rough edges of the dictatorship were excused by a
concentration on the future. Louis Fischer reported that the goal
was to establish the first socialist democracy, and even Sherwood
Eddy, who sharply criticized the dictatorship, could still speak of
its democratic aims. Not only were the aims beneficial, but as Marx
had predicted, the dictatorship would eventually "wither away."
Thus Roger Baldwin wrote in 1934 of the early disappearance of
the proletarian dictatorship, and Harry F. Ward indicated that it
was aiding in "its own dissolution."[16]

The indirect argument sought to transfer attention away from
the dictatorship itself. Some liberals, usually fellow travelers, went
beyond this feinting technique to focus directly on the dictatorship, citing either its good qualities or its necessity. Roger Baldwin
claimed more liberties for the Russian people under the dictatorship than anywhere else in the world: the "fundamentals of liberty" were established on economic grounds—"the only ground on
which liberty really matters." Beyond this, was the claim of a
causal connection between repression and "good": the dictatorship was *necessary* to accomplish the ends of the Revolution. In
an argument brought up to date by advocates of "guided democracy" and rationalizers of colonialism, Walter Duranty stated that
the Russian masses were not ready for independent self-govern-
ment and that the dictatorship was acting as a "tutor and guar-
dian" while they prepared themselves for it. Similarly, Jerome
Davis asserted that under democracy, "a fickle populace" might
be "lured away" by the "bright promises of charlatans and dema-
gogues." Hence the dictatorship was necessary to achieve "any
brand of socialism."[17]

To a large extent, these positive justifications were only exten-
sions of the indirect rationalizations. Thus the argument for the
necessity of dictatorship to accomplish socialistic and democratic
ends was the extreme of the indirect argument that those ends
excused the dictatorship. And the argument for the "positive good"
of the dictatorship was a logical extension of the indirect justifica-

tion in terms of a crueler Czarist past. The fellow traveler also carried to an extreme the rationalization that the Soviet was a party, not a personal, dictatorship. Jerome Davis' comparison of Stalin to an American party boss was symptomatic of this tendency. Harry F. Ward went further in redefinition: the dictatorship of the proletariat was "the control of activists over the rest of the population." It was minority control, but control which succeeded by obeying majority wishes. This, he said, was "the general nature of social control everywhere." Anna Louise Strong carried the process to its absurd limits. Denying the similarity between Stalin and Hitler and Mussolini, she insisted that those close to Stalin knew him as a "comrade" and "leader." Stalin did not "impose his will" on the people. He and the Central Executive Committee of the Communist Party were simply "interpreters" of the people's wishes and demands. It was not Stalin against the peasants; he had not ordered the kulaks exiled. That had been done by "meetings of poor peasants and farm-hands." The Party's and Stalin's job was "to correlate and guide" the "scattered initiative of the masses" according to the dictates of the Revolution. The Party did not "rule," nor was Stalin a "ruler." The Party was simply "the most energetic part" of the population helping to create a new order, and Stalin, who had no parallel in other governments, was "chief analyst of the 'party line.'" He gave his "summing up of the important next steps." This Orwellian redefinition, in which a dictatorial order became an innocent "summing up" of the situation, went further than the Russian sympathizers were generally willing to do. They were willing to excuse by various convoluted arguments the existence of the dictatorship, but they declined to call it a "higher form" of democracy.[18]

The political dictatorship was hard enough for liberals to rationalize, but, to many liberals, the general absence of civil liberties was even more disconcerting than the particular form of government. The fellow traveler, however, faced the problem with little apparent difficulty. Anna Louise Strong denied that anyone had been punished after the Kirov assassination "merely for political views." Others were more cynical: Louis Fischer, in 1930, admitted the G.P.U. could find nonexistent counterrevolutionary plots which it used for "discrediting unpopular factions, or keeping non-Communist state specialists in line." Even more cynical was Walter Duranty's comment in 1930 when a group of Russian engineers and technical experts were on trial for counterrevolutionary activity and for conspiring with capitalist powers against the government. Maintaining that the proof of the government's case against them was "beside the mark," he said that the important thing was that the trial helped to unite the masses behind the government and thus gave the government a free hand in dealing with internal and external enemies and "doubters." At the time of the Kirov assassination, Duranty conceded that many of those executed had not plotted to murder Kirov. They were " 'hostile elements' whose elimination was meant to strike terror; it was not an act of revenge, but a symbol and a warning."[19]

But other liberals, sympathetic to different aspects of the Russian system, could find no such delight in "symbolic" murder. Sherwood Eddy vehemently censured the secret arrests, secret trials, and general terror, and Alfred Bingham and Selden Rodman wrote of the "horror" of the post-Kirov executions, which they compared to the Nazi purges of June 30. During the early thirties the editors of *The Nation* were also critical of the Russian record on civil liberties. In 1933 an initial impulse to believe the charges of sabotage against a group of British engineers in Russia soon developed into a condemnation of the unfairness of the trial and of Soviet justice in general. The Communist, they wrote, proclaimed the impossibility of "an impartial trial and a classless justice" and argued for justice to be "prejudiced in his favor." Reaffirming the traditional "liberal" position of "classless impartiality," the editors found the Russian theory filled with the "dangers of a medieval method of trial." After the Kirov assassination, the editors protested that murder did not justify execution without trial; the legal safeguards were a fraud. And they held that the executions had upset the picture of a progressive Russia in contrast to a terror-ridden Germany. *The Nation,* however, was speaking as a "friend" of Russia, and when the danger of Fascism seemed greater and Russia seemed the chief bulwark against it, it too would temporize on civil liberties.[20]

The editors of *The New Republic* were willing to temporize earlier. Bliven and Soule did not like the absence of civil liberties, but they refused to make any outright condemnation of Russian justice. They usually made a gesture at independent thought and then accepted a position close to the Communist one. This is apparent in their attitudes toward the civil trials in Russia during the early thirties. In its first notice on the trial of Russian engineers in 1930, *The New Republic* pleaded for suspended judgment until definite evidence was available (a device subsequently used during the Kirov executions and later the Moscow trials), but stressed the incredibility ("too perfect to be real") of the capitalist plot theory. But two weeks later the editors moved closer to the official Communist position. The defense testimony was still incredible, but, on the other hand, why would they lie? "Already dead men" don't lie, they wrote. And since verification was easy, one could assume the charges were true. No longer finding it hard to believe in capitalist intervention, the editors pointed to the groups desiring to overthrow the Russian regime. The following week they announced that the theory of confessions by torture had collapsed—a victim of "its own implausibility." Thus they concluded: "As against the theory that the story of counterrevolutionary plots is part of the necessary myth of Communism, there is as good or better reason to believe that the repudiation of such stories is part of the necessary myth of capitalism." There matters stood until the series of arrests and executions following the Kirov assassination in 1934. Perplexed at the vast purge, the editors had "doubts." They assumed those executed had been "implicated in a plot against the Soviets," but noted that a public trial could have eliminated any doubts. The whole situation seemed to them reminiscent of the 30th of June in Germany. The evidence implicating Germany in the assassination was "pretty flimsy" and the implication of Trotsky seemed "groundless." Russia had a right to destroy conspiracies against the regime, they asserted, but what was open to question was "the guilt of particular persons" who had not been tried "in an open court of law."[21]

This critique of the trial—and especially the comparison with Nazi Germany—was not lost on the Communists, who condemned the comparison as "sheer obfuscation" and linked the editors of *The New Republic* and Oswald Garrison Villard with William Randolph Hearst. This was characteristic of the Communist attack on liberals who questioned the executions. When the International Committee for Political Prisoners, including Roger Baldwin, George S. Counts, John Dewey, Arthur Garfield Hays, John Haynes Holmes, and Robert Morss Lovett, protested the executions "in a friendly spirit," the *New Masses* accused them of helping the enemies of Russia. Even Waldo Frank, who couched his criticism of the executions in declarations of loyalty to Russia, was accused of dangerously splitting hairs. These were the "myopic American liberals" who placed "a few score White Guards, Hitler agents, and confessed assassins" above the marvelous achievements of the Soviet Union.[22]

By the time the *New Masses* had leveled its guns at the International Committee for Political Prisoners, the editors of *The New Republic* had begun to temporize. By mid-January 1935 they were saying that the supporters of Trotsky (supposedly behind the assassination of Kirov) had not been executed for their ideas, but for their "active campaign to disorganize the Soviet Government by killing off its leaders." The defendants had not been shot without trial; they had been tried before the "military tribunal of the Supreme Court of the Soviet Union." Fairness to the Soviet Union required suspension of judgment until all the facts became available. By the end of January they had accepted, for all practical purposes, the official interpretation. There was "no evidence" for a "reign of terror" against "mere political opponents." The people

executed, they said, had been connected with direct acts of conspiracy and with assassination. The editors had found their resting
place.[23]

Toward an Explanation

It is the position of liberals like Bliven and Soule that has led
to the denunciation of liberal capitulation to Russia and Communism in the 1930's. But the editors of *The New Republic* did
not speak for all liberals. As the above analysis makes clear, there
was no one liberal opinion on Russia. There were many issues
and many opinions. There was an articulate group of liberals, like
Dewey, Villard, or Kallen, ready to condemn the suffering under
the Russian economic and political system. There was a group of
liberals, sympathetic to Russian economic progress and Russian
foreign policy, but anxious about the dictatorship and the lack of
civil liberties. Some of these, like Eddy, were critical of the political system; others, like Bliven, rationalized it. Finally, there was
a group of fellow travelers set off from the Russian sympathizers
by their acceptance of *all* aspects of the Russian regime. The
totality of this commitment was never more apparent than when
they were defending Russia against the criticism of other less dedicated liberals and radicals. In 1930 Reinhold Niebuhr, the noted
theologian, visited Russia and wrote a series of mixed, but certainly not unfavorable, articles. These articles elicited a sharp
attack from Maxwell S. Stewart, a subsequent editor of *The Nation,*
who at that time was living in Russia. Stewart charged in a letter
to *The Christian Century* in December 1930 that Niebuhr had been
listening to "whispers." Stewart denied any food shortage and supported the restrictions as generally "beneficial." But his principal
concern, he said, was not with Niebuhr's "inaccuracies," but with
his "disproportionate emphasis" on the defects in the Russian system. What Stewart apparently found most exasperating was Niebuhr's confirmation of the charges of unreliability against Russian
tourist guides. The guides, Stewart asserted, were usually right

and were certainly more reliable than the "rumor mongers." Thus all attempts at a balanced judgment were reduced to rumor mongering; honest analysis was impossible except through "regular channels."[24]

If this totality of commitment distinguished the fellow traveler from the Russian sympathizer, the two groups, nevertheless, shared two principal patterns of thought. Soule, Bliven, Fischer, Duranty, Chase, Hindus, and even Bingham all believed that production qua production was "progressive." Growing out of naturalism, with its accent on the technological basis for societal advance, and instrumentalism, in so far as it emphasized growth and process over ends, this belief was the inverted form of the businessman's philosophy of "growthmanship." The liberals who idealized production demonstrate the phenomenon of a group in revolt becoming antibusiness without shedding the businessman's mode of thought. The forerunners of those whom Irving Howe and Lewis Coser were later to call the "left authoritarians,"[25] these liberals were possessed by a fascination for physical growth, for rising factories and growing towns.[26] They were drawn to Russia by her economic expansion, and they contrasted her staggering economic progress with the deterioration of the American economy. Russian planning, making possible this rapid growth, became an end in itself. They did not always believe that the United States should adopt Soviet methods, but, in terms of Russia and in terms of their evaluation of her, planning acquired a value of its own. There was no question (or at least too little question) of how, at what price, and for whom: it was enough that Russia was planning.

In addition to this faith in the mystique of production, many fellow travelers and Russian sympathizers also shared a bias toward action and power. This attitude evolved from the old American penchant for "getting things done," the behaviorists' emphasis on action rather than theory, and a corrupted form of pragmatism which made action per se more important than the ends in view. This is not to deny social idealism to these liberals. Certainly their enthusiasm for Russia would have been much less if they had not believed it to be a "people's economy," if they had not believed social justice was being created. But it is impossible to understand the attraction Russia held for liberals without understanding this predilection for action and power. It can be explained historically as growing out of their frustrating ineffectuality of the twenties. The thirties offered them opportunities, and Russia seemed to offer types of action. The attraction again provides another example of a group in revolt maintaining the mode of thought of those against whom it had rebelled, the business class with its image of action and power. Hence they were attracted to an "active" Russia in contrast to an "inert" America, and many rationalized Russia's use of force: she was "acting." The process culminated in an admiration for "powerful" Stalin and his ability to "get things done." It reached its height in Duranty's explanation that Stalin deserved to win because he was the strongest and most fit.

These two patterns of thought help explain why the fellow travelers and Russian sympathizers were attracted to Russia, but they do not explain why so many were willing to overlook, or at least to tolerate, the terror and repression of the Communist regime. There was, of course, simply irrational, blind faith in the aims of the Revolution—much more prevalent in the fellow travelers than in the Russian sympathizers. An analysis of the more rational attitudes of the Russian sympathizers, however, reveals two specific reasons. The first was the tendency to regard Russia as an experiment (a tendency often sneered at by the Communists, who apparently believed her "proven"). Like Dewey in 1929, they were misled by their belief in pragmatism and instumentalism. It was the resulting emphasis on the application of the scientific method to social problems that caused them ultimately to mistake mass control for social experimentation. They did not mean to equate the two, or they would have referred to Fascist Italy and Nazi Germany as experiments. Their use of the terms "experiment" and "social laboratory" implied a scientific quality: the Russian rulers were scientifically testing their economic and political theories. The laboratory, however, implies a specific testing before a general application, and Russia was playing for keeps. But because they believed Russia was an experiment, these liberals mistook the Five-Year Plan and collectivization for tests.

The very fact that they believed Russia to be an experiment removed them from the need to evaluate it. As an experiment it was not in its final state, but in the process of achieving it. Hence any "imperfections" in the Soviet system could not be criticized in the same way as in another system. Final judgment could be suspended until the experiment was over and the system, like any scientifically developed phenomenon, had been perfected. In another sense the value was implicit. Since science itself was "progressive," and since Russia was scientifically experimenting, the experiments were "progressive." If the concept of Russia as an experiment seems to conflict with the recurrent war images used to describe the struggle for collectivization or with the idea that Russia was waging a life and death struggle, the disparity is only superficial. As an experiment Russia was "progressive," and those forces holding back the experiment must, therefore, be eliminated. Thus arise the battle images. This fetish for scientific experimentation was also related to the glorification of economic production. Both were "progressive" processes. The former, if practiced, furthered the latter. Again ultimate values were buried beneath the lava of process.

The second mistake of the Russian sympathizers in approaching Russia was to assume, as Roger Baldwin did in 1928, that liberty could be divided into political and economic liberty. The separation of the two, and the attendant devaluation of political liberty, resulted from the historical approach to culture that tended to make political and civil liberties relative to particular environments and from interpretations of Marx that seemed to liberals to make economic rights primary. The bifurcation of political and economic democracy appears to make sense on the surface, for it might be argued that the American worker had political rights before he had economic rights. Did not political liberty exist without economic liberty and could not the reverse be true in Russia? Yet the

Russian sympathizer would not have granted that there could be real political liberty in the United States without economic liberty. The American worker might think he had won political liberty before he had won economic liberty, but it was only pseudo-liberty. The sympathizer's argument was not that political and economic liberty were "separate but equal," but that economic liberty was of primary importance. Political liberty was dependent upon it. Since there was no economic liberty in the United States, political liberty was, at best, jeopardized and, at worst, unreal. Russia, on the other hand, was building an economic democracy; therefore, the foundations were being created for a future—and true—political democracy. In the meantime, however, political democracy was relegated to an inferior position in the sympathizer's evaluation of Russia.

There was a connection between this division of democracy and the accent on production. If there were two kinds of democracy (economic and political), and if the former was more important (all political rights ultimately depended upon economic rights), and if Russia, through her increased economic production, was working toward the former, then judgment could be "suspended" on the lack of political rights. First things first. The division of liberty became a refusal to judge the absence of liberty. However, if economic democracy means anything, it means not merely a voice in economic policy, but a check on the political administrators carrying out that policy. To admit degrees of both within the same society is permissible; to chop democracy or liberty in half makes a mockery of the ideal of economic democracy. It implies that workers or a people can control the economy of a state in which they are politically subjugated.

In the depression world of the early thirties, however, political rights did not seem so important to many liberals. Living in a period of economic crisis, they were primarily concerned with economic problems. When they did turn their attention to political repression, it was not the Communist dictatorship that most distressed them. The worldwide rise of Fascism seemed to threaten the basic values of liberalism. The depression was the impetus in turning the liberals' eyes toward Russia. But the rapid rise of Fascism, more than anything else, increased and maintained the prestige of Russia even after her internal practices increasingly came to resemble those of the Fascist nations. Indeed, the rise of Fascism caused a fundamental and far-reaching reorientation in Communist-liberal relations after 1935.

5

THE FASCIST TIGER AT THE GATES

The Threat

The depression corroded the liberal's faith in piecemeal reform and shocked him into a basic questioning of capitalism. But as the thirties progressed, a new force, even more terrifying than the inadequacies of capitalism, entered the arena. This was Fascism. The strange mixture of disbelief, fear, hysteria, and confusion that gripped many liberals during the rapid rise of Fascism in the early thirties is reflected in the pages of *The New Republic*. In the winter of 1931 Bruce Bliven diagnosed the political situation in Germany. The striking thing about his analysis was not his conclusion of a lessened threat of Nazi or Communist revolution, but the combination of disbelief and fear with which he responded to the Nazis: disbelief that a party with "no real plan" should have an attraction for so many people and fear of what that attraction might mean in terms of external war and internal revolution. That a philosophy of "madness" with the "mental horizon" of the Ku Klux Klan should have a wide appeal was a strange and foreboding phenomenon.[1]

Such a phenomenon deserved close scrutiny, and throughout 1932, as indeed throughout the thirties, the editors of *The New*

Republic kept a vigilant eye on the growth of National Socialism in Germany. They noted its ominously increasing power and arrogance; they diligently recorded its setbacks and lost opportunities; they warned of possible civil war; continually they pleaded for labor unity. There was always uncertainty and confusion about what was really going on. Sometimes German big business was reported reluctant to support Hitler; at other times Hitler was described as its instrument. When Hitler at last emerged triumphant in power, the editors watched aghast as he proceeded to destroy trade unions, suppress political opposition, and persecute the Jews. But there was always hope: they were quick to report any small sign of restlessness in Germany. Enthusiastic over the "moral" defeats of Nazi candidates in shop-council elections, they announced in June of 1934: "The fantastic spell that lay over Germany's workers is breaking. Life is becoming real once more." After the June 30 "plot" against Hitler was crushed that year, *The New Republic* expressed a paradoxical opinion: Hitler was stronger than ever and labor was disorganized, but there was unrest in Germany and Hitler's political influence was dwindling. The key to the future was German economic affairs; Fascism would be unable to solve the chronic ills of capitalism, and eventually Hitler would be deposed and the whole system would go under. But as 1934 continued into 1935, wishful thinking was forced to give way to the unhappy recognition of Fascism's growing strength. Liberal recognition of this fact coincided with the beginning of the Communist shift to a united front. Already convinced of the danger of Fascism —it meant eventual war—*The New Republic*'s editors and many other liberals were ready to join in a maneuver that made anti-Fascism a central part of its philosophy.[2]

Paralleling and augmenting the growing fear of external Fascism was the increased fear of domestic Fascism arising out of the activities of various groups in the United States. Bliven and Soule were typical of the liberals in recognizing that Fascism was not an isolated European phenomenon. Throughout the early thirties— mainly after 1932—editorials and articles on various Fascist and semi-Fascist groups began appearing in *The New Republic*. Organizations such as the Silver Shirts and Khaki Shirts were subjected to careful observation. Americans were warned not to laugh off Art Smith's plan to march on Washington and make Roosevelt dictator. Business leaders' speeches were examined for signs of Fascist philosophy. Fascism and Red-baiting were linked. Communities where vigilantism ran wild were castigated for Fascist tactics. The Imperial Valley in California and San Francisco during the longshoremen's strike were cited as areas where Fascism could be witnessed in action. And "the Kingfish," Huey Long, was regarded as a potential leader of a native Fascist movement. As frequent victims of this incipient American Fascism, the Communists naturally received their share of sympathy. As apparently staunch opponents of Fascism, they also received their share of praise. Domestic forces as well as the threat of Fascism abroad were pushing many liberals toward an accord with the Communists. To the editors of *The New Republic* and other liberals in the mid-thirties, a united front with the Communists and with all "progressive" elements to fight Fascism at home and abroad was beginning to appear the wise course of action.

The Theories

What were they really fighting? What was the *nature* of Fascism? What came to be an academic question in the Popular Front elicited bitter controversy in the early thirties. In the debate, two clear positions stood out: the Communists believed Fascism to be an extension of capitalism; but Alfred Bingham, the most articulate spokesman for the opposing view, maintained that it was a misdirected revolt against capitalism. This basic disagreement derived from the different role that each theory assigned to the big industrialists in a Fascist movement. R. Palme Dutt, the British Communist theoretician, believed that the big industrialists had always supported the Fascist movements from the beginning, and John Strachey, a British Communist influential in liberal circles in the

United States, described Fascism as "merely the militant arm of the largest property owners." The editors of the *New Masses* called it "the open terrorist rule of the most reactionary elements of monopoly capitalism," and in the 1934 Report of the American Communist Party, Fascism was defined as the dictatorship of "finance capital." But Bingham, in his book, *Insurgent America*, answered that Hitler had been the industrialists' "second choice" in Germany. They had turned to Hitler only when they discovered that he alone could protect them against revolution. Although Fascism in Germany had always had a few wealthy supporters, nevertheless its mass support had come from the middle classes. Bingham saw Fascism arising when the middle class reached "the point of desperation in the crisis of capitalism." It was, then, a revolt of the middle classes against capitalism. But the revolt became misdirected because, although the middle classes called for "revolution" and a "new system," in reality they suggested only reforms. The middle-class mind, he said, hated the insecurity under the capitalist system, hated monopolistic power, and hated the power of the wealthy bankers and industrialists. Because the middle-class mind also feared the disorder and violent change accompanying any disturbance of the status quo, it demanded a dictatorship to preserve order. It demanded "the advantages of economic planning and control," but did not wish to surrender the capitalist system. "Hence," Bingham concluded, "in reacting *against* capitalism it ends by *saving* capitalism."[3]

The role attributed to the middle class by Bingham was nonsense to the Communists. They agreed, of course, that Fascism ended by saving capitalism (temporarily). For them Fascism was an attempt by the capitalist class to save capitalism; for Bingham it was "the last stand of the middle-classes for capitalism." Obviously, an interpretation viewing Fascism as a genuine middle-class movement accepted by the capitalists only after all else had failed ran counter to the Communist claim that Fascism was a capitalist plot in which the middle class was merely manipulated. John Strachey, Dutt, and the 1934 Report of the Party all denied that Fascism was a "revolutionary movement" of the middle classes against both the capitalists and the workers. Both Strachey and Dutt agreed that the lower middle classes supported Fascism, but they believed these supporters were, as Strachey said, "hired mercenaries" of the capitalists. There was simply no room in the Communist theory for a middle class in revolt. Fascism as a movement never had had to conquer power. Since it was always controlled by the "bourgeois dictatorship," it was the latter that had everywhere placed Fascism "in power from above." Again, however, Bingham rejected as drastically oversimplified any view of Fascism as a "vast plot on the part of the capitalist interests" to destroy the proletarian revolution. Such reasoning, he said, was the consequence of a two-class view of society. He acknowledged that the Fascist revolt served to help the capitalists, but insisted that it was not a "plot" directed by them from the beginning with the deliberate use of a demagogue to manipulate the middle classes. Fascism, according to Bingham, was a genuine revolt of the middle classes against both capitalism and the revolutionary proletariat.[4]

In addition to quarreling over the nature of Fascism, Bingham and the Communists also disagreed over the future of Fascism. The Communists regarded Fascism as a form of heightened imperialism leading to war, while Bingham believed it to be a movement for economic self-sufficiency with war as only a possibility. The Communists argued simply that capitalism led to imperialism and imperialism necessarily led to war. When capitalism began to fail, according to Strachey, the capitalists attempted to preserve the system through intensified imperialism abroad and by a Fascist dictatorship at home. Thus Fascism was "imperialism raised to a pitch of frenzy hitherto unknown." At the end of the road lay another imperialist war. Bingham agreed with one part of this analysis: Fascism, as it stood (planned capitalism), could not solve the ills of capitalism. But he did not agree with the Fascism-cum-imperialism theory. Rather, he believed that Germany was moving toward a self-sufficient economy, toward autarchy. Despite imperialist forces in Germany, the "main trend" of Fascism was inclined toward "self-contained nationalism." It had moved toward "discipline, control, regimentation, toward a national self-contained collectivism," not toward imperialism. This made war a possibility, not a certainty.[5]

To the Communists, however, Fascism pointed directly toward war, and the only way to meet this threat was through revolution. The Party's 1934 Report criticized those who would divert the workers from the "revolutionary way out." According to Strachey, the aim of the working class should be the overthrow of capitalism before Fascism triumphed or of Fascism where it had already triumphed. Strachey's view was based on the belief in continued capitalist oppression under Fascism until the working class revolted. But Bingham did not believe in this continued direct domination under Fascism. He viewed Germany's system as neither socialism nor pure capitalism. It was State Capitalism: the capitalist system had been maintained, but the system moved toward subsidized monopoly whereby the state, "acting as capitalist," became the whole or partial owner and administrator of industry. This meant that, although certain industrialists received favors, it was the politicians who controlled the state. The capitalists retained power, but they retained it "on the sufferance of the powers-that-be." The future of Fascism was open too; unlike the Communists, Bingham foresaw a number of possible future developments. The Fascist state might stagnate into a kind of feudalism or might disintegrate into a dog-eat-dog primitive society. A proletarian revolution was also a possibility, but he was inclined to regard this as wishful thinking. The most probable future of Fascism was an evolution into socialism and eventually Communism. Bingham found striking parallels between the German and the Russian economies. Pointing to the corporate or totalitarian state as "much closer to Socialism than was its predecessor, competitive capitalism," he predicted the likelihood of increased similarity: "In my judgment there is more than an even chance . . . that Fascism will develop into a true cooperative and classless society." If this seems "soft" on Fascism, it is true that Bingham never completely grasped the oppressive character of the totalitarian state. Yet in fairness to him it should be pointed out that he did not want this future for the United States. Even if Fascism should become a classless society, he said, it would have blundered into "an intelligent and humane social order" by "an accidental back-door path through near barbarism." It was up to the United States to find a better path. However, the better path was not Communist revolution: the Communist accent on purely working-class action worked against the necessary unity in the face of Fascism. Bingham's concern for unity was not for a unified working class—Communist and socialist—but for the unity of the laboring class and the middle class. A split between the two would create the breeding ground for Fascism; if labor attempted its own revolution, as the Communists advised, the middle classes, frightened by the class struggle and revolution, would turn to Fascism. Thus Bingham constantly cautioned against relying solely on labor as a defense against Fascism. Such a defense, rather than preventing Fascism, would further its development. What represented for the Communists during this period the only "way out" was for Bingham a dangerous device likely to backfire into a Fascist regime.[6]

Bingham and the Communists presented two antithetical theories of Fascism. These two extreme positions reflect the poles of liberal opinion on Fascism. Between them, most liberals fluctuated. Max Lerner and Frederick L. Schuman, for instance, made analyses similar to the Communists'. Though Lerner stressed certain patterns of behavior in Fascism unrelated to the Communists' position, his economic analysis of Fascism was close to their view. He criticized those who, because Fascism "found fertile soil" in middle-class despair, believed it to be a middle-class movement that was anti-proletariat and anti-capitalist. This was "to mistake fertile soil for an effective force." Big business, according to Lerner, had backed the Fascist movement in Germany. The middle class had been susceptible to the Fascist emotional appeal, but "the real stakes" were those of big business. Lerner's point was the same as that of the Communist theoretician, A. B. Magil, who, in a review of a book on Fascism by Raymond Gram Swing, one of *The Nation*'s editors, wrote: "Swing's basic error is that he confuses those classes (the farmers and city petty-bourgeoisie) that are the chief dupes of fascism and form its mass base with the classes (the big capitalists and landowners) whose interests it represents and whose economic and political power it seeks to maintain."[7]

A similar analysis was made by Frederick L. Schuman, although he accented a psychological aspect of Fascism—mass neurosis— not central to the Communists. Like Lerner's, his economic interpretation paralleled the Communists'. From the start, Schuman said, the big industrialists had viewed the Nazis "as a useful tool with which to win the masses to reaction . . . to crush not only Marxism and a pernicious democracy, but the entire German labour movement." Whereas Bingham had used the German industrialist Thyssen's departure to South America as proof of tension between Hitler and big business, Schuman viewed Hitler as "unshakably loyal" to Thyssen and the other German industrialists and financiers. Citing Strachey and Dutt, he declared that Fascism was "the social philosophy of the State-form of the bourgeoisie in the monopolistic epoch of late capitalism." Schuman did grant slightly more initiative to the lower middle classes than did the Communists: the origins of the Fascist state lay partially in "the neuroses of a lower middle class and a peasantry reduced to desperation by social insecurity and impoverishment." Unlike Bingham, he did not consider the middle class the dominant force in Fascism. Here he distinguished between Fascism as a "mass movement" and Fascism as a "dictatorial state-form." As a mass movement, it was "the expression of the neurotic insecurities of lower middle class people," and both Hitler and Mussolini symbolized these insecurities. But as a dictatorial state-form, Fascism was "created by a conspiracy of monopolistic industrialists and monopolistic agrarian aristocrats, aided by professional militarists and self-seeking politicians." While Hitler and Mussolini symbolized middle-class neuroses, they had been "raised to power" by a combination of big business, the army, and the landed aristocracy. In power they obeyed these forces and not the middle class. Once the Fascist state had been established, it moved toward economic disaster and was forced to turn to "imperialistic aggression." Schuman's writings, then, contain the essential elements of the Communist interpretation: the initial capitalist influence, the capitalist "plot," and the inevitable imperialist war.[8]

Among the liberals agreeing with Bingham's essential position were Stuart Chase and John Chamberlain. Discussing the possibility of Fascism coming to America, Chase wrote in 1934 of the two current theories of Facism. There was the "last-stand-of-capitalism" theory in which big business bought the "Purple Shirts to prop its tumbling house, clean out the reds and make capitalism secure." This was the Communist theory paraphrased in Chasean manner. The other theory portrayed Fascism as a middle-class dictatorship, neither Communist nor anti-capitalist, but composed of various middle-class groups "growing sullenly impatient with Wall Street, profiteers, trusts . . . and big business generally." Leaning toward the second theory, Chase declared: "The potential fascist will throw out the brain trust joyfully and dance over reds as such, but bankers and brokers will go into the dust bin along with Tugwell and Foster. . . . Fascism is an *alternative* for an abdicated capitalism, not a prop." Although these were random thoughts and not a detailed theory of Fascism, Chase echoed Bingham's most important point: Fascism was not an extension of capitalism, but constituted a "third" way. Chamberlain, too, made certain points that Bingham was to develop more fully later. Reviewing John Strachey's *The Menace of Fascism* in 1933, Chamberlain agreed with Strachey that Fascism was the "maintenance of capitalism by violence." He criticized as superficial Strachey's definition of Fascism as a contrivance of big business. Chamberlain argued for the ruling classes' preference for democratic forms as long as possible, and he supported Bingham's "second choice" thesis of big business' backing of Hitler and Mussolini. Like Bingham, he believed the original vital impulse of Fascism was "definitely revolutionary." Also similar to Bingham's view was Chamberlain's picture of the middle class: it wished to be radical, but not Communist. The lower middle class might eventually combine with the capitalists, but it believed itself revolutionary, though the capitalist class directed these revolutionary feelings "to its own ends." Finally, like Bingham, Chamberlain believed Fascism to be in the process of evolution. It might return to feudalism or it might turn out to be "a necessary phase of a revolutionary process that will ultimately result in economic democracy." In fact, he said, Fascism must either disintegrate into "an industrial feudalism" or progress into a "form of communism."[9]

Between the extremes of these two antithetical positions moved other liberals like the editors of *The New Republic* and *The Nation*. The editors of these periodicals were close to the Communists on events in Germany (especially after Hitler became chancellor), but on the internal development of Fascism in the United States they differed from the Communist position in significant ways. Before Hitler became Chancellor, *The New Republic* reported that he filled German big business with "horror." Like Bingham, the editors believed he was the second choice of the industrialists. "German big business will never willingly permit Hitler to form a cabinet of his own," they affirmed. As late as July 4, 1934, *The New Republic* was reporting the industrialists' dissatisfaction with Hitler. By this time, *The New Republic*'s liberal co-weekly, *The Nation*, was speaking as if Hitler were the tool of the big industrialists. All the original "socialistic inclinations" had been eliminated and Hitler's middle-class followers were in bondage to the capitalists. Hitler was working "hand in glove" with big business. After the June 30 purge of the S.A., *The New Republic* joined *The Nation* in viewing Hitler as the puppet of the German industrialists, their "willing tool" before and after he became Chancellor. Both periodicals reported Thyssen and other German industrialists as the true masters of Germany. In August of 1934 the editors of *The New Republic* declared that Hitler was "held in power by . . . the heavy industrialists who financed and nursed the National Socialist party and placed its chiefs in the seat of the mighty."[10]

Although this last statement was close to the Communist position, neither *The Nation* nor *The New Republic* agreed entirely with the Communist interpretation. Unlike the Communists who saw the capitalists pulling the strings from the very beginning of any Fascist movement, both periodicals seemed to feel that Fascism began as a radical movement. Only later did it become conservative and reactionary. Diverging from the Communist theory on this essential point, *The New Republic* and *The Nation* played down the capitalist plot theory of Fascism when applied to the American scene. Although they were quick to point out connections between American industrialists and semi-Fascist movements, they minimized the significance of the Wall Street plot revealed by General Smedley Butler in the winter of 1934. As Butler reported the plot, he was to have led a Fascist army of veterans on Washington to take over the government. But neither periodical feared this "capitalist" plot. The editors of *The Nation* warned that if Fascism came to America, it would not be "cooked up in Wall Street," but would be a "pseudo-radical movement" having popular support. Similarly, the editors of *The New Republic* argued that a Fascist movement in the United States would not arise from the wealthy resisting change, but from the masses' demand for change. Since Fascism grew out of a revolutionary situation, its leaders would be anti-banker and anti-big-business. Fascism, according to the editors, began as a rival, not as an opponent, of the labor movement and the older revolutionary movement. Fearing it at first as a "dangerous enemy," the capitalists soon perceived its possible conversion to a "useful ally against organized labor and true social revolution." It was then that they moved to gain control. Without their eventual backing, it was doubtful if a Fascist movement could succeed; when the right moment came, the Fascists seized the government "with the approval of the capitalists already in power behind the scenes."[11]

There are two important differences between this and the Communist interpretation. The Communists argued that Fascism originated as a capitalist plot; Bliven and Soule, in this respect closer to Bingham, believed it to be anticapitalist in origin. The Communists maintained that the Fascists never "seized" power; they were placed there by the capitalists. But Bliven and Soule believed the Fascists seized power, though with the acquiescence of the capitalists. Both interpretations, however, held that it was the capitalists who determined the success of the movement, and that, once in power, the Fascist leader served the needs of the capitalists. Ultimately, then, as the editors of *The New Republic* wrote in 1935, Fascism became a movement "to preserve capitalism in its dying struggle by enslaving the working masses of the people."[12]

This view was close to—indeed, these last words echoed—the Communist position. Although the editors of *The New Republic* and *The Nation* differed significantly from the Communists on the origins of the Fascist movement, both tended to accept the Communist view of it as a capitalist-run system: its aim was to preserve capitalism by violence. It should not be assumed, however, that either was merely following the Communist line on Fascism. The theory of Fascism as an extension of capitalism was in the air and was accepted by many anti-Stalinist intellectuals. The independent radical, Sidney Hook, for example, saw Hitler as foreshadowing the future of capitalism in crisis: "Hitler is not merely an individual; he is the incarnation of a principle, a system, which seeks to bolster up the hegemony of finance-capital with properly administered doses of myth and blood and iron."[13] The problem is much more complex than a simple one-for-one relationship in which liberals were manipulated by the Communists. Faced with the growth of Fascism in Germany, liberals like the editors of *The Nation* and *The New Republic* were haunted by a fear of its possible development in the United States. Drawing from an intellectual milieu in which the writings of such people as Strachey and Dutt were considered intellectually respectable, they sought to understand Fascism. Just as one did not need to be a Communist or a fellow traveler to write panegyrics on Russia, so one did not need to be either to interpret Fascism partially in their terms. Hence it is a mistake to see only the influence of Communism at work; but to overlook all Communist influence on such liberals is equally incorrect.

That the thinking of liberals like Bliven and Soule was independent of the Communist line on Fascism, but not of Communist influence, is most clearly apparent in their ambiguous relation to the Communist doctrine of "social Fascism." The theory of social Fascism was based on the view that Fascism and Social Democracy were "twins." The latter was "the moderate wing" of Fascism. The Report of the Central Committee of the Eighth Convention of the Communist Party in 1934 said that it was impossible for Fascism to win the support necessary to defeat the workers without receiving aid from within the working class. Since it could not win direct support of the masses of workers, it had to gain indirect support. It found this aid and support in the Socialist Party leadership and in the reformist trade union leaders. These leaders restrained the revolutionary activity of the workers and caused them to submit to the introduction of Fascism, or to steps leading to Fascism. "That is why we call these leaders 'social-Fascists,' and their theories 'social-Fascism,'" the report said.[14]

Among liberals like Bliven and Soule, the theory of social Fascism did not appear in any direct form. Yet their editorials on Germany (the German Social Democrats were a chief target of the "social Fascist" charge by the Communists) contain no general criticism of this Communist theory or the Communist tactics. Such criticism was left to the radical anti-Communist press. Indeed, there was often a tacit acceptance of certain aspects of the theory. On the one hand, the editors of *The New Republic* reported the Communist Party's attempts to break up the Social Democrats in Germany without comment on its methods or the possible disastrous consequences of such action. On the other hand, they criticized the Social Democrats for being overly cautious in the face of Hitler's ascendancy and contrasted them with the more aggressive Communists. Similarly, they diagnosed the Belgian Socialists' 1934 "De Man Plan for revitalizing European Socialism" as further enmeshing the Socialists "in the machinery of the capitalist-parliamentary states." These charges of cautiousness and parliamentarianism followed the same general pattern as the Communist charges contained in the social Fascist theory. Again it is important to note that independent radicals who did not agree with the theory of social Fascism made similar charges. Reinhold Niebuhr, for example, wrote of the German socialists becoming "lost in the mazes of parliamentary manipulations and engulfed by the caution of bureaucratic statesmanship." That *The New Republic* did not combine its criticism of the Social Democrats with an equally forthright criticism of Communist tactics in Germany, however, indicates the acceptance of the general outlines of the social Fascist theory.[15]

Behind the editors' tendency to pull their punches when dealing with the Communists lay their hope for a united labor movement in Germany with the Communists and the Social Democrats working together. If this had been coupled with a critique of German Communist tactics, it might have been akin to the Trotskyites' demand for a united front. But since outright criticism was blurred, it was more in line with the general hazy appeal of the later Popular Front in America. The editors simplistically reasoned that since both groups opposed Fascism in Germany, they should unite. The Communists were gently chided for their divisive tactics, although it was their treatment of the Social Democrats as "social Fascists" that prevented any united front. These disastrous Communist tactics were written off as "fanaticism," and *The New Republic* became a mediator pleading for the contestants each to "give a little." Wanting unity, the editors did not analyze the obstacles to that unity nor the question of whose terms should prevail in any united effort. It seemed enough to call for unity. Thus they bemoaned labor differences and labor disunity, urged mutual toleration by German Communists and socialists, and acclaimed the formation of an underground united front. In short, although they were not prepared to criticize the Communists for the "fanaticism" of their "third period" position on Fascism, they were ready and eager for a united front against Facism before the Communist line shifted on that point. When the call came, they were ready.

6

BEHIND THE POPULAR FRONT

Ideology

The formal call for a People's—or Popular—Front was issued at the Seventh Congress of the Communist International, meeting from July 25 to August 20, 1935. After the Seventh Congress the Communists began to urge a united front on all "progressives" against Fascism. This move was the result of a shift in Russian foreign policy to a position favoring cooperative action by the democracies (including Russia) against the Fascist nations; at home and abroad collective action was necessary to meet the threat of Fascism. With this change in the Communist line, the ideas of revolution and of the dictatorship of the proletariat were curtailed, and, after a brief interlude with a labor party, the Communists joined in support of the New Deal. Indeed, the whole issue of socialism was put off into an indefinite future. Earl Browder summed up this aspect of the Popular Front: "This is not a program of revolutionary overthrow of capitalism. It can be realized within the framework of the present economic system by a people's government backed by the organized masses, determined to fight to keep Wall Street and its fascism out of power."[1]

The rationale for this back-tracking on socialism was the impossibility of establishing socialism if Fascism were not defeated. The Popular Front would preserve "the possibility for the American people to choose the socialist path." Thus the Communists argued that the Popular Front was creating the necessary conditions for socialism. Yet, paradoxically, they also urged its lack of socialism as being in its favor. Browder declared: "The People's Front program is not socialism. It has the merit of making no pretensions to that effect. It is openly and frankly a joint platform of non-socialists. But the realization of this program creates the most favorable conditions for gathering and organizing the forces of socialism. No one can seriously pretend to fight for socialism, without fighting stubbornly by all means to create those most favorable conditions." The new policy side-tracked the conflict between capitalism and socialism; democracy and Fascism were now the antagonists. With this dichotomy ever present in their prose, the Communists went forth into the liberal world with their clarion call for all progressives to unite. They formed new, or extended old, committees and organizations to back collective security, to aid Spain, to whitewash the Moscow trials. Permeating this bustle of activity was a sentimental appeal to the "American tradition," to "democracy," and, above all, for "unity."[2]

Many liberals were prepared to answer the call. They felt Fascism was growing in the United States, and they saw its alarming growth abroad. Hitler and the Rhineland, Mussolini and Ethiopia, the Fascist rebellion in Spain, Japan's constant nibbling at, and eventual attack on, China, and the impotence of the League in checking Fascism—all these convinced many liberals that Fascism was not only growing, but that nobody could or would stop it. Moreover, many of the Fascist aggressive statements were aimed at Russia, a country in which many liberals had an emotional stake. This seemed doubly dangerous, for not only was Russia the first socialist "experiment," but she was believed to be the one great country sincerely opposing war. The danger of a combined Fascist attack, with the capitalist democracies looking contentedly on, appeared great in 1936 when the Fascist nations formed their anti-

Comintern front. With the one "peaceful" nation in danger, it seemed to many liberals imperative that they unite with those advocating cooperative action against the Fascist aggressors.

To understand this solicitous concern with Russia, one must understand the increasing sympathy for Russia between 1935 and 1937, resulting from certain developments in Russia. The old foundations for Russian sympathy were, of course, present. Corliss Lamont, Mary van Kleeck, Anna Louise Strong, Jerome Davis, and George Soule all had high praise for Soviet planning and Soviet economic progress during the Popular Front period. In *The New Republic,* George Soule reported on Russia's peaceful foreign policy, and in *Soviet Russia Today* Corliss Lamont, Upton Sinclair, Sherwood Eddy, Malcolm Cowley, Max Lerner, Robert Morss Lovett, and Harry F. Ward hailed Russia's peace effort and her defense of democracy. "In the future, as in the past," wrote Lamont, "it will ever be the strongest of champions on behalf of world peace." To the two previous bases for sympathy, however, was added in 1936 an apparent move toward political democracy in Russia: the new Soviet Constitution. Louis Fischer told the readers of *The Nation* in June of 1936 that the new Constitution revealed that the dictatorship was "voluntarily abdicating" in favor of democracy. Despite a few minor differences with Fischer, the editors of *The Nation* saw "a liquidation of the dictatorship of the proletariat in the civil sphere and its replacement by constitutional democracy." *The New Republic* also joined in the praise. Although neither periodical argued vociferously along with *Soviet Russia Today* and Anna Louise Strong that Russia was a democracy (in fact, they would have admitted that she was not), they still believed, or at least tried hard to believe, that she was moving in that direction. Thus they did not raise their voices to protest when Fischer asserted that those who did not believe in the reality of Russian democracy were "either ignorant or malicious."[3]

To understand the success of the Popular Front ideas with liberals only in terms of fears of the advance of Fascism and of attacks on Russia, however, misses the most significant causes: the "internal" causes within liberalism. By 1936 liberalism had reached an impasse in its attempt at redefinition; it was therefore faced with a "crisis" in ideology. Liberalism had moved, as a result of the depression, from an awareness of the inadequacies of liberal reform to an apotheosis of the idea of planning, an apotheosis in which planning became almost synonymous with liberalism. It became almost an "ideology," but an increasingly irrelevant groping at ideology. For a liberalism stressing central planning leading to some form of socialistic collectivism was applicable only so long as liberals were primarily concerned with the re-formation of society. Certainly, to apply planning to the world of action meant working toward a radical transformation, not simply preserving the basic structure of society. However, when the rise of Fascism seemed to threaten society, these ideas were pushed into the background. Some liberals like Dewey and Bingham continued to believe in the adequacy of planning as a social philosophy, but others, like Bliven and Soule, while not abandoning planning and social change, came to feel that a larger philosophy was necessary to meet the new world conditions. This need was supplied by the Popular Front, which seemed directly applicable to the immediate problem. Immediately it was an anti-Fascist philosophy; it was also a minimal ideology for comprehending the world. That liberals should be in such a desperate search for an ideology should dispel the idea that most liberals had an ideology in the sense of a politico-social philosophy whose theories, aims, programs, and assertions were integrated. They may have been "ideological" in much of their writing—in the use of Marxian insights into capitalism, the depression, imperialism, and war, for instance. George Soule's *The Coming American Revolution* came the closest to being an integrated philosophy of social change, but even it was largely a rationalization of previous positions taken in response to immediate situations. The impasse in liberal thought arising from the increasing irrelevancy of *only* planning, the lack of a completed ideology and the search for one accounts for much of the success of the Popular Front. In short, it was not any ideology of history that led liberals into this union with the Communists; it was their lack of ideology.[4]

By answering this need, the Popular Front succeeded. It is important to recognize, however, that this was an ideology consisting not of a well-developed philosophy of history and social change, but of a series of phrases, slogans, and catchwords furnishing only a bare schematic picture of society. It was an ideology that blurred theoretical differences and well-articulated philosophies. Reflecting the liberal impatience with what seemed to them minute differences of political theologians (*The New Republic* had commented in 1934 that letters received on a Sidney Hook-Herman Simpson debate on Marxism had a "faint aroma of theology, battling at best over concepts and sometimes even over words"),[5] the slogans of the Popular Front obscured such theoretical differences. There was only one big split in society—Fascism and reaction as opposed to democracy and progress. It was necessary for all those who believed in democracy and progress, despite their differences, to unite against reaction and Fascism. "Progress," "forward-looking," "democracy," and "unity" became the catchwords of the Popular Front. And it was these catchwords and their counterparts—"retrogression," "reaction," and "Fascism"—that provided the "rudimentary ideology."

All of these slogans appeared constantly in the liberal press. In 1936 Harry F. Ward argued in *The Christian Century* for a common ground between the liberal and the radical: they were both interested in the future—"looking forward not backward." Though they might disagree on the question of reform versus total change, he said, this economic question was no longer the real one. The real question to be asked of liberals was, "Will they join with them [the radicals] in opposing the attempt of the reactionaries to stop the democratic process?" *The Social Frontier*, an educational magazine edited by George S. Counts, subscribed to the Popular Front ideology in 1936 and 1937 (later it became critical of the Communists). In January 1936 it commented that formerly each radical group had been pursuing "its own 'correct' way." This mistaken

attitude had caused disunity in the "forward looking social movements," and Fascism had engulfed Europe and was threatening
the United States. With its rise, the issue was no longer capitalist
democracy or socialism, but cooperative democracy or Fascism.
Previously separated radical and liberal elements, therefore, must
unite: "A United Front of all forward looking forces is necessary."
Similarly, the editors of *The New Republic* were convinced that
the "luxury of factionalism" could no longer be afforded: Fascism
in the United States had grown rapidly while radical groups had
been making "faces at one another." Whatever the past issues dividing the left, the situation had changed so that now there was only
"one test" for participation in a united front: "Are you for fascism
(under that or some other name) or against it? . . . If you are against
it . . . that is enough." It was better to risk cooperation with people
one did not like or did not agree with on every point than to run
the risk of a Fascist dictatorship: "against a common enemy you
need a common army." Here were the battle lines—for or against
Fascism. Differences in approach did not matter. Even procedural
differences did not matter. As the editors said in a statement revealing much of the fatuousness of Popular Front thinking: "If you
agree with this diagnosis, then you must, we think, agree with Mr.
Browder that common action is imperative and that the way to
unite is to unite; and with Mr. Thomas that the way to begin is on
specific issues." It did not make any difference that there was a
serious matter of debate between Browder and Thomas. Both
were right.[6]

The Popular Front supplied many liberals with a bare scaffolding
of ideology designed to combat the onrush of Fascism. Yet, at its
base lay a simple Manichaean view of the world, indicating that it
was also a substitute for thought. It was closer to an emergency
technique for fighting Fascism than a carefully developed ideology.
The typical liberal writings of the period consisted of *ad hoc* demands—demands to lift the Spanish embargo, demands for labor
unity, demands for collective security. There were, however, two
attempts to create a larger rationale for the Popular Front: one at

the start of the period by Frederick L. Schuman, professor at Williams College, and one in 1938 by Max Lerner, an editor of *The Nation.*

In the fall of 1936 Schuman wrote "Liberalism and Communism Reconsidered." The article was based on the assumption of the common roots of liberalism and Communism—not just their current opposition to Fascism. Communism had developed from a "matrix of liberalism": Marx built his philosophy on the "foundation of Ricardo and Adam Smith." Both liberalism and Communism believed in reason and the common man, he said. The liberal democracies had "reluctantly perpetuated economic and social inequalities through democratic forms of political power" in the hope that political democracy could result in social and economic democracy. Communism had "reluctantly adopted non-democratic forms of political power" in order to end economic and social injustice and inequality. The Communists hoped that in a "classless society," political democracy might be restored. Therefore, Schuman insisted, though the means differed, there were no irreconcilable differences in the fundamental "values and objectives" of the two theories. On the other hand, the ends of both systems were "wholly irreconcilable" with those of Fascism. "The great cleavage between contemporary societies," he wrote, "is not between 'capitalism' (democratic or fascist) and 'communism,' but between those (whether in Manchester, Moscow, Marseilles, or Minneapolis) who believe in the mind and in the government of, by, and for the people and those (whether in Munich, Milan, or Mukden) who believe in might and in government of, by, and for a self-appointed oligarchy of property and privilege."[7]

In order to argue in this manner, it was necessary to show Russia's belief in democratic government, and Schuman offered the writings of Sidney and Beatrice Webb as proof. They had shown that political responsibility in Russia, as in the democracies, moved from superior to inferior while "political authority" moved from inferior to superior. Furthermore, Communists governed not for themselves, but for the masses. Schuman's conclusion? The dictatorship of the proletariat was not even a dictatorship. In terms of mass selection of officials, of mass criticism, and of mass participation in politics, Russia was "democratic." Since both Communism and liberalism were on the "democratic" side, Schuman said, they might profit from each other's experience. He saw a quality of faith in Communism that was lacking in liberalism; but he also saw "brutality" accompanying Russia's advance toward democracy. Thus liberalism needed the faith of Communism; Communism could, in turn, profit by a liberalizing of brutality. But, along with all democratic values, both of these developments depended on peace. And since the shared values of liberalism and Communism could be achieved only if there were peace in the world, it was necessary to form a united front for peace, a front that might even do more than win the peace. Working in common cause, liberalism might gain a new faith and Communism might undergo a further liberalization. If liberalism refused Russia's offer of collaboration, the future would bring barbaric Fascism and a doom of Western civilization. This was Schuman's larger rationale for the defensive movement of the Popular Front—peace and a common exchange of values. Reiterating these views a year later, he wrote: "In ultimate ideals and immediate interests, democracy and sovietism are not enemies but brothers. In closer union and in gradual assimilation between these faiths, freedom may yet find salvation."[8]

Schuman enumerated the reasons for the Popular Front: the shared values, the shared needs, and, above all, the urgency. The urgent note was still present in 1938 when Max Lerner wrote *It Is Later Than You Think*. His book called for a "militant democracy," but it was in large measure a justification of the Popular Front. Lerner advocated enough reform to allow the progressive to feel "advanced," but also rationalized gradualism and tempered demands. This was the period, he said, of "the collapse of high radical hopes, of the mortal fear of fascism." However, it was necessary to demand more than small gains. Lerner's "more" was economic planning, democratic collectivism, and a gradual approach to democratic socialism. He was also for the New Deal, as well as for an eventual Labor Party. Here, all in one package, was the peculiar mixture of reform and radicalism characteristic of Popular Front thinking.

Lerner's book also demonstrates the flexibility and criticism possible within the confines of the Popular Front. Lerner wrote of the "six errors" of Marxism, and contrasted democratic planning with German and Russian planning. He defended the two-party system against the two totalitarian systems. Yet he always avoided fundamental criticism. Admitting resemblances between "the corruption of power" in Russia and in Germany, he insisted that they lay not in the economic or cultural areas, but in "the organization of power." Moreover, the similarities, like "the cult of the leader" and "the suppression of opposition," were "semi-truths . . . far more false than true." The corruption of power in Russia derived from her past: the too-sudden transfer of power from one class to another and the encirclement of Russia by enemy powers. Thus, he wrote, "the current tendency to identify the Soviet system with the fascist regimes is unfair." It only aided those fighting socialism in the United States.[9]

It Is Later Than You Think, however, was more than a compendium of Popular Front attitudes; it was a specific defense of the whole Popular Front tactic. Lerner explained the problem of "sheer survival" that came with the collapse of radical hopes and the increase in the Fascist threat. The radical's hopes for power had been "pushed into the indefinite future." This was where the Popular Front entered the picture. It was a "peace pact" among radicals, liberals, and labor, and a defensive pact against Fascism, but it was also a pact capable of later use in an offensive battle to win socialism. For the present, however, the Popular Front was necessary to preserve democracy. Hence it was "not a choice," but "a necessity." After stressing the need for "sheer survival," Lerner then attempted to make the whole technique seem like a radical maneuver. He warned that socialism could not be won "by the negative slogan of avoiding fascism or even saving democracy." The former was "a resistance to reaction," the latter "a conserving of the best in our past." These were necessary, he said, but not enough. After these goals had been attained, it would be necessary for the militant democratic forces to battle for positive ends: "The basis of a Popular Front must be not only a pact with the middle class against fascism, but a pact of all progressive groups for the privilege of sharing in the adventure of democratic socialization." Thus Lerner's book illustrates how the Popular Front provided all things for all people: radicalism was mixed with reform, and a defense of democratic capitalism was a brilliant flank-attack upon it.[10]

Schuman concentrated on a rationale for international coopera-tion between Communists and liberals, while Lerner provided a justification for the domestic Popular Front. Both were attempting to provide a larger intellectual framework for the Popular Front than the day-by-day practical endeavors of its supporters. Neither, however, went far beyond the basic outlines of the general Popular Front ideology: the strict dichotomy between democracy and reac-tion and the apotheosis of unity. In this dichotomy, Russia and Communism were clearly aligned with democracy and against Fascism and Germany. The belief that one could distinguish morally between Fascism and Communism as repressive social systems, of course, predated the Popular Front. In 1933, Ernest Sutherland Bates, a later critic of Russia during the Popular Front, took Walter Lippmann to task for suggesting that Fascism and Communism were similar in being dictatorships. "As if," Bates wrote, "the personnel and aims of the dictatorship made no essen-tial difference!" He concluded: "The anonymous author of the popular adage that it makes a difference whose ox is being gored was a more realistic philosopher than Mr. Lippmann who pretends that the only essential factor is that there is some goring going on." During the Popular Front period, it seemed that democracy's ox was being gored by Fascism and that Russia, always on the side of "progress" and now backing the democratic ox, was *ipso facto* the enemy and opposite of Fascism. This belief became a corner-stone, indeed the foundation of Popular Front thinking. Harry F.

Ward distinguished between the transitional "group" dictatorship under Communism and the perpetual "personal" dictatorship of the ruling class under Fascism. Maurice Hindus and I. F. Stone emphasized the economic difference between the two regimes: one had eliminated private property, the other attempted to preserve it. Ward, Hindus, and the editors of *The New Republic* all insisted that Fascism glorified war and was a threat to peace while Communism opposed war. *The New Republic* editorialized simply: "Fascism constitutes an international danger, and Communism does not." *The Nation* summed the whole matter up: Fascism and Communism were as different as "night and day."[11]

If the ideology was simplistic, dealing in dichotomies of black and white, it nevertheless succeeded in winning the allegiance of many liberals. This can be understood only in terms of its appeal to certain qualities in the liberal mind. The dire threats of Fascism, even the fact that the Popular Front provided an ideology, could not have compelled liberal acceptance if the nature of the ideology had not appealed to liberal feelings and attitudes. Above all, the appeal to unity struck a responsive chord. "Sectarianism," the editors of *The New Republic* had written in the winter of 1934, "is the heaviest handicap of those who want to change the world." It was sectarianism—the putting of one's particular creed above the common cause—that disturbed them as well as many other liberals. Three years earlier, in 1931, the N.A.A.C.P. and the Communist Party had feuded over the handling of the Scottsboro case. At that time, *The New Republic* suggested that the two organizations "compound their differences, cease battling each other and devote their whole energies to saving the eight lives at stake while there [was] still time to save them." If they did not, the editors said, the International Labor Defense and the N.A.A.C.P. would have only corpses to struggle over.[12]

If one substitutes the Socialist Party and other left-wing groups for the N.A.A.C.P., and thinks in terms of Fascism as the threat, rather than judicial hanging, then one can see what these liberals were asking—that rival "progressive" organizations "compound" their differences in the common cause. If they did not, the corpse of democracy would be trampled over by Fascist hordes. Only in "unity" could the anti-Fascists win. This accounts for the constant applauding of unity among progressive groups and the constant urging of further unity by such liberals as the editors of *The New Republic*, Max Lerner, Roger Baldwin, and Frederick L. Schuman. But these Popular Front liberals were not alone in crying for "unity." Alfred Bingham, although he excluded Communists, called for a "united front" of the laboring and middle classes—the "millions of people." John Dewey wrote in 1935 in support of liberal unity, and Norman Thomas, who knew the hazards and pitfalls of any cooperation with the Communists, was willing in 1934 to make the attempt at a "united front" between Socialists and Communists on specific issues. Although Bingham, Dewey, and Thomas did not support the Popular Front, their attitudes demonstrate the deep response that appeals to unity would find in liberals less knowledgeable about "cooperating" with the Communists.[13]

The appeal to unity was closely related to the stress on "cooperation." Freda Kirchwey, editor of *The Nation*, although not speaking directly of the Popular Front, put this liberal attitude into words a few months before the Popular Front was to collapse: "We must believe, and fight to make our belief valid, that in a democracy people of many minds and varied backgrounds can get together on some area of common ground. From the New Deal down to the smallest and poorest defense committee, we work in that belief." It must have seemed to many liberals that, in the principle of the Popular Front, regardless of its immediate aim, to check Fascism, they were watching democracy in action. Here were people of varied political backgrounds uniting in a cooperative cause. This appeal to men of "good will" to come together reveals the sentimental idealism of the Popular Front. I am not speaking here of the Communists' emotional evocation of Abraham Lincoln and the Founding Fathers. Although Heywood Broun defended it, other Popular Front liberals found this sentimentality hard to swallow. The sentimentality I have in mind can best be suggested by a report by Malcolm Cowley on the American Writers' Congress of 1939. Cowley wrote of the changed intellectual climate since the early thirties and told of a previous writers' meeting of that period when a writer, lost in revolutionary dreams, had slammed a door in a pregnant woman's face. The moral for the intellectual in relation to the working class was, of course: "You can't lead them toward a better society by slamming the door in their face." But all of that had changed, he said. Writers were no longer lost in revolutionary dreams. Cowley applauded the new "interchange of ideas," the new tendency to think of fellow writers not as "rivals," but "as partners in the same undertaking and as human beings to be treated with consideration." It is this sentimental appeal to "partners in the same undertaking" that accounts for much of the success of the Popular Front. It appealed not to what was worst in man—his ego and his selfishness—but to his "best" qualities—his selflessness and his capacity to cooperate.[14]

Cowley's little tale suggests another reason for the favorable response to the Popular Front: it de-emphasized revolution. The liberal had always been frightened by this concept. Soule's *The Coming American Revolution,* for example, had tempered the picture of violent revolution by making revolution essentially an evolutionary process. Although they had seriously challenged the economic base of society in the early thirties, the liberals had always shied away from revolutionary proposals as far as the United States was concerned. The whole idea of starting planning under the existing system kept one foot securely in the door of reform. The Popular Front merely reinforced this tendency. It allowed the liberal to keep one foot, and sometimes two, firmly in that door, while at the same time, it seemed radical enough to enable him to criticize mere "reformers." The liberal could be a New Dealer and a critic of the New Deal all at once. Heywood Broun revealed this characteristic logic of the Popular Front when he declared: "I am an ardent New Dealer but with the reservation that in my opinion Mr. Roosevelt and his policies are by far too conservative."[15]

Unity, cooperation, the coming together of men of good will—
liberals had always accented these ideas, just as they had always
played down the idea of revolution. Thus when the Communist
line changed, it seemed to many liberals that the Communists were
coming over to their position. As Upton Sinclair said, in trying to
explain to Eugene Lyons why a man once branded a "social Fascist"
was cooperating with the Communists: "I do not mean to be ego-
tistical and imply that they have taken my advice, but it is a fact
that they are now saying and doing what I urged them for many
years to say and do: to support and cooperate with the democratic
peoples." The political commentator Quincy Howe made the same
point in 1939. Speaking of various "front" organizations, he wrote:
"All this confusion serves chiefly to conceal the simple fact that the
liberals have taken over the Communists. . . . It is the Communists
who have changed."[16] Howe's and Sinclair's statements suggest the
absence of a sharp break in past liberal thinking. The Popular
Front was, in many ways, simply an extension of it—another reason
for its success. These statements should warn against facile assumptions of Communist domination of Popular Front thinking, a
different thing from domination of a specific front organization.
The Communists did not change liberal beliefs by manipulation,
nor did they "control" liberal thinking. They can only be said to
have dominated Popular Front thinking in the sense that, by providing a schematic ideology, they gave old modes of thought new
meaning. Their slogans permeated liberal thought; the ideology
crowned liberal activity with a meaning. But the slogans and the
ideology "worked" only because they were attuned to the liberal's
previous thought patterns.

In reply to a letter by Max Eastman, the editors of *The New
Republic* argued that the Communists had come over to their
position of "a united front of leftward and progressive forces . . . for
immediate gains, the building of a labor movement and resistance
to fascist tendencies and war." The editors explained that they
"welcomed" the Communists' "conversion" as ardently as they had
criticized their past "disruptive tactics." If this had been literally

so, the "welcome" would have been tepid indeed, for their claims of past criticisms were exaggerated. *The Nation* also welcomed the Communist conversion. Though the editors recognized the self-interest involved in the shift by the Communists, they believed that, since the issue had come to be Fascism or democracy, "the revolutionary lions and liberal lambs" could cautiously come together against "the universal enemy," sustained by "the compelling logic of self-preservation."[17]

The Contours

Drawn together by this logic, the liberal and the Communist did not necessarily merge into a unanimity of belief. There was agreement on certain principles, but within the framework of the Popular Front there could be disagreements and areas of criticism. Earl Browder spoke of the freedom of Popular Front groups to propagandize their economic positions. Harry F. Ward urged Christians to join the United Front, explaining that the right to criticize Communism would not be forfeited, although it would be done with "a different spirit." The Popular Front was not a closed monolithic system of thought. Its very semiautonomy was what was attractive to the liberals, and was another reason for its success. It gave the appearance of freedom and at the same time prevented the disunity that would result from outright disagreements in doctrine. For example, there was agreement on the need to combat Fascism, but there was no need to subscribe to the theory of the "capitalist plot." Bruce Bliven sounded very much like Alfred Bingham when he wrote in 1938 of Fascism's confiscation of private wealth and that the wealthy supporters of Hitler and Mussolini "got it in the neck." Archibald MacLeish, who participated in Popular Front causes, criticized the Communist theory that Fascism derived from a *coup d'etat* of the capitalists. When the Communist writer A. B. Magil attacked MacLeish's statement, the real reason for the attack was not MacLeish's theory (although Magil said that his mistakes derived from it), but MacLeish's audacity in questioning the Communists' basic Popular Front policy: the defense of the status quo.[18]

Even Russia could be criticized as long as her basic institutions were not challenged. Max Lerner criticized her political methods, and George Soule criticized her restricted liberty and the "wide inequalities of income and power." But both cooperated in Popular Front causes. The Popular Front also tolerated criticism of the American Communists. Freda Kirchwey criticized the phoniness of the Communist Party's appealing to Jefferson, Lincoln, and "American democratic institutions," while maintaining an "intolerable control" over its membership as far as cooperation with other Marxist groups was concerned. Van Wyck Brooks, in an address to the Connecticut Writers' Conference in 1939, challenged the Communist members to say whether freedom could exist in the United States under a Stalin. Yet Brooks and Miss Kirchwey participated in the Popular Front. It was not that the Communists did not answer these criticisms. MacLeish, Lerner, Bliven, Miss Kirchwey, and Brooks were all duly chastised, but not in a way that would end all possibility of cooperation. They were not labeled "social Fascists" or liberal defenders of cops and capitalists as they would have been before 1935. It was as if the Communists knew they must defend the purity of their line, but did not have their hearts in it. In fact, there was even a touch of pathos in some of their criticism. When A. B. Magil reviewed Lerner's *It Is Later Than You Think*, he wrote pettishly: "Communism is part of the mainstream of the democratic thought and action of the world. It should be treated as such."[19]

But such "defensive" criticism was only for the critics who had not challenged the basic assumptions of the Popular Front. The principal assumption was the dichotomy between Fascism and Communism and the consequent necessity of anti-Fascist unity. Those who did attack this assumption were subjected to sharp censure. Writing in *The New Republic*, Heywood Broun said that those who yoked Hitler and Stalin and called Communism and Fascism "twins" were acting like reactionaries, and were aiding the

Mayor Hagues of the world. In answer to an attack on the Communists by Max Eastman in 1938, the editors of *The New Republic* wrote that it was "nonsense" to say that Communists were "more on the side of fascism, than of democracy." Of the liberals who co-operated in the Popular Front, Archibald MacLeish came as close as anyone to challenging its basic assumptions, and his challenge really signaled the end of his cooperation. In 1939 he criticized the Communists' defensive anti-Fascist front and urged an "offensive" pro-democratic policy. A defense of the status quo was unrealistic, he said, because the status quo had created Fascism. Therefore, instead of defending the status quo along with the Communists, the liberal should attempt to extend democracy. Not content with this blasphemy, MacLeish went so far as to compare the Russian and German artistic suppression. MacLeish was threatening the basis of the Popular Front. It was possible to reject Communism and Fascism alike, and many Popular Front liberals did so, but to attack its anti-Fascist defensive position and to suggest parallels between Russia and Germany threatened its very foundation. And the Communists realized this. A. B. Magil made an extended attack in the *New Masses* on MacLeish's criticism of the Popular Front's defense of the status quo, and John Garnett set forth the implications of MacLeish's statements in *Soviet Russia Today*. Statements comparing the artist in Russia and Germany, Garnett said, were like those of Hearst—they linked Germany and Russia as "the common enemy of democracy." But the nations had nothing in common, he insisted; Russia stood for peace and was an enemy of Fascism. He concluded by urging on MacLeish and those like him the realization that in the fight between Fascism and democracy, Russia was "definitely and irrevocably on the side of democracy."[20]

Another area off bounds for criticism was labor. For labor provided the acid test of Popular Front concepts. If different groups with the same progressive aim could not work together in labor unions, then democracy seemed jeopardized. The point was made in a report by George Counts and Reinhold Niebuhr, who, acting as mediators, urged that the charter of the New York City Teachers' Union not be revoked and replaced by a new one barring Communists: "The forces of reaction seem to be in the ascendant in our country, as well as in many parts of the world. If liberal and labor forces cannot form a united front, if they weaken themselves in bitter factional and sectarian strife, there is no hope." The Communists were slow in siding with the C.I.O. in its fight with the A.F. of L., but by 1937 they were active in C.I.O. unions. Many liberals felt that they were playing a vital role in the new industrial unionism. Max Lerner defended their "energy and zeal and discipline" in the unions; their influence came from "their responsiveness to the needs and desires of the union members." Even John Chamberlain, a critic of the Popular Front, placed the Communists "among the best trade unionists." If the Communists were "good" trade unionists, there seemed to the Popular Front liberal to be no reason for not cooperating with them in the unions to win progressive measures. Consequently, the gravest threats to union harmony were the "Red-baiters," for, according to liberal theory, Red-baiting only played into the hands of the conservatives. The editors of *The Nation* expressed the standard argument: "There is no reason why Communists should be exempted from the eternal vigilance that trade unions must always exercise against factional controls. But once you begin attacking Communists as such, your next step . . . is to attack progressives for 'following the line.' The step after that . . . is to attack all progressives. And beyond that looms a reactionary trade-union movement."[21]

In the interests of unity, the Popular Front liberal decried union factionalism. But generally factionalism meant anti-Communist factionalism. The editors of *The New Republic* criticized Homer Martin for giving aid to the employers in his feud with the Communists in the United Auto Workers Union. In January 1938 they suggested the greater likelihood of factionalism and "disruptive tactics" coming from anti-Stalinists rather than Stalinists because of the former's "irreconcilable revolutionary position." Thus those who persisted in criticizing the Communist influence in the C.I.O. were subjected to bitter attack. When Benjamin Stolberg wrote a series

of articles on the issue, Heywood Broun reported that Stolberg's
method was "to try and sneak over a punch immediately after
the handshake." The proletarian novelist, Robert Cantwell,
charged Stolberg with supporting antiunion forces, while *The
Nation*, kinder to an old contributor than Broun or Cantwell,
granted Stolberg's interest in the welfare of the working class, but
ultimately came around to Cantwell's point: Stolberg's writing
aided the Hagues, Fords, and Girdlers.[22]

The common tendency to label as Red-baiting all criticism of
Communism in the labor movement had the effect of justifying all
Communist tactics within the unions. But it also suggests the
larger dimension of the Popular Front: the abuse heaped on all
people, left and right, who challenged the basic assumptions of
the Popular Front. As Earl Browder said, there was a "discipline"
involved in the Popular Front. Those failing to keep the discipline
underwent scathing criticism. In 1938 Malcolm Cowley accused
Louis Adamic's *My America* of "smelling of Stolberg and red her-
ring." The same year he wrote of the anti-Stalinist *Partisan Review*:
"Put a green cover on it and today you could hardly tell it from
the *American Mercury*." In *The New Republic* columns of Heywood Broun, Norman Thomas was "strictly a gymnasium fighter,"
the Lovestoneites and Trotskyites were making "common cause"
with the Girdlers and Sokolskys, and the isolationist speeches of
Phil LaFollette "smacked" of Hitler and Mussolini.[23]

Broun, of course, carried vilification to an extreme. But his attitude does indicate the intolerance of divergent opinions underlying
the superficial tolerance of the Popular Front. An episode in
Broun's career is significant here. He left *The Nation* after getting
"tired" of that magazine's policy of "fair play." This was no "ama-
teur tennis match," he warned; it was a fight. Safely encamped in
The New Republic, which never allowed as many divergent opinions to appear as *The Nation*, Broun touched off a debate on free
speech in 1938 when he criticized the Civil Liberties Union for
offering to defend the notorious Red-baiter, Mrs. Elizabeth Dilling,
in a slander suit and for offering to ensure employers' rights of free
speech. Broun suggested that such organizations should "limit

their activities to the services of the underdog." Arthur Garfield
Hays of the Civil Liberties Union replied that Broun's position
would mean surrendering the fight for civil liberties and taking up
the fight for one class. The editors of *The New Republic* joined in
the fray in support of Broun: "Somehow we cannot believe that
aiding the causes of Mrs. Dilling, the Constitutional League, antiunion employers or Representative Hoffman is going to do much
to safeguard civil liberties in the long run." Apparently free speech
too was a matter of whose ox was being gored. Roger Baldwin saw
the implication and wrote that the defenders of civil liberties
could not "play favorites and expect to be taken seriously." The
editors replied that they agreed with his statements, but defended
their position on Mrs. Dilling: "To rush to the protection of someone who is notorious for untruthful attacks upon individuals is
leaning over backward." They were right back where they had
begun.[24]

Broun and *The New Republic* reflected the Popular Front
liberals' ambivalence toward civil liberties. All liberals who participated in the Popular Front did not subscribe to the belief in "Civil
Liberties for Our Side only,"[25] but many of them did help to undermine the concept of civil liberties for both sides. This derived
largely from the division of society in half: democratic and antidemocratic. When one's view of society is complex enough to
include a variety of conservative, reactionary, liberal, and radical
forces, it is easier to recognize the need for civil liberties for all.
But with society simplistically bifurcated, there was a great tempta-
tion to deny, or partially deny, civil liberties to the most extreme
antidemocrats. The genial face of democracy that the Popular
Front wore masked a hidden cynicism concerning civil liberties.
The contours were potentially repressive.

Those Who Said "No"

The Popular Front was established as a defense against Fascism.
Believing that Communism and Fascism were antithetical, the
Popular Front liberal called for unified action of all progressive

people, including the Communists. However, there were liberals who did not respond to this call. The concept of the Popular Front was openly criticized by Alfred Bingham and Selden Rodman in *Common Sense*. Bingham and Rodman believed unity to be impossible among those who had different objectives. Opposing the Communist aim of a proletarian dictatorship, they saw no basis for unity except on "minor incidents." In December 1935 they criticized those wishing only to "defend" democracy against war and Fascism, and urged instead a "vigorous offensive" for a new system: "We are trying to build a new world, not save the old one." As their own demands for revamping the economic system were curtailed, Bingham and Rodman lessened their criticism of the reformism of the Popular Front. But they continued to criticize the idea that the world conflict was between democracy and Fascism. "How can democracy be an issue," they asked, "when it is the Soviet dictatorship that opposes the Fascist dictatorship, and capitalist imperialism in the democratic states that opposes Fascist imperialism?" John Chamberlain also challenged the Popular Front with his analysis of the "limited" as opposed to the "strict" racket theory of government. A strict racket government was the instrument of one class; a limited racket government sought to balance conflicting interests. According to Chamberlain, the democratic liberal should give his allegiance to the latter. Hence the Popular Front was a doubtful technique in preserving democracy, for he suspected the Communists' use of it was "a mere prelude" to establishing a strict racket government—the dictatorship of the proletariat.[26]

Liberals also criticized Russia. In 1937 Charles Beard classified Russia as a despotic government; in 1938 John Dewey denied that democratic ends could result from a class dictatorship; in 1939 John Chamberlain stated the incompatibility of Russia and democracy. Bingham and Rodman maintained a mixed attitude toward Russia, but one that was hardly satisfactory to the supporters of the Popular Front: they mixed high praise for her economic achievements with sharp criticism of her political dictatorship. Occasionally they used arguments similar to those of the editors of *The New Republic* to rationalize repression, e.g., they contended that the economic achievements required the political dictatorship. But if Bingham and Rodman seemed to equivocate sometimes on Russia, it was not the result of incipient Popular Frontism. Rather they seemed to be moved by a desire to temper the sharp edge of both Fascism and Communism in order to avoid American involvement in European wars. And they could not surrender the idea that increases in economic production were "progressive."[27]

However, there were no such limitations on their attacks on the American Communist Party. In 1938 Bingham and Rodman declared it undemocratic and hypocritical on the issue of free speech and toleration. Its original "social idealism," they said, was threatened by "regimentation." That same year they refused to join in the liberals' wholesale condemnation of the Dies Committee. They also repudiated the Popular Front liberals when the latter characterized all criticism of the Communists as Red-baiting. To refuse to criticize Russia or the Communists on the grounds that liberals would "be the next victims of vilification and possible suppression" was also "a form of suppression." Moreover, they thought the American Communists' subservience to Russia ensnared them in "Jesuitry." The Communists were forced to defend at the same time "the Leninist revolutionary theory, the idea of 'collective security' with the great imperialist powers, the American progressive tradition, civil liberties, and the Moscow trials." The effects of this Jesuitry were felt in the labor movement. Whereas the Popular Front liberals argued that the Communists were good trade unionists, Bingham and Rodman suggested the impossibility of being a good unionist if one's main efforts went toward committing one's union to economic sanctions against Japan. The allegiance of the Communist in the unions was divided between the Russian foreign office and the immediate economic necessities. Though they found the Communist movement as a whole "a healthy stimulant to thought and action," it was damaged by "intolerance" and "crooked thinking." In short, the non-Communist progressive could learn little from the Communist.[28]

Finally the liberal critics of the Popular Front went to its roots: they compared Fascism and Communism. The liberal journalist

Elmer Davis spoke in 1937 of the Communists' and Fascists' common belief in the "imperative necessity of liquidating the opposition." In a critical review of Walter Lippmann in the same year, John Dewey agreed with Lippmann that Russia and the Fascist states were becoming identical. George Counts, in *The Prospects of American Democracy* in 1938, and Arthur Garfield Hays, in *Democracy Works* in 1939, rejected Communism and Fascism alike as undemocratic, while John Chamberlain saluted Counts for leading the "counter-offensive" against all totalitarian systems—left and right. And elsewhere Chamberlain praised Bertrand Russell's dissection of the similarities of all dictatorships. Alfred Bingham also drew parallels between the Communists and the Fascist states. He believed that the world was undergoing a transition to collectivism and that both the Russian and the German systems were part of this trend. Thus the "man in the street" who lumped the two together was closer to the truth than the radical who regarded them as opposite. Both systems, Bingham said, had established economic collectivism and had shackled free business enterprise. There was no democracy in either country, and each had a one-party dictatorship controlling all aspects of life. Both had pushed militarization; both had deadened culture by suppressing liberty. There was a positive side, however, to Bingham's picture. By moving toward economic collectivism, both systems had begun national economic planning and had eliminated or "hog-tied" the capitalist class. He also saw the possibility of democracy eventually emerging in both states. Communism aimed at democracy and the new Constitution was a gesture, "but not an empty gesture." By eliminating class distinctions, Germany too might eventually move toward democracy. In either case, though, the hope was remote, Bingham said, and he urged the United States to avoid "absolutist creeds." She should stay out of European absolutist wars and should create a "democratic collectivism" of her own.[29]

In these opinions, Bingham betrayed his mixed feelings toward European affairs: his belief that Fascism and Communism were not unmitigated evils, combined with a criticism of political absolutism and the hope that the Unted States would discover a different path to an abundant economy. However ambiguous his attitude may have been toward Fascism and Communism, it was unfavorable to the concept of the Popular Front. If the difference between Fascism and Communism in economic and political practices was shrinking, there was no necessity for a system of collective security against Fascism or, for that matter, for the Popular Front itself. The formulation of such a conclusion was what the Popular Front liberal feared would happen if one drew parallels between Communist Russia and the Fascist states. If it were once admitted that German and Russian practices were too similar to make much difference one way or another, the whole notion of a Popular Front would collapse.

This examination of the Popular Front's attitudes and ideas, abstracted from the issues of the day, reveals that it supplied liberals with the framework of an ideology. That there were few attempts to synthesize the ideas of the Popular Front indicates that its ideology was a potpourri of slogans and catchwords in place of well-developed thought. It presented a dualistic view of the world in which the liberal had only to choose the progressive side. It spoke in the name of unity and cooperation and, in doing so, appealed to the liberal's sentimental and "cooperative" mind. It seemed to indicate that the Communists had come around to the liberal position and that cooperation with them would be fruitful. It was nourished and sustained by an abiding faith in Russia. Within its confines the Popular Front allowed for minor disagreements, but to those who challenged its basic assumptions it revealed its intolerant side. The presence of liberal critics of the Popular Front demonstrates its failure to rule liberal culture completely. The degree of liberal-Communist agreement or disagreement, however, cannot be fully understood on the basis of ideology alone. It requires an examination of the liberal and Communist confrontation on the crucial issues of the period: Spain, collective security, and the Moscow trials.

7

LIBERALISM FIGHTS
THE "LITTLE WORLD WAR"

The View from America

In February of 1936 a Popular Front government was elected in Spain. In July of that year there was a rebellion of the armed forces and a quasi-Fascist government was organized at Burgos. This was the beginning of a struggle which for three years commanded the attention of liberals and radicals throughout the world. Three thousand Americans joined thousands from other nations to fight against the German- and Italian-backed armies in Spain. Thousands more in the United States anxiously followed the tragedy that was Spain's. The Spanish Civil War was well constituted to engage the emotions of American liberals. A democratically elected reform government had been attacked by a rebellious minority supported by Fascist powers. This was a clear-cut conflict between a "progressive-democratic" cause and the forces of reaction. American liberalism responded by giving its almost unanimous support to the Loyalist government. "I am one hundred one per cent against Franco and fascism," wrote George S. Counts in 1938; "I am one hundred per cent for the legal government of Republican Spain." Even Alfred Bingham, holding serious reservations about the war, was convinced that the Loyalists were fighting for "humanity's highest aspirations." William Faulkner, usually apolitical, joined a host of political novelists in "unalterably" opposing Franco, and Ernest Hemingway journeyed to Spain as a reporter for the Loyalist side. A third writer, an Englishman, George Orwell, joined the Loyalist army, was wounded in the throat by a Fascist sniper, and ultimately learned how the cause he had come to defend had been corrupted by its professed friends, the Communists. But most Popular Front liberals were to remain ignorant of Orwell's truth. Undisillusioned until the end, they remained "unqualifiedly" behind the Loyalist government.[1]

Thus the Spanish Civil War helped to bind the Popular Front together. It emphasized the necessity of unity to meet the Fascist threat. Other issues tended to become secondary to the war; part of the reason for liberal failure to speak out unequivocally on the Moscow trials was the fear of partisan dispute disrupting the unity necessary to support the Loyalists. Liberals were afraid that a Fascist triumph in Spain would mean the worldwide defeat of democracy. Because the Communists also supported the Loyalist cause, liberals and Communists met on the question of Spain. Earl Browder summed up the Communist position: "In Spain the great issue of our day, democracy or fascism, has come to a head." Week after week the *New Masses* diligently printed the same interpretation of the war. *The Nation* and *The New Republic* also reflected this point of view. In August 1936 the latter described Spain as "the battleground of the reactionary versus the progressive forces of the entire world." This attitude, however, should not be attributed simply to Communist influence. It derived from the belief that a democratically elected government had been subjected to a revolt by a group of reactionary plotters aided and abetted by Hitler and Mussolini. Hence it was based on fact and was a legitimate view to hold. Nevertheless, the parallel interpretation resulted largely from the liberals' concurrence in the Popular Front mode of thought. To the Popular Front liberal, the Spanish civil war was even more than a "little world war" between democracy and Fascism. It was a heroic demonstration of the Popular Front principle in action. The fight for democracy by the Spanish Popular Front, according to the editors of *The Nation*, was "a dramatic example" for all popular fronts. At the same time, the Popular Front liberals saw the war as America's war. The conflict in Spain was an extension of the division between pro- and antidemocratic forces existing in the United States, they thought. The attitudes of Americans toward Spain, *The New Republic* reported, followed the lines of their sympathy toward "the same struggle" in America. Spain was the outpost of democracy; a similar conflict might soon take place in the United States. But if the Loyalists won in Spain, Americans might be spared the literal battle. "How . . . can we, who profit by . . . victory, not claim the war as ours?" Archibald MacLeish asked the American Writers' Congress in 1937.[2]

There were some liberals, however, who quarreled with the Popular Front interpretation of the war. In 1937 John Chamberlain denied MacLeish's contention that the Spanish war was "ours." It menaced European democratic institutions, he said. Hence it was a European war. Since it did not menace American democracy, the United States should stay out. Alfred Bingham challenged the Popular Front view that the war was between democracy and reaction. Like the editors of the *New York Times*, Bingham felt it had developed into a war between Fascism and Communism. Democracy was no longer the issue.[3]

But to the Popular Front liberals, democracy was the issue. They believed that the United States should remove the embargo on arms to Spain, an embargo hurting the Loyalists. *The Nation* and *The New Republic* had both favored the nonintervention agreement in the beginning because they foresaw a Loyalist victory if neither side received arms. Unlike the *New York Times*, which called nonintervention "the finest piece of statesmanship," the editors of both periodicals soon opposed it when it became apparent that England and France had no serious intention of enforcing the principle on Germany and Italy. They then concentrated their efforts on having the government lift the embargo.

The Communists also maintained that the embargo simply aided the Fascists under the mask of neutrality. It was illegal—"a gratuitous act of war against a friendly nation," Browder called it. But the Popular Front liberal was not merely accepting the Communist assessment in demanding that the embargo be lifted; the very breadth of criticism rules out only Communist influence. Advocates of collective security like Max Lerner, Frederick L. Schuman, Louis Fischer, Lewis Mumford, and the editors of *The Nation* singled out the Spanish embargo for special condemnation as part of an "unneutral" foreign policy which helped Fascism by depriving the democracies of aid. Fischer summed up their opinion of the embargo when he called it "one of the major atrocities of a cruel age."[4]

Bruce Bliven and George Soule, supporters of strict neutrality, also joined the advocates of collective security in opposing the embargo. They urged a "cash-and-carry" plan under which Loyalist Spain could be supplied with her rightful arms without the risk of United States involvement in war. Charles Beard, an arch-foe of collective security and also an anti-Communist, argued that the embargo was illegal because it violated a treaty with Spain. It was also against the principles of neutrality, he said. The embargo was an insult to the Spanish government and only served the interests of Hitler and Mussolini. Furthermore, it did not even promote the cause of nonintervention, but constituted an "intervention in European affairs." The opposition to the embargo by all ranges of opinion on foreign policy indicates that the Communist drive to remove the embargo was only one influence among many in determining liberal opinion. That it was an unjust embargo was the main reason.[5]

Nevertheless, there were some liberals who did not believe that the embargo should be lifted. John Chamberlain felt that private citizens might aid the Loyalists, but was afraid that government interference in Spanish affairs would result in a new world war. Alfred Bingham agreed with the Popular Front liberals that nonintervention was a farce, but, like Chamberlain, argued against the removal of the arms embargo. In July of 1937 he made a detailed examination of why the United States should not ship arms to Spain. He based his position on the nature of the war: it was not between democracy and Fascism, but was a religious war between Communism and Fascism in which atrocities were committed on both sides. He criticized the American liberals who forgot their own slum children while they participated in "orgies of indignancy . . . for the orphans of Guernica" and for the Spanish children who had "suffered a comparatively merciful fate by bombing." Atrocities were bound to happen in a religious war, he said, and they were not something to cause the United States to go to war. Unlike the Popular Front liberal, Bingham argued it was not a matter of American democracy's sitting idly by while democracy in Spain was slaughtered by a Hitler- and Mussolini-backed reactionary minority. The rebels had become a "real Fascist" movement, a form of collectivism not run solely by reactionaries. Italy, Germany, and Russia were all becoming increasingly alike. It is apparent that the particular form of collectivism did not make enough difference to Bingham to cause him to feel the need for America to choose sides. Though he said that the Popular Front government stood for "progress," he felt that the stakes in Spain were no longer democracy, a new social order, or even Spain itself. Therefore he urged neutrality and the maintenance of the embargo by the United States.[6]

Inside Spain

Whereas the Popular Front liberals' interpretation of the war and their attitude toward the Spanish embargo were not necessarily dependent upon the Communist position, there is less justification for their distortion of internal events in Spain. It is here that the real Communist influence on liberalism is apparent. The distortions were partly due to plain ignorance: the Popular Front liberals were victims of correspondents in Spain who received their information from official, i.e., Communist, sources. These correspondents, who, as Anita Brenner charged, "milked" the "Stalin-ist sources" in Spain, deserve a large onus of blame.[7] But this does not excuse the Popular Front liberals who ignored the informa-tion in the Socialist and anti-Stalinist left press. As much victims of their sympathies as of their ignorance, they did not look beyond the Communist interpretation of internal events in Spain. One of the chief reasons for this was the prestige given the Communists by Russian support. If Neville Chamberlain, because of his role in the nonintervention agreement, was the Popular Front liberals' villain in the Spanish drama, Russia was their hero. Russia alone called the world's attention to the duplicity of "non-intervention." Russia alone lent substantial support to the Loyalists. Hence they refused to inquire "At what price?"

In addition, the Communists' particular line on Spain helped create the passive acceptance of their distortions of Spain's internal news. Their cry of "unity at all costs" and "win the war first; make the revolution later" found a ready response in the Popular Front liberal. Whereas the anti-Stalinist left criticized the Communists for having sabotaged the Revolution in Spain, many liberals praised as eminently sane the policy of placating small business-men and farmers in order to gain the unity necessary to win the war. If the Communist policy had been economically reactionary, of course, they might not have accepted it. But it seemed to blend the right amount of change and preservation so appealing to the Popular Front mind in the United States. The Spanish cause seemed "progressive," but it did not sacrifice in any premature attempts at revolution the unity needed to defend democracy. It was with this in mind (its surrender of immediate revolution and forced collectivization, and its reversion to "liberal principles") that Sherwood Eddy, in 1937, described the Spanish Communist Party as "by far the most tolerant and statesmanlike Communist party in the world."[8]

Attracted by this "liberal" Communist position in Spain, the Popular Front liberal tended to follow the Communist line on internal events. The principal feature of this aspect of the Communist line was its abuse of the groups in Spain whose advocacy of immediate revolution and workers' control of the army departed from the official Communist position of cooperation and compromise. Chief targets of the attack were the Anarchists and the P.O.U.M., a dissident Communist group branded "Trotskyist" by the official Communists. After the first few months of the war, it was almost impossible for the reader of *The Nation* and *The New Republic* to get more than a slightly mellowed Communist interpretation of internal events. Louis Fischer, *The Nation*'s correspondent in Spain, reported the cowardice of the Anarchists at the siege of Madrid, and the editors placed him on their Honor Roll for "unprejudiced reporting" of the war. *The New Republic* consistently opened its columns to Communists and fellow travelers on Spain. John Cornford, a young English Communist, reported that the P.O.U.M. was disorganized and labeled it "semi-Trotskyist."* Ralph Bates, the English novelist, told how the P.O.U.M. troops and the Fascists played football together between the lines. Malcolm Cowley referred to "the brave stay-at-homers of the FAI and POUM." Herbert L. Matthews, the *New York Times*'s Loyalist Spain correspondent, who told the same stories of football games and of the cowardly actions of the P.O.U.M. and the Anarchists, was always praised in the Popular Front press for his objectivity.[9]

The Communist interpretation was never more unquestioningly accepted than with respect to the May 1937 fighting in Barcelona and the subsequent resignation of Premier Largo Caballero and

* Cornford's charges were not necessarily false—he served in a P.O.U.M. regiment. But the label "semi-Trotskyist" for an organization which, although it admired Trotsky as a revolutionary leader, was unconnected with and criticized by Trotsky, implies some bias. The labeling of the P.O.U.M. as "Trotskyist" was common among Popular Front liberals. Herbert L. Matthews wrote of the P.O.U.M.: "A small and dissident-Communist party which for convenience sake is branded with the designation 'Trotskyist.'" See Matthews, *Two Wars and More to Come*, p. 287. This was misleading. The Communists had a purpose in branding the P.O.U.M. with this label: it raised the disruptive connotations which were associated with Trotsky's name in liberal circles.

suppression of the anti-Communist left. Early in 1937 the Communists began their suppression of the Anarchists in Spain. As part of its campaign, the government sought to disarm the Anarchists in Catalonia. Tension between Communists and Anarchists mounted and on May 3 a move, interpreted by the Anarchists to mean a government and Communist take-over of the Anarchist-run telephone exchange in Barcelona, touched off street fighting lasting several days. During the struggle the Anarchists were supported by the P.O.U.M. In the end the government dispatched 4,000 troops to ensure the quelling of the riot. The official Communist version of the event was that the P.O.U.M. and a minority of Anarchists—the "uncontrollables"—had consciously planned the revolt (a "putsch") with the aid of Fascists in order to stab the Popular Front government in the back and seize power. Browder wrote that Franco had expected to destroy the Popular Front army in Spain with the aid of the Barcelona revolt staged by the "counter-revoluntionary Trotskyites of the P.O.U.M." Filling his report with inaccurate information on the strength of the P.O.U.M., the number of dead, and the origin of the fighting, James Hawthorne in the *New Masses* concluded that the revolt demonstrated Trotsky's "chosen" side—with Hitler.[10]

The New Republic and *The Nation* were more moderate than the Communists, but their views clearly reflected the official Communist interpretation. Bliven and Soule reported that the "Anarchist revolt" had augmented the Fascists' hope. They saw the related issues as the Anarchists' insistence upon the collectivization of agriculture against the wishes of the peasants and their determination to withhold arms from the government. The dispute between the "Socialists" and Anarchists over the weapons had resulted in charges and countercharges, the editors said. Finally, the Anarchists had rolled out their "tanks and machine guns." The whole episode, they concluded, might have been worse for the Loyalist cause than the Fascist offensive against Bilbao. The editors of *The Nation* discussed the stockpiling of heavy weapons in Catalonia, the Anarchists' desire to force collectivization, and the generally noncooperative actions of the Catalonia government in the war effort. When the Valencia government had ordered all military equipment to the front, they said, the Anarchists and the P.O.U.M., including the "Trotskyist wing," had openly revolted. This "little civil war" had aided the Fascists: "The dissidents could not have done a better job in Franco's behalf had Hitler and Mussolini paid them." The only "wholesome" result was that the independent Catalonia province had been brought under government control. Such subordination was necessary, they believed; otherwise, "What good are farm collectives if Franco wins?"[11]

When Bertram D. Wolfe, a follower of Jay Lovestone, leader of a dissident Communist group, challenged *The Nation*'s version, the editors reaffirmed their support of the Loyalist government and its action. They based their views, they said, on "first-hand information" from Louis Fischer, their Spanish correspondent. Fischer, in his answer to Wolfe, accused the Anarchists and the P.O.U.M. of "infantile leftism" in their desire for immediate revolution and collectivization. He repeated the Communist charges against the Anarchists: they had failed to supply arms and had been generally noncooperative during battle. He justified labeling the P.O.U.M. "Trotskyist" on the basis of its "violent anti-Soviet attitude." He placed the initiative for the revolt solely on the Anarchists and the P.O.U.M.: the Valencia government had tried to be cooperative; it had pleaded with the Anarchists to surrender their arms before it finally demanded them. But the Anarchists had answered by mounting the barricades and the government had had to suppress the revolt. Concluding with the usual protest that unity was needed to win the war, Fischer asserted that by spreading dissension the result had aided Franco.[12]

Perhaps *The Nation* and *The New Republic* did not portray the fighting in Barcelona as so much of a conscious plot as the Communists did. They made no attempt to duplicate the Communist picture of a web of intrigue leading directly from the P.O.U.M. to Trotsky and from there to Rome, Goebbels, and Hitler. But they did follow the main outlines of the Communist version: it was a *revolt* by the Anarchists and the P.O.U.M. Furthermore, the editors of both magazines accepted the government's case against the dissidents with no consideration of the possibility of legitimate Anarchist and P.O.U.M. grievances. Unity was all that mattered. And, in disrupting unity, the Anarchists and the P.O.U.M. had greatly aided the Fascists. Nor did the Popular Front liberals revise their opinion of Barcelona as the war progressed. In August 1937 Malcolm Cowley, citing as his source an "official of the Propaganda Ministry," blandly reported the Communist version as if it were the truth. Herbert L. Matthews wrote in 1938 that Fascist money had "engineered" the revolt.[13]

After the Barcelona "revolt" had been crushed, the Communists succeeded in forcing Largo Caballero to resign as Premier of the Loyalist government and replaced him with Juan Negrin. They accused Caballero of failing to pursue the war effort wholeheartedly, of not taking action against traitorous generals, and of failing to move against the P.O.U.M. and the "uncontrollables" who were helping Fascism under the mask of "revolution." Although the editors of *The New Republic* and *The Nation* did not join the Communists in heaping abuse upon Caballero, their bias was apparent in their silence. *The Nation* was more concerned about the ouster than *The New Republic*, but neither journal protested when the Communists began their slander campaign against a man whom they had both previously supported uncritically. And the general charge against Caballero—his failure to prosecute the war thoroughly—was voiced without discussion frequently enough in liberal circles to warrant the imputation that the Popular Front liberal accepted at least this Communist charge. In 1937 Ralph Bates expressed this view in *The New Republic*, Herbert L. Matthews seconded it in his writings, and Louis Fischer made similar charges in *The Nation*. Although Caballero's conduct of the war was not necessarily above criticism, the Popular Front liberal's amazing discovery of his incompetence only after he had resigned can be attributed to an acceptance of the Communist charges, rather than to any "objective" analysis of Caballero's record.[14]

By the summer of 1937 the Barcelona fighting had been extended into a larger issue. The Communists were conducting a reign of terror in Spain against their Loyalist opponents. But the

Popular Front liberal press said very little about the government's use of terror. It is true that *The Nation* and *The New Republic* never celebrated the suppression of the P.O.U.M. and the Anarchists like the Communist press. Nor did they openly misstate the facts as Edwin Rolfe did in the *New Masses* when he said that Andrés Nin, the P.O.U.M. leader who had been executed by the Communists, had escaped into Fascist territory. But they did little to bring attention to the growing terror in Loyalist Spain. In *The Nation* Louis Fischer spoke of Negrin's "rigorous campaign" against the Anarchists' "arbitrary acts," but he gave no hint of what that campaign entailed. *The New Republic* was silent on the terror. In November of 1937 Felix Morrow, a follower of Trotsky, wrote to *The New Republic* to criticize a series of articles by Ralph Bates and the editorial policy of the magazine. He accused the editors of ignoring the government's crushing of revolution and its reign of terror against the P.O.U.M. and the Anarchists. The editors answered that the Spain of 1937 was not the Russia of 1917, and that, in any case, the main outlines of the revolution had been achieved. It was not the revolutionaries, but the counterrevolutionaries, who were attacking the Loyalist government behind the lines. Thus dodging completely Morrow's charge of a reign of terror, the editors retained their "progressive" image of the government and tagged its opponents with the slur of helping Fascism.[15]

The Nation did somewhat better in facing the issue of terror. However, the editors argued that war precluded political liberty; war demanded cooperation. They pointed out also that Russia, in her attempt to win Britain and France to a program of collective security, had pressured the Spanish government to deemphasize revolution. Hence "social control" and centralized organization had replaced immediate revolution, and "some degree of repression" was therefore to be expected. But they warned the Communists against terrorist tactics. The government had gone too far in its use of force instead of cooperation, they said, and unless it controlled the "vigilantism" of its supporters, the cooperation of the dissident left in Spain would be jeopardized. Without such cooperation victory "would be an empty triumph." But after this editorial in August 1937, there were no further statements on the suppression. There is no evidence in the magazine of any change in interpretation of Spanish events, which was due probably to Louis Fischer's continuation as its Spanish correspondent throughout the war. Fischer could mention the "unhealthy possibilities" of a Communist-dominated Loyalist government, but, like the Popular Front liberals, in general, he never discussed them frankly.[16]

There were a few dissenting voices among the liberals over the Communist suppression of opponents. John Dos Passos, moving away from the Communist orbit, returned from Spain in 1937 to tell the readers in *Common Sense* something of what was going on behind the Loyalist lines. Alfred Bingham and Selden Rodman were not taken in by the "democratic" pretensions of the Communists in Spain. They acknowledged that the Communist emphasis on control was right in respect to winning the war, but asserted that it only demonstrated that if the Loyalists did win the government would not be democratic. They pointed to "Moscow political methods" being transferred to Spain: suppression and liquidation had already begun. Although they did not condemn liquidation in violent terms, they did provide a glimpse of the internal terror.[17]

But the Popular Front liberal was driven by the need to believe in the uncorrupted nature of the Loyalist cause. In 1938 Waldo Frank, close to the Communists since the early thirties but recently censured for proposing an investigation of the Moscow trials, still could not bring himself to criticize the analogous terror in Spain. His report in *The New Republic* was largely a rationalization of the role of the Communist Party in Spain. According to Frank, the Communists had brought discipline, order, organization, and action to a Spain traditionally characterized by its "national inaction." Their function was altruistic in Spain. The Russian government did not want "future power," but was interested only in helping Spain fight Fascism. It only wanted "a democratic Spain" to serve as a barrier against Fascism. In this spirit, the Popular Front liberals remained loyal to the Negrin government to the end, condemning the revolt of Casado and Miaja, which precipitated the end of the war. Echoing the Communist charges, Louis Fischer asserted: "Defeatism and anti-communism are twin brothers." But with final defeat, it was necessary to face the question of whether the whole war had been worthwhile. The editors of *The New Republic* attempted to pick up the pieces: the defense of Spain had been worthwhile because it had increased the opposition to Fascism. In supporting Spain, people had discovered what Fascism was and who its "friends" were in America. The defense of Spain had symbolized, and thus had justified, the Popular Front. It had demonstrated the necessity for unity. Insofar as the Spanish government had been unified, they said, it had been successful. When unity had been shattered, defeat had followed. The Spanish Popular Front had accomplished the unity of political parties, but it had been unable to achieve trade union unity. This had greatly hampered "the organization of resistance."[18]

The important point here is not so much that the editors were supporting the Communists, who had demanded trade union unity in Spain, but that by clinging to the Popular Front ideology of unity, they were able to avoid reexamining the Spanish civil war. In the spring of 1939 General Krivitsky, an ex-Soviet secret agent, charged in a series of articles that O.G.P.U. agents had engineered the Barcelona uprising in order to enable the Communists to suppress the other parties and the trade unions. Although Krivitsky may have erred in some of his details, his testimony was important. Yet the editors of *The New Republic* refused even to reconsider the Barcelona question in light of the new information. They asserted that the P.O.U.M. had long urged its followers to turn their guns against the Loyalist government, and they denied Communist suppression of the trade unions or parties other than the P.O.U.M. Moreover, they said, the P.O.U.M. was suppressed only after it had "publicly accepted" the responsibility for the Barcelona uprising. When Luis Araquistain, the former Loyalist ambassador to France, accused the Negrin government of having served the interests of the Communists, Bliven and Soule reaffirmed their faith in Negrin. He had stood "for unity and faith in the victory of the

Spanish Republic." Because the Communists had seemed to stand for the same thing, it was inadmissible that they might have had other interests or aims.[19]

Old myths die hard. After the Nazi-Soviet Pact, Ralph Bates was ready to denounce as "utterly unscrupulous" the Communist accusation of a P.O.U.M. alliance with France and the Fascists. But Malcolm Cowley continued to paint an idealistic picture of the Communists in Spain. He attributed their prominent role to their hard work and sacrifice. To preserve this ideal, it was necessary—for Cowley had come to realize the self-interested nature of Soviet diplomacy—to separate the activities of the Comintern from those of the Kremlin. The latter had supplied much help, but only in an "experimental fashion." The Comintern, however, had fought the war "with all its heart and all its resources." Stalin had become a villain, but the Communists in Spain remained unblemished. In January 1940 Cowley was still defending this position. In a review of General Krivitsky's *In Stalin's Secret Service*, he characterized as unfair the charge that the Communists had used the prestige gained by Russian aid "to extend their influence at the expense of other parties." Nor was it fair to accuse the Negrin government of having been Stalinist.* According to the Spanish war veterans that

---

* Both David Cattell and Hugh Thomas deny that Negrin was a fellow traveler or, as Thomas says, "a mere instrument of Soviet policy." Cattell points out that he successfully resisted the Communist attempt to unify the Socialist and Communist parties and that he supported Prieto in eliminating the "Communist-dominated political commissars" from the Army. Thomas cites, among other things, his attempt—kept secret from the Communists—to secure a negotiated peace in the early summer of 1938. Thomas also writes that "the Communist party increased its power far less under Negrin than under Largo [Caballero]." Both agree that Negrin was forced to work with the Communists because Russia was the only source of arms: Thomas comments, "He had no alternative than to sup with the devil." All this may be true, and it furnishes a good argument against the American embargo on Spain. But it does not change the fact that Negrin was "used" by the Communists. He may not have been a fellow traveler, but he did not measure up to the image that was presented to American liberals. See Cattell, *Communism and the Spanish Civil War*, p. 169; Thomas, *The Spanish Civil War*, pp. 433-435, 551.

he had talked to, Cowley reported, the Spanish Communists had "loyally and unselfishly" backed the Popular Front. They had attempted to reach an accord with the other parties and had opposed Caballero and supported Negrin on military grounds alone. Denying Krivitsky's contention that the Barcelona uprising had been engineered by O.G.P.U. agents to discredit Caballero and "pave the way for Negrin, a tool of Moscow," Cowley argued that the Anarchists and the P.O.U.M. had long prepared to revolt and that the P.O.U.M. had subsequently taken responsibility for it. The war veterans had told him of a series of such revolts staged by Anarchists desiring the immediate abolition of government and by politicians seeking peace. Hence these plots, which had been kept out of the newspapers, accounted for the "arrests by the secret police."[20]

Undoubtedly there had been "peace" plots, but what had really been kept out of the Popular Front press were the "arrests by the secret police." In order to retain his former view of the Loyalist government, Cowley was forced to rationalize the terror. The idealistic picture of Spain remained even after the general disillusionment over the Nazi-Soviet Pact.

More than any other issue, the Communist and Popular Front liberal positions overlapped on the Spanish Civil War. Even liberals opposed to the Popular Front did not challenge its point of view with respect to Spain. When Oswald Garrison Villard wrote that Herbert L. Matthews' coverage of the war had been "extraordinarily objective,"[21] he probably did not realize that he was endorsing views obtained from the Communist-run official government sources. But he was. Most probably there were many liberals who opposed the behind-the-lines events in Spain, but, afraid that their remarks would be interpreted as criticism of the whole cause, they hesitated to speak out. It was left to the Socialists, the anti-Stalinist radicals, and a few liberals like Dos Passos and Bingham to publicize the terror.

The Spanish Civil War was emotionally agonizing for all liberals. It was a war which they believed should have won, but which had been lost only because Chamberlain, with the concurrence of Blum, had "sold out" to Hitler and Mussolini. For the liberals the Loyalist cause, as Villard said, was "not only a just one but compelling in its appeal." The two went together. It appealed to the liberal because it was a just cause. It was precisely because the Loyalist cause was a just one—because a desperate stand was being made against Fascism—that it deserved the support of liberals. Norman Thomas was right when he said: "To aid Loyalist Spain is not an act of generosity; it is a debt of honor."[22]

Yet one cannot help feeling that the liberals who supported the Loyalists blindly did the cause no particular service. It is not that the Anarchist or the P.O.U.M. policies were necessarily right, but these groups deserved more consideration than to be dismissed by the Popular Front liberals as disrupters of unity—of a unity which, in its basic features, meant Communist control. Norman Thomas, who disagreed with the Anarchists and the P.O.U.M. in general, could still see the necessity of not abandoning all reforms during the war and of not having Spain "subjected to the dictation of any nation, be it Russia, England, or France."[23] But, in the name of a spurious unity, too many liberals were willing to forfeit all criticism. By refusing to inquire seriously into the possible validity of the charges of suppression raised by the anti-Stalinist Left, these liberals acquiesced in the terror taking place behind the Loyalist lines. To say that they did this because they were under Communist influence states only part of the truth. What was more important was the peculiar composition of the Popular Front mind. If Fascism were literally battling democracy in Spain, it was necessary that there be unity on the Left. Any dissension on the Left aided the Fascists. Moreover, if it was admitted that the dissenters' cause was itself legitimate, it placed the whole democratic cause in jeopardy. For the Popular Front mind could not tolerate ambiguity; it did not understand "critical support."

8

COLLECTIVE SECURITY: PEACE POLICY
OR WAR POLICY?

World War I had left the liberals shell-shocked. Believing that
nonidealistic reasons had led the United States into war—a belief
reaffirmed by the Nye Munitions Investigation in 1934—and disillusioned with the peace, liberals were convinced the United
States must not again be drawn into war. Liberals, international-
ists and isolationists alike, desired peace. They disagreed only on
the method of ensuring it. As Fascism grew in the thirties, the
issue of war became increasingly relevant, and America was faced
with the problem of what foreign policy to follow. The answer of
the American public was decidedly isolationist. Supported by public opinion, Congress passed a series of strong neutrality measures
between 1935 and 1937 in order to assure that the United States
would not be dragged into war in the process of aiding any belligerent.

While the United States was moving toward stricter neutrality,
the Soviet Union was moving away from isolation. Communist
theory during the third period had looked on Fascism as the last
stage of capitalism; the only way to destroy it was to destroy capitalism. But Hitler was growing stronger, and there was no sign
of a Fascist collapse in Germany. Along with Japan, Germany

began making verbal threats against the Soviet Union. Russian foreign policy, therefore, underwent a transformation and she began seeking alliances with previously scorned capitalist nations. In 1934 she entered the League of Nations; in May of 1935 she completed a mutual defense pact with France. And in the summer of 1935 the Communists announced the Popular Front tactic of aligning with liberals and socialists in an anti-Fascist front. In foreign affairs this meant urging the democratic nations to join with the Soviet Union in a system of "collective security" for joint action against aggressors.

Alliance

In the United States collective security was the most important part of the Communist line. The Communists urged collective security as the only true peace policy; Earl Browder said that the Communist Party's program alone would keep the United States out of war by keeping war "out of the world." They labeled "neutrality" and isolation "self-deception" and a "cowardly retreat" before the onrush of Fascism. Russia was "the reliable bulwark of peace" in a world of aggressors; to reject her program would mean to surrender to the Fascists. "Those who will not stand with the Soviet people," wrote John Garnett in 1939, "sooner or later crawl into the camp of fascism." If the United States was to avoid such an ignoble surrender, she would have to join Russia and the other democracies in a system of collective security. The Communists were joined by the fellow travelers in support of collective security and Russian foreign policy. Harry F. Ward called Russia "the largest single factor" in preventing war; Corliss Lamont said that she was "the chief protector" of international cooperation. *Soviet Russia Today* launched hostile attacks on the isolationists for failing to realize that peace for the United States was "inseparably connected" with world peace: peace was indivisible. Despite its warning that America needed collective security for her own interests, Russia's interests were uppermost in its mind. This is demonstrated by the ease with which most of the editors defended the Nazi-Soviet Pact—the antithesis of collective security.[1]

Collective security was a bitter issue; its opponents often lumped all proponents together as the war party or warmongers on the left. The charges derived from the belief that collective security was designed to bring the United States into the next war on the side of Russia. The effect was to make the collective security program solely a Communist program and its advocates merely Communist dupes. This was unfortunate because it simplified a complex matter: though many supporters of collective security were deeply influenced by their Russian bias, the issue should not be understood solely in these terms. It is necessary to examine a number of liberal proponents, some biased toward Russia, in order to see the spectrum of liberal thought.

Frederick L. Schuman was very helpful to the Communists because he brought to the side of collective security the prestige of supposedly impartial scholarship. In Schuman's writings collective security became the "price of peace." At the same time, he urged on the United States an independent policy (embargoes on nations breaking the Kellogg Pact). But he also argued that American interests were the same as the interests of Britain, France, and the Soviet Union. Characterizing the League of Nations as "a grand alliance of liberalism and communism" against the Fascist aggressors, Schuman did not hesitate to smear anyone favoring neutrality and opposing the League. With a sweep characteristic of the Communists' own writing, in December 1935 he placed the isolationist *New Republic* in the same camp as Father Coughlin, Hearst, and the Croix de Feu. Peace could be attained only through collective security: a liberal-Communist alliance against Fascism. But as Schuman surveyed the European situation in 1938, he saw the democracies in retreat. With Britain and France rejecting collective security and attempting to appease Hitler, the outcome could only be war. This retreat discouraged Schuman's hope for collective security, and in June of 1938 he wrote that both isolationist neutrality and collective security had "become irrelevant to the problem." In a review of Lewis Mumford's *Men Must Act* in 1939, Schuman admitted the collapse of selective security: "America is alone and must act alone. But isolation is a myth and collective security is a memory."

However, this disillusionment meant no rejection of Russian foreign policy. For Schuman had a bias in favor of Russia that made his writings largely a rationalization of Russian foreign policy. In his world view, among the barbarians of the Fascist Triplice, the irresponsible isolationists of America, and the Machiavellis of London, only Russia held out a solution for peace. Schuman continually pictured Russia as the only true advocate of collective security. England's attempts were always "phony." Nowhere did England appear so infamous as in Schuman's writings. Munich was a "hoax," a conscious arrangement by Chamberlain and Hitler to give Hitler hegemony over the European continent and force him eastward. But Hitler had decided to move westward first. According to Schuman, the belated attempts of Chamberlain to win Russia to a "stop-Hitler" campaign were attempts to embroil her in a war with Hitler in Poland while England neatly ducked out of the picture. At the same time that he was condemning English power politics, however, Schuman portrayed the Soviet Union as a clever *Realpolitik*er in a world where *Realpolitik* was necessary for survival. Stalin was too wise to be maneuvered into Britain's traps and was rejecting Chamberlain's "stop-Hitler" campaign. The bias is obvious: England's attempts at power politics were not only futile, but "bad"—they were aimed at destroying Russia. But Russia's power politics was praiseworthy and realistic. With such a bias, Schuman was well prepared to excuse the Nazi-Soviet Pact.[2]

Even when a liberal obviously duplicated the Communist position, it should not be assumed that his motivation came only from his agreement with all things Russian. During the Popular Front period, Louis Fischer voiced the typical fellow traveler position: peace was indivisible, Russia was the bulwark of peace, American neutrality legislation was wrong, and the proponents of neutrality played into the hands of the Fascist aggressors. In April 1939 he wrote: "It is collective security or fascist aggression, either all for each and each for all or chaos and defeat." Somewhere along the line, however, Fischer divorced his belief in collective security from the *specifics* of the Communist line. Thus when the Nazi-Soviet Pact reversed the policy, he broke with the Communists. If he had supported collective security only because of sympathy with Russia, he would have defended the Pact.

Unlike Fischer, other liberal critics of American neutrality and supporters of economic sanctions against aggressors never accepted the Communist line. John Childs, a critic of the Communist activities in the New York City Teachers' Union, was an advocate of collective security. Reinhold Niebuhr criticized American neutrality legislation, advocated collective security, and even participated in meetings of the American League against War and Fascism, but he did not refrain from criticism of Russia and the Communists. Archibald MacLeish, in backing collective security, lent his name to various Popular Front organizations, but, at the same time, he criticized the Communist defense of the status quo. One can argue that by lending their names to front organizations, these people automatically furthered Stalin's political interests. But this does not dispose of the question of motives, or the question of Communist influence. MacLeish and Niebuhr might have been willing to participate with Communists in collective security endeavors, but their position seems to have been arrived at without any particular Communist influence. Certainly it was not a simple relation between manipulator and manipulated. Even *The Nation,* which called Litvinov an "international touchstone of sanity" and whose advocacy of collective security was buttressed by the belief that Russia stood for peace and for collective action against Fascism, cannot be said to have derived its support of collective security from Communist influence. The Communists' support of collective security no doubt helped sustain *The Nation* in its belief, but of itself did not determine that belief. Freda Kirchwey's quick condemnation of the Nazi-Soviet Pact indicates that her support

of collective security and opposition to American neutrality legislation had other sources.[3]

If critics of collective security were over-ready to interpret
support of it as Communist-inspired, there was also confusion in
the isolationist left between advocacy of collective security and
criticism of American neutrality legislation. The two were often
related: *Soviet Russia Today* consistently urged the adoption of
collective security and the repeal of the neutrality acts. But the
editors never indicated that the United States could have an anti-
Fascist foreign policy independent of Russia. However, there
were advocates of an independent aggressive American foreign
policy who opposed neutrality legislation, but thought collective
security no longer viable. In an article in *The New Republic* in
1938 and in his *Men Must Act* in 1939, Lewis Mumford criticized
isolationists and backed a bold policy of complete nonintercourse
with all Fascist nations and a withholding of arms from the appeas-
ing governments of France and England. It is true that Mumford
arrived at this position after becoming disillusioned with collective
security and that he made no condemnation of Soviet foreign policy; however, his "call to arms" was accompanied by a specific
rejection of collective security. Though the critics of collective
security may have missed this difference between opponents of
American neutrality, the Communists did not. Theodore Draper,
in his *New Masses* review of Mumford's book, had high praise for
Mumford's plea for action against Fascism but serious reservations
about his go-it-alone solution: "As long as he cries 'J'accuse,' he
is magnificently eloquent, but neither his analysis nor his solution
does justice to his passion."[4]

In discussing "war mongering on the left" in 1938, Eugene Lyons
declared: "It is no accident . . . that those . . . who play the
Stalinist game are vehemently for Collective Security. Paradoxically those who are most ready to explain away totalitarianism in
the Soviet Union are most ready to fight a war against totalitarianism."[5] However, the issue was much more complex than that.
Reinhold Niebuhr, who criticized the purge trials, was for collec-

tive security, while Mauritz Hallgren, who lent his name to a smear of the Dewey Commission and a whitewash of the trials, opposed collective security. *The New Republic* apologized for the trials, but opposed collective security; *The Nation*, which apologized to a lesser extent, was for collective security.

Lyons' statement was obviously true of many fellow travelers. But of many liberals it would be fairer to say that, though they favored collective security for non-Communist reasons, they were brought into the playing fields of the "Stalinist game." People like Archibald MacLeish and Lewis Mumford did not advocate collective security or direct American action because they were playing the Stalinist game or because of a readiness to "explain away totalitarianism in the Soviet Union." MacLeish, Niebuhr, and Mumford had, apparently, no misconceptions about the basic nature of Russian foreign policy. They did believe, as Mumford said, that Communism was a "false bogey" and Fascism "the real enemy." But there is no evidence that they believed that the Soviet Union stood *permanently* for peace, as Ward and Lamont insisted. These people were brought to support collective security through normal world pressures. They were willing to cooperate with the Communists because Soviet foreign policy, given the growth of Fascism, made more sense to them than the isolationism of many liberals. But since they entered into it consciously and with some awareness of what they were doing, they cannot be said to have been mere "dupes" of the Communists. Nor were they simply serving the interests of Soviet foreign policy. What did happen to people like MacLeish and Freda Kirchwey was that their support of collective security brought them into relationships with those whose allegiance to it was directly connected with their Stalinism. This forced them to modify their criticism of, and sometimes almost to exonerate, the Soviet regime.[6]

But the basic trouble with views like Lyons' is that they treat collective security as only a Communist issue when it was a much larger issue. The proponents of collective security ranged from League of Nations advocates to calculated *Realpolitik*ers. Largely an understandable reaction to the rise of Fascism—it seemed logical that anti-Fascist nations combine in their own defense—the idea of collective security would have had a large liberal following even if the Communists had never adopted it as part of their program. That they did, of course, brought them into the forefront. Their support increased the number of adherents, and they mobilized many of the organizations supporting collective security. They channeled the collective-security emotions into a series of front organizations and, at the same time, provided a glaze of slogans and catchwords. Most unfortunate, the relationships that were established between them and the collective-security liberals caused many of the latter to equivocate in their attitudes toward Russian totalitarianism. The relationship was close enough and the effects morally ambiguous enough without making the issue solely a Communist issue.

Isolation

The alliance for collective security was at no time as monolithic as it appeared, but its adherents all believed that the neutrality policy of the United States did nothing to prevent war and, indeed, aided countries provoking war. Standing in opposition to these collective-security liberals were a number of liberals who believed that America's peace cause was better served by strict neutrality. These opponents of collective security did not all have the same beliefs, but their attitudes and ideas reveal a shared pattern of thought. Composing the so-called "peace party" were the magazine editors Bruce Bliven, George Soule, Alfred Bingham, and Selden Rodman; the popular economists Stuart Chase and John T. Flynn; the journalists John Chamberlain, Oswald Garrison Villard, and William Henry Chamberlin; the political writers Elmer Davis, Quincy Howe, and C. Hartley Grattan; and such leading liberals as Charles Beard and John Dewey.

Among the shared beliefs of these men was the feeling that America's problems were not the same as Europe's. Charles

Beard supported this view when he wrote of Europe as a land of "ambition" and "caprice," with "a wide ocean" separating the two continents. John T. Flynn seconded Beard's opinion, declaring that there was not "a single issue" between the United States and any other country that could get America into war. This meant that if America went to war, it would be over somebody else's problems; hence it should be somebody's else's war. America's job was to avoid these foreign problems. Alfred Bingham voiced the same belief when he opposed the United States' intervention in Europe's religious wars; she should rebuild her own institutions and pursue her own path toward democratic collectivism. The old frontier attitude was right: "Europe's quarrels are not ours. America has its own faith. It is a faith which requires no venomous religious wars for its fulfillment." Closely related to this isolationism was disbelief in the ability of the United States to solve Europe's problems even if she wanted to. Beard wondered how America was expected to solve Europe's problems if Europe itself was incapable of doing so. And John Chamberlain approved Beard's remark that America was not "smart enough" to solve the problems of Europe—"a continent . . . encrusted in the bloodshed of centuries." In November of 1935 the editors of *The New Republic* said that the United States lacked "the power" to reorganize Europe's economic and political life even if she had "the will." Buttressing these views was the idea of American economic self-sufficiency and American safety from invasion. Beard called himself a "continentalist" because he believed in a self-sufficient continental economy. Stuart Chase wrote a whole book in 1939 to prove the self-sufficiency of the American economy, and Alfred Bingham supported Chase in a review of his book. Chase also wrote that unless America were forced to fight with "bare hands," any conceivable invasion of the United States would fail. And Oswald Garrison Villard, John T. Flynn, and John Chamberlain all voiced the opinion that there could not be a successful invasion or attack upon the United States.[7]

The legacy of World War I provided another major stimulus for the opponents of collective security. Embittered by the experience of the last war, they wanted the United States to stay out of the next one. They recalled a United States manipulated into war by false idealistic slogans used to cover up the real economic motives. In May of 1937 Alfred Bingham asserted that during World War I Americans had gone to die for a slogan—"make the world safe for democracy"—manufactured for them by wealthy exporters and financiers desiring to maintain profits. Charles Beard, although he claimed to reject the "devil theory of war," also was convinced that the United States had not entered the war for her professed reasons, and the experiences of the war made him cynical about the big words for which wars were supposedly fought. The American people had gone to war to make the world safe for democracy, but they had received "wounds and death. . . . A false boom. A terrific crisis." The editors of *The New Republic* were similarly cynical about the noble motives and lofty ideals of World War I rhetoric, and were convinced that economic interests had played an important part. Distrustful of militarists, munitions makers, and big industrialists, suspicious of war propaganda, and convinced that any reason for America to go to war would be nonidealistic and entangled with economic and imperialist reasons, these liberals were ready to affirm, as C. Hartley Grattan did in April 1939, "No American shall ever again be sent to fight and die on the continent of Europe."[8]

The isolationist liberals' feeling that American participation in World War I had been a mistake was reinforced by the belief that the Treaty of Versailles had created an unjust settlement. Beard wrote that the Treaty had "made an impossible peace." The editors of *The New Republic* argued that the unjust peace treaty, by mistreating the German people, had been "largely responsible" for the rise of Fascism. And Alfred Bingham viewed European disagreements as results of the unjust status quo. England and France were trying to preserve it, Germany to upset it. But the greatest lesson of the war was that democracy and war were incompatible. As C. Hartley Grattan said, war was the "enemy of democracy."

The New Republic editorialized that the last war had taught Americans that democracy was "suspended" during war, and Oswald Garrison Villard predicted "a fascist dictatorship" if the United States intervened in a European war. Villard, John Haynes Holmes, Elmer Davis, John Chamberlain, C. Hartley Grattan, Stuart Chase, and John Dewey all believed that democracy would end the minute war began. Perhaps the best expression of this prevailing mood was made by an independent radical, Sidney Hook: "The day war is declared the fascist emblem will flutter over the nation's capital—be it France, England, or our own United States."[9]

Since the next war would not be fought for democracy, it would be fought for something else. Some believed that it would be fought for Britain and France, others for Russia. Beard argued that collective security was designed for British, French, and Russian purposes. Villard, Flynn, Elmer Davis, and especially Quincy Howe believed the policy was designed to compel the United States to defend Tory Britain and her empire in her imperialist wars and her "sell-outs" of Spain and Czechoslovakia. The editors of *The New Republic* were consistently distrustful of Great Britain and doubted her dependability in any system of collective security. On the other hand, Stuart Chase, Villard, and John Chamberlain were suspicious of collective security involving the United States in a defense of Communist Russia. The editors of *Common Sense* feared both. Selden Rodman wrote that the call to make the world safe for democracy would mean a defense of British imperialist interests, and Alfred Bingham felt that in the next war the United States would be fighting for British and French colonies—not Britain and France. At the same time, Bingham saw the battle in Spain as a war between Communism and Fascism. This was becoming the issue in Europe, he said, but it was not "America's battle." She should keep out.[10]

According to Bingham and Rodman, therefore, the fight in Europe was a battle for the status quo, a defense of imperialism, a religious war between the two rival political religions—not a fight between Fascism and democracy, as the advocates of collective security said. In September 1938 they illustrated this point by saying that the conflict in Europe was between Russian and Fascist dictators and capitalist imperialism and Fascist imperialism. Even the editors of *The New Republic*, generally subscribers to the Popular Front division of the world into democratic and Fascist camps, went so far as to refute this doctrine in their rejection of collective security. It was too "black and white to be true," they wrote in 1936. The struggle could just as easily be described as a conflict between the democratic nations who had what they wanted and the Fascist nations who were still "hungry," a division of the world into "haves" and "have-nots" that the Communists always condemned.[11]

The opponents of collective security also set forth a very practical argument: the economic sanctions that collective security would entail would not work and might easily lead to war instead. John Dewey had written in 1932 that economic sanctions, instead of forcing a belligerent to retreat, would cause him to rebel in anger. And in 1938 Charles Beard argued that collective security ran the risk of backfiring—it was liable to antagonize the aggressor into war. *The New Republic* led these pragmatic attacks on sanctions and collective security. In 1932 the editors opposed League sanctions against Japan as designed to incite war; the way toward peace was through the elimination of the causes of war. In 1936 they argued that economic sanctions were "a mild bluff" unless supported by military sanctions. Unlike the editors of *The Nation*, they did not believe economic sanctions alone, "honestly applied," would ensure peace. Since no one seemed willing to back economic sanctions with military sanctions, it was better not to risk the use of any sanctions at all. Moreover, they argued, there was no evidence of even a serious application of economic sanctions (England and France were already negotiating with Hitler). There was no evidence that Hitler would refrain from war if he were certain the League would apply sanctions. In 1937 Bliven wrote of the uselessness of taking part in a "bluffing game" with Fascist nations. The United States was being asked to threaten a war that she had no intention of waging, and this would not work. Hitler was willing to fight and would "always outbluff the democracies." Therefore, it was preferable for the United States not to pretend that she was willing to fight when, in fact, she was not: "Any half-hearted attempt at coercion is worse than none."[12]

Unlike the proponents of collective security, who endorsed Roosevelt's post-1937 moves toward stronger policy against Fascism, the liberal opponents were critical of the New Deal foreign policy. Beard denounced Roosevelt for his armament spending, for his steps toward a policy of collective security, and for generally meddling in European affairs. The editors of *The New Republic* condemned Roosevelt for trying to loosen the neutrality legislation and for wanting to help Britain in the post-Munich period. In place of a policy of collective security and involvement in European affairs, these liberals supported stricter neutrality legislation. Most of them favored tightening the 1935 and 1937 neutrality legislation to remove the President's discretionary power in putting it into effect: Beard, Villard, Flynn, and Chase all favored mandatory neutrality. *The New Republic* supported the neutrality acts of 1935 and 1937, in spite of the imperfection of allowing the President too great a discretion in applying embargoes. The ideal neutrality legislation, as set forth by the editors in February 1937, would include a complete embargo on war material and would forbid American citizens to travel in belligerent countries or war zones, not simply allow them to travel at their own risk. They would allow a "cash-and-carry" policy on raw material useful to warring countries. Alfred Bingham and Quincy Howe went even further than Bliven and Soule. Howe opposed the "cash-and-carry" provision and urged a disallowance of all trade with warring nations. And Bingham thought "cash-and-carry" proposals might provide a fatal loophole. The implication was that he, too, desired a complete embargo on trade with nations at war.[13]

None of the anti-collective security liberals wanted to aid Fascism by their neutrality position, and the editors of *The New Republic* were particularly concerned on this score. They argued that, in practice, the neutrality acts would help the democracies while they kept the United States out of war. Although neutrality would damage English and French trade (the Soviet Union was "nearly self-sustaining"), it would be "ruinous" to Japan (she had more American trade than China) and would reinforce a British blockade against Germany. Moreover, the "cash-and-carry" policy would aid England and France—they had the monetary supplies and the control of the seas. Thus the editors refuted the supporters of collective security who said that neutrality legislation aided the Fascist nations. Instead, they wrote in October of 1938, the Neutrality Act made the United States "virtually an economic ally" of the enemies of Hitler and Mussolini.[14]

That *The New Republic* was so anxious that neutrality legislation not be interpreted as pro-Fascist, or even as antidemocratic, indicates that there were tensions and cleavages within the "peace party." Oswald Garrison Villard, Elmer Davis, Bliven, and Soule all criticized Munich severely, but Alfred Bingham and William Henry Chamberlin defended Munich for having avoided war. The latter also regarded Russia as a potential aggressor, but John Chamberlain, a frequent critic of Russia and Communism, believed her to be sincere in desiring peace. The clearest division was between the editors of *The New Republic* and the editors of *Common Sense*. Bingham and Rodman refuted the Communist position that the world division was between Fascism and democracy. In 1937 Bingham accused the Communists of attempting to drag America into a new war under the old slogan of a defense of democracy. The Communists, he charged, had refused to discuss their policy honestly: they were for the defense of the Soviet Union, but they had skillfully coined the slogan of democracy versus Fascism. Dangerous because the United States' entrance into the next war would not be for democracy, the slogan was also false because it avoided the primary conflict in Europe: Communism versus Fascism. Bingham viewed this as a strange conflict since Russia and Germany, as participants in the worldwide movement toward collectivism, were becoming so alike that their differences were not worth fighting over. Hence the "anti-Fascist" liberals with a double standard of morality where Russia and Germany were concerned were wrong. Ridiculing the liberals who believed that there was an essential difference between Germany and Russia and thus were fearful of a German attack upon Russia, he wrote in 1938: "A triumphant Hitler would have no more incentive to attack the vast strength of the Soviet Union, after establishing himself in Southeastern Europe than the Soviet Union . . . has today of attacking Hitler."[15]

This statement was characteristic of *Common Sense*'s constant minimization of the external dangers of Fascism. It described world conquest by the Fascist nations as "dream stuff." Hitler, the editors said, only desired the necessary territory and resources to make Germany self-sufficient and Mussolini only wanted "a new Roman Empire" in the Mediterranean region. Nor did they regard Fascism as reactionary. It was autocratic collectivism to be sure and the United States should avoid taking the same path, but it had the potential to make possible a more humane life. Thus Bingham and Rodman did not assign Fascism to perdition; the "blood-dripping monster" of Fascism was a myth. It was simply the result of tension arising in the world trend toward collectivism and could be explained in terms of "have" and "have-not" nations. It was not the "aggressor powers" that were at fault, but the status quo. A solution required revision of the status quo, and revisions required economic appeasement guaranteeing Germany her raw materials and food supplies. They proposed peace conferences to solve the economic problems of the world: world economic planning was necessary to prevent war. Yet they were not alarmed at the advances of the Fascist nations. Brushing aside Czechoslovakia as a monstrosity created by Versailles and maintaining that the possible German conquest of the Balkan peninsula was no threat to civilization, the editors were unperturbed by the possibility of Hitler's success in his designs: "What if Hitler does extend his crazy swastika to the Adriatic and Aegean? Mad dictators in the past have occasionally swept away a lot of rubbish in their brutal conquests. But they make mistakes. And they die." There were even possible advantages in such a conquest. An integrated Europe, a program they favored, required the disappearance of small countries. Thus in May of 1939 they wrote that the extinction of Austria, Czechoslovakia, and Albania might be "worth the price of temporary horrors." They added: "Certainly those horrors are less than would follow a general war. Hitler will not live forever, but an integrated Europe is essential to civilization."[16]

This moral obtuseness and complacency in the face of Fascist aggression clearly distinguishes Bingham and Rodman from Bliven and Soule, whose alarmed reaction tolerated no such possibility. Bliven and Soule did agree with Bingham and Rodman that the best way to fight Fascism was to make the American economy work, and they even suggested economic terms for the appeasement of Hitler. But they were much more critical of Fascism and much less sanguine about economic appeasement. They accepted the barbaric and reactionary character of Fascism and believed in its designs on Europe, especially Russia. It was the pro-Russian aspect that most clearly differentiated Bliven and Soule from Bingham and Rodman. *The New Republic* constantly reported the danger of a Fascist attack on Russia. It portrayed Russia as being desirous of peace and described her foreign policy as the only honest one in Europe. In fact, their views on European affairs were similar to Frederick L. Schuman's contention that the English and French leaders were playing ball with Hitler, that they were trying to isolate Russia and turn Hitler against her. Russia and Germany were not two similar nations, as in Bingham's opinion. They were opposites.[17]

In criticizing the Communists' support of collective security, Bliven took the Communists "more seriously" than other supporters, but he rejected their program. In 1937 he acknowledged that it was a good policy for Russia (*European* collective security would work), but held that it was not a good one for America. Unlike Bingham, Bliven did not reject the policy as a warmongering program designed to ensnare the United States in a new war under a false slogan. Instead, he spurned it largely for the pragmatic reason that it was not good advice: it would not work. The way to stop Fascism was not by collective security and sanctions, he said, but by following Russia's own lesson: the United States should begin to move toward a socialized economy. Although Bliven and Soule had not attacked the Communists violently, their support of neutrality and concentration on internal reform were bound to bring them into conflict with the Communists. Moreover, in rejecting collective security, the editors went so far as to suggest that the issue was not between Fascism and democracy, but between "a group of elderly burglars and another group of young ones." They were not, of course, denying Russia her place on the side of democracy; their whole point was that French and English democratic professions (because of their imperialism) were in doubt. Nevertheless, the editors had questioned the world view presented by the Communists.[18]

The Communists were aware of this crack in the Popular Front: mandatory neutrality and a "divisible" peace were not designed to sit well with them. In an article in the *New Masses*, Theodore Draper charged Bliven with "defeatism." Earl Browder, writing in *The New Republic*, criticized its adherence to neutrality—"the Hamlet-like paralysis that has gripped the minds of *The New Republic*'s editors under the hypnosis of fascism." Elsewhere he linked Bliven with the Trotskyites and "the fascist *American Mercury*." Bliven and Soule answered these charges, but their tone was one of friendly dissent. The Communist supporters of collective security were entitled "to respectful consideration," although their program would ultimately be rejected by "realistic American pacifism." What is most significant about *The New Republic*'s treatment of the conflict is that the editors raised no basic question as to the Communists' aims in advocating collective security. Despite an occasional query as to whose interests it was serving, the editors generally accepted the Communist support of collective security at face value. They acknowledged that the Communists were supporting it because of Russian interests, but did not acknowledge that they were under "orders" to support it. To have done so would have been to destroy the myth that the American Communist Party was not under direct orders from Moscow, but was only in general agreement. Thus, when Bliven used the issue of collective security to deny that *The New Republic* was a Stalinist organ, he overstated the differences it had with the Communists. Unlike the Moscow trials, the issue of collective security did not necessarily affect larger attitudes toward Russia and Communism; during the Popular Front period, *The New Republic* was sympathetic to both. On the other hand, Bliven was correct in pointing to *The New Republic*'s disagreement with the Communists on the most important part of their program. Designed to further the interests of Russian foreign policy, the Popular Front lost much of its meaning if the participants could not be dragged into line on the foreign policy plank—collective security. Therefore, while the differences should not be overstated, neither should they be ignored. It was a large crack in the Popular Front, and it provoked the Communists enough to make them use their "guilt by association" technique against Bliven. [19]

If one cannot draw a direct line from Stalinism to the supporters of collective security, neither can one draw a line from anti-Stalinism to its opponents. In fact, there seems to have been little correlation between opposition to collective security and opposition to the Russian regime. Most of the isolationist liberals were critical of Russia, but this did not lead them into their opposition to her foreign policy. Villard's opposition to collective security derived more from his World War I experience than from his dislike of the Russian regime. Stuart Chase recognized the dictatorship in Russia—though he was not an outspoken critic—but his opposition to collective security stemmed from his belief in American self-sufficiency. Beard and Bingham both disliked much about Russia, but their isolationism largely resulted from the traditional fear of Europe's wars, which they believed would corrupt American progressivism. Bliven's and Soule's opposition to collective security, of course, was unrelated to their attitudes toward the Russian regime. What one can say about Bingham, Beard, Villard, and Chase is that their recognition of the dictatorship in Russia confirmed their opposition to collective security. But there was no root relationship between the two attitudes.

The case of *The New Republic* requires further consideration. In 1938 the social critic James Rorty noted the contradiction between *The New Republic*'s opposition to collective security and the rest of its pro-Stalinist outlook, saying, "In explanation one can only suppose that the *New Republic* suffers from editorial schizophrenia."[20] If one accepts the view that the Popular Front was monolithic and that the liberals were puppets manipulated by the Communists, then one is forced to accept such "psychological" explanations for disparities within the Front. It is true that *The New Republic*'s attitude was schizophrenic, but the disease is not the explanation. If it is understood that, except in certain crucial areas, the Popular Front was not a closed system for the liberal and that the real pressures were not from the Communists' planted cells (though they played a distinct part), then partial explanations for this odd behavior are possible. The real pressures on liberals were the world and domestic pressures which were troubling all thinking men: the rise of Fascism abroad and the threat of reaction at home. The Popular Front ideology offered a means of coping with these threats. The liberals who accept the ideology were brought into close association with the Communists, where manipulation was possible. At the same time, however, because the ideology was not monolithic, the liberal continued to feel the pressure of old attitudes and ideas. Communism, in other words, was not the only force working on the Popular Front liberal. The explanation of *The New Republic*'s schizophrenia lies in the editors' disillusionment with World War I and their indignation at the unjust Treaty of Versailles. The new catchword ideology could not erase these memories. Where the Popular Front did not touch on an issue that had been emotionally and bitterly rejected, the editors accepted its ideology. Only the issue of collective security had these acutely bitter connotations; for this reason it was rejected. However, for other liberals, like the editors of *The Nation,* the previous disillusionment with World War I had been overcome by the rise of Fascism and they were able to accept collective security as an idea making good sense in a world where Fascism was on the rampage.

Collective security was an old issue. Ever since Wilson had declared war, the liberals had been fighting the battle of internationalism as opposed to isolationism. In the late thirties the program became associated with the Communists, but it was larger than just a Communist issue. At the same time that the question of collective security was being debated, another issue was reverberating throughout liberal and radical circles. The Moscow trials were directly a Communist issue (though they contained broader political implications), and in the 1930's they constituted a new experience for the liberal.

9

THE MOSCOW TRIALS ON TRIAL

From August 1936 until mid-1938, American intellectuals watched in consternation and wonder as a series of trials and executions took place in Moscow. Zinoviev, Kamenev, Radek, Piatakov, Bukharin, Rykov, Rakovsky—the names read like a roster of the Revolution—poured out their confessions of sabotage and treason, of plots to assassinate Stalin, and of an incredible conspiracy with Fascist powers to overthrow the Soviet regime. The succession of secret arrests and "private examinations," followed by the dramatic "overconfessions" at the open trials, left the Popular Front liberal dazed and perplexed. Charged with having masterminded the fantastic plots was Leon Trotsky, the exiled co-leader with Lenin of the Russian Revolution. The issues raised by the Moscow trials and the general purges in all areas of Russian life severely challenged the Popular Front. If Trotsky were not guilty and the trials were a monstrous frame-up, one could not distinguish morally between Communism and Fascism. And if the Russian system was not only without political and civil liberties, but was also characterized by systematic terror, there remained little basis for including Russia in a "democratic" anti-Fascist front. The cumulative effect of the trials could not but disturb the "progressive" image of Russia in the liberal mind. If sympathy for Russia survived the trials to a remarkable degree, even the sympathizer was no longer willing to say, as Edmund Wilson had once remarked, that Russia was the "moral top of the world."[1]

The Enthusiasts

But if the Communists were gnawed by inner doubt, it was not for public view. Their public performance consisted in a verbal back-slapping of Stalin's magnificent acumen at rooting out traitors; the applause was deafening. Earl Browder declared it useless to doubt Trotsky's guilt because of the confessions in "open court" and the Soviet government's verbatim reports of the trials. According to the *New Masses,* only an "out-and-out counter-revolution-ary" would believe that the defendants had lied. "The confessions are there; Trotsky's guilt is there." It was as simple as that. In lieu of more convincing evidence, the American Communists were eager to cite supporting opinions by non-Communists. Particularly useful, for it evoked a semblance of rationality, was the reasoning of Mauritz Hallgren. An editor of the *Baltimore Sun,* Hallgren had joined the American Committee for the Defense of Leon Trot-sky only to resign when he concluded that the appeal for Trotsky's right to be heard masked Trotskyist propaganda designed to harm the Soviet Union. Writing after the second trial, Hallgren argued that since the defendants at this trial knew both their fate and their inability to make a deal their confessions must be true. Moreover, the unanimity of testimony, far from proving the trial a frame-up, proved the opposite. At least one innocent person would have "blurted out" the truth. And finally, if the verdict of the second trial was just, then it stood to reason that the same was true of the first trial.[2]

Even more useful, in terms of quelling questioners and persuad-ing doubters, was the argument of Frederick L. Schuman. Schu-man's analysis of the trials of 1937 was valuable to the Communists because he superficially concealed the official version with protestations of his neutrality and of the objectivity and "tentativeness" of his conclusions. But his conclusions were neither tentative nor objective: in spite of discrepancies, the testimony "unmistakably" proved the defendants' guilt. The defendants, confronted with definite proof of their guilt, had confessed. Schuman's "unprejudiced" examination revealed the existence of "a treasonable conspiracy." As for Trotsky himself, Schuman conceded that he was not necessarily guilty of the "specific charges" against him. This was Schuman's show of objectivity. He went on to say that it was implausible that the confessions accusing Trotsky were "all pure fabrications." But even if they were, Trotsky was not innocent: "Should all the allegations against him be disproved, Trotsky must remain under suspicion of complicity until he has demonstrated convincingly that he proposed to remove Stalin and to organize revolution against 'bureaucracy' by methods other than those he is said to have employed." In short, he could not clear himself of having plotted murder with an ax until he could prove that he had actually planned to use poison. By Schuman's strange logic, Trotsky could be innocent and still be guilty.

Schuman's main effort was directed at persuading liberals that a choice between Stalinism and Trotskyism was not a moral choice, but a practical one. According to Schuman, Trotsky stood for world revolution, class war, and opposition to "liberal 'bourgeois' democracy." His fanatical doctrines were a threat to peace and an incitement to violence. Hence, Schuman argued, whether or not he had actually conspired with the defendants, Trotsky must be held responsible for their criminal actions. Again in Schuman's eyes, Trotsky could be guilty even though he was innocent. In contrast to Trotsky, Stalin stood for peace and cooperation with liberalism. Although Russia was not a Utopia, Stalin was pursuing a pragmatic, constructive path. Therefore, he concluded, liberals and Western democracies should ally with Moscow against Fascism. What Schuman's analysis amounted to was a vindication of the official verdicts and an assertion that the issues raised by the trials were unimportant. It did not matter whether Trotsky was guilty or not. The real questions were political and it was politically expedient to side with Stalin.[3]

Others less cerebral than Schuman in their attempts to validate the trials simply appealed to "authority." Prominent names were paraded across the pages of *Soviet Russia Today* in support of the trials: Dudley Collard, a British barrister who had attended the Radek trial; D. N. Pritt, a member of the British Parliament who had been present at the Zinoviev-Kamenev trial; Leon Feucht-wanger, the French novelist. After reading the verbatim reports, Sherwood Eddy had become convinced of the defendants' guilt, and the editors published his views. The veteran crusader for social justice, Upton Sinclair, endorsed the trials and his opinions were duly printed. Especially useful was the corroboration of the verdict by Newton D. Baker, the former Secretary of War who had ordered American troops into Siberia in 1918. Here was an anti-Communist, a friend of the Morgans, a Liberty Leaguer who saw nothing fraud-ulent in the trials.[4]

Hallgren's "logic," Schuman's "objective" analysis, the oft-cited "confessions" and "corroborating testimony," together with an attempt to rewrite history to prove the defendants had never been Bolsheviks, had always opposed Lenin, and had been traitors from the beginning were all that composed the Communists' case for the state. Yet not only did they consider this sufficient but they went on to affirm the beneficial results of the trial in strengthening the Soviet Union. Having rid herself of the "vermin," Browder wrote, Russia was rapidly advancing toward a new life. The trials, therefore, were not a tragedy. According to Browder, it was "un-American" and "anti-American" (Trotsky was another Aaron Burr) to suggest that, though the verdicts were just, such treason in high places proved the Soviet system unsound. In order to allay fears of the demoralizing effects of the trials on the Soviet Union, the Communists and fellow travelers were at great pains to maintain the "progressive" image of Russia. In 1938 Jerome Davis, without once mentioning the trials, reported on Russia's great advances.

In the same year Corliss Lamont denounced as "agitated brain-fantasies" the reports of demoralization spread by "Trotskyists and . . . wavering New York liberals." The *New Masses* spent much time and effort to disprove similar reports by Harold Denny in the *New York Times*. This emphasis upon Russian progress reached its zenith (should one say nadir?) in Maxwell S. Stewart's attempt to connect the trials and purges directly with Russia's constructive advance. In September 1938 Stewart wrote in *The Nation* that the "average worker" had been pleased by the purges, for they had come "exclusively from below." Supporters and doubters of the verdicts, he reported, placed the origin of the trials "in an irresistible popular tide of anti-bureaucratic feeling." The young people in the party leadership had conducted the purges in order to appease this popular discontent. Hence the purges revealed the political pressures of the common man in Russia. Although Stewart said that "as an American" he could not excuse the ruthless treatment of individuals whose crime was "inefficiency, mistaken political views, or—at worst—sabotage," he had signed statements which did excuse the Moscow trials. His whole picture of Russia was of a progressive country, and the purges and trials were part of that progress. They were part of the forward march toward democracy in Russia; the people's voice was beginning to be heard.[5]

The Communists moved in two directions: they not only affirmed the trials and their forward-looking character, but they sought to disarm the trials' critics. According to the Communists, the defendants had been confederates of Trotsky in league "with Hitler against the Soviet Union and the people's front movement." Sam Darcy, a Communist organizer, wrote: "The cheap and facile Trotskyist agents of fascism must be rapidly eliminated from decent democratic society." But this meant more than an exposé of supporters of Trotsky. It meant condemnation of all those even remotely disagreeing with the official version. The bitter attack on the doubting Thomases erupted with the formation in 1936 of the American Committee for the Defense of Leon Trotsky, an organization of liberals and followers of Trotsky wishing to give him a chance to be heard. The original statement by the committee was signed by a number of prominent liberals including John Dewey, Horace Kallen, and Freda Kirchwey (who later resigned). And as part of their appeal, they circulated an editorial from *The Nation* stating that it was Trotsky's turn to present his case. The *New Masses* responded by indignantly attacking the editorial for encouraging "the serious libel that the Moscow trial was not genuine." What had *The Nation* found so "mysterious" about clear confessions in open court, the editors asked. They concluded that perhaps *The Nation* had become "a Trotskyite mouthpiece" and was "the organ of a band of counter-revolutionary conspirators and assassins."[6]

This was the beginning of a long attack by the Communists and fellow travelers on the Committee and the later Dewey Commission which heard Trotsky's side. In January 1937 the editors of *Soviet Russia Today* charged the Defense Committee (because it questioned the clearly valid verdicts) with making "an attack on the Soviet courts and on the Soviet government." Liberals joining the committee were therefore "serving the cause of fascism." Two months later "An Open Letter to American Liberals," signed by a group of liberals and printed in *Soviet Russia Today* with an introduction by Corliss Lamont, affirmed the validity of the verdicts and warned the American liberals who were being approached by the Defense Committee that they were being asked to join a movement opposing the Russian "progressive" program and aiding the worldwide reaction supporting Trotsky. When the Dewey Commission's hearing began, it was immediately attacked with charges of "Trotsky Investigates Himself." In May of 1937 *Soviet Russia Today* printed an article by Carleton Beals, a member of the Commission who had resigned because, he said, the Commission was not conducting a thorough and impartial investigation. Providing welcome ammunition for the attack on the Commission's findings, Beals accused it of treating Trotsky with kid gloves. He called the investigation "utterly ridiculous" and labeled it "a schoolboy joke."

Frederick L. Schuman concluded that if the Dewey Commission were "honest," it could only report an insufficiency of information to reach a decision. But, he sneered, it would probably find Trotsky innocent. And in 1937 Corliss Lamont expressed "regret" that Dewey had turned against Russia, and urged "friends of progress" to support the Soviet Union. When the Commission returned a verdict of "not guilty," the editors of *Soviet Russia Today* accused Dewey and fellow commission members, John Chamberlain and Benjamin Stolberg, of embracing reaction and of Red-baiting. Writing in the *New Masses* under his Communist pseudonym of Robert Forsythe, *Colliers'* drama editor, Kyle Crichton, coupled innuendos on Dewey's intelligence and honesty with charges that he was being used by the Trotskyites and Fascists. In the December 7, 1937, *New Masses,* Michael Gold defended the trials against the Commission's findings: "The Soviet system is indivisible, and if Soviet nurseries, libraries, and schools are a sound development, Soviet justice must be as sound, for it comes from the same source as the Soviet cultural renaissance." Speaking over the radio on December 13, 1937, Corliss Lamont took the same approach as Gold: "The Soviet regime and its achievements" could not be divided. The Commission, he said, had always intended to "whitewash Trotsky." By February 1938 the editors of *Soviet Russia Today* had cast Dewey into "the ranks of black reaction." He had "embraced" Hearst.[7]

Total acceptance is the key to an understanding of the Communists' and fellow travelers' attitudes toward the trials. Not only did they attack forthright critics of the trials like Oswald Garrison Villard and John Haynes Holmes, the prominent minister of the Community Church of New York City, but every divergence from the official position was subject to criticism. When the editors of *The New Republic* wrote that the trials revealed the "Tartar beneath the skin of the Russian" and thus had no meaning for Americans, John Garnett, in *Soviet Russia Today,* attacked the statement as part of their "isolationist illusion." Soule and Bliven had hardly challenged the verdicts, but the mere suggestion that something was wrong about the trials required refutation. In May 1938 the editors of *The New Republic* suggested an explanation of the trials which viewed the defendants as "unsuccessful statesmen." *Soviet Russia Today* pounced upon this hint that the official version required interpretation: "The trials do not need to be explained. They *were* an explanation." To offer interpretations was not "liberalism," it said, but "the worst sort of reaction." At the same time the *New Masses* was attacking both *The New Republic* and *The Nation*, the former for suggesting the trials' damage to Russian prestige and the latter for saying that the trials indicated the "final demoralization of the whole government apparatus" and had jeopardized collective security. Hitler hoped these charges were true, the *New Masses* said, but happily they were not. They simply revealed the "panic and fright," the "doubts and confusions" of the type of liberalism the two magazines had always represented. But, it concluded, clarity and faith were "indispensable" at this time: "Faith in the Soviet Union and in the people's front movement in all countries—if mankind is to be saved from catastrophe."[8]

In May 1938 after the third major trial, 150 "American Progressives" signed a statement vindicating the trials. It warned liberals not to be misled by anti-Soviet propaganda and appealed to them to support the Russian efforts to eliminate "insidious internal dangers." The statement was a call for liberals to preserve their unity in the face of the Fascist threat. But even the signers of this document were not safe from censure, as Malcolm Cowley discovered when he departed ever so slightly from the official version. Accepting the verdict of the Bukharin trial, Cowley noted in a review of the trial record that the defendants had turned to treason and wrecking after "the disappearance of avenues of legal work." To Jessica Smith, the editor of *Soviet Russia Today*, this was too close to Bruce Bliven's suggestion for a legal opposition in Russia. A legal opposition, she said, would mean the "legalization of counter-revolution." She suggested to Cowley a re-reading of the statement by American Progressives (which he had signed). The implication was that Cowley had come close to doing exactly what the statement warned against: aiding the Fascists through anti-Soviet propaganda.[9]

Suspended Judgment

The criticism directed at *The New Republic* and *The Nation* indicates the existence of differences between the Communists' version and the reaction of the Russian sympathizers. When the verdict of the first trial was announced in September of 1936, the editors of *The New Republic* saw no apparent reason "to take the trial at other than face value." Dismissing as "labored hypotheses" the charges of a "staged" trial and forced confessions, they saw—although the evidence against Trotsky himself was not "conclusive" —no doubt of the guilt and Trotskyism of the defendants. The editors of *The Nation* were somewhat less willing to accept the government's version of the trial. Referring to the defendants as "Old Bolsheviks," they attributed the trial to Russia's need to establish unity against her enemies and considered it proof that dictatorships died slowly. Yet they were convinced the Russian dictatorship was dying and considered it equally difficult to believe or to doubt the charges. More evidence was necessary. By October their criticism of Russian judicial procedures and their demand for a hearing for Trotsky had become sufficient to provoke the *New Masses* to call *The Nation* a "Trotskyist" tool. But soon Freda Kirchwey resigned from the American Committee for the Defense of Leon Trotsky and *The Nation*'s criticism diminished.[10]

After the Radek-Piatakov trial in January 1937, Bliven and Soule were not as dogmatic in their pro-government stand. They noted Walter Duranty's (the *New York Times*' Moscow correspondent) acceptance of the verdicts, and they felt that the evidence supported Duranty. But they did not believe that anyone in New York could pass a meaningful judgment on the trials. The editors of *The Nation* agreed with this call for suspended judgment. Still claiming insufficient evidence, they were inclined to regard as "quite plausible" the charges of terrorism and conspiracy, but found the specific conspiracy with the Fascist powers difficult to believe. Slightly more critical than Bliven and Soule, they wrote that although the trials did not cancel out the great economic and cultural achievements of Russia, liberals could not put their trust in such a conspiracy-ridden society. But what disturbed some of *The Nation's* old contributors was the editors' rationalizations: they seemingly excused the dangers of Soviet judicial proceedings on the basis that Russia's judicial system differed from the West; they seemingly excused the political purposes for the trials—the charge of Trotskyism was being used to eliminate all opposition— on the ground that Russia needed "complete unity" in the face of war threats.[11]

By mid-February 1937 *The New Republic* had firmly established its official "know-nothing" attitude. Although the literary editor, Malcolm Cowley, appeared certain of the defendants' guilt, Bliven and Soule said that only speculation was possible. Anti-government theories could be balanced by pro-government arguments, and all one knew was that the defendants had confessed and had been condemned. Therefore "fair-minded persons" should suspend judgment until more facts were available. Although both *The New Republic* and *The Nation* adopted this position, neither was truly "agnostic." *The Nation* tended to give the benefit of the doubt to the government: since opposition to the government's program had certainly been present, it was probable that some had "translated their resentment" into direct conspiratorial action. *The New Republic*, by saying that all one knew about the trials was the defendants' confessions, implicitly gave weight to those confessions.[12]

The New Republic coupled its plea for suspended judgment with a plea for unity. Refusing to see in the trials any evidence of a violation of civil liberties requiring liberal protest, the editors wrote in February of 1937: "The simple fact is that we do not know enough to be sure of our ground; we should therefore be content to let opinions differ and turn our attention to matters near at home." Unity was needed among liberals to achieve domestic measures,

measures unrelated to the guilt or innocence of the Moscow defendants. The contestants were not battling over liberal democracy,
they argued, and it was the job of liberals living under a liberal
democracy to defend it at home. Therefore, the liberals lining up
with Trotsky were letting Russian politics take precedence over
the needed unity at home. To back up their position, Bliven submitted the evidence on the trials to Professor Fred Rodell of the
Yale Law School. From his report of "no real information" on
which to render a judgment, the editors drew the moral: American
liberals should not take sides over an issue where evidence was
lacking at a time when unity was necessary for domestic programs.
There is no reason to doubt Bliven's and Soule's sincerity in wanting unity among liberals or their concern with domestic problems.
But their principal aim was to quell partisanship. Seeking to
discredit dissenting opinion, they insisted that the type of investigation demanded by Trotsky would be worthless because Trotsky
would be the sole witness. Their whole argument for unity was
loaded against the defenders of Trotsky's right to be heard. If, as
they maintained, their own position of refusing to question the
verdicts was the neutral one, then the liberals who were engaged
in partisan activity were those demanding a hearing for Trotsky.
Given Bliven's and Soule's previously announced belief in the
defendants' guilt, and no explicit retraction of the statement, their
position amounted to an appeal to the liberals on the Trotsky
Defense Committee to resign. [13]

That their appeals for an end to partisanship were aimed at the
defenders of Trotsky's right to be heard is particularly apparent in
their atttiude toward the Dewey Commission. Both *The New
Republic* and *The Nation* genteelly sought to undermine the Commission and to discredit its verdict. The editors of *The New Republic* claimed that the partisans of Trotsky were using the trials for
"political purposes," and they wrote that Carleton Beals's resignation had "somewhat impaired" the Commission's usefulness and
had thrown doubt on its impartiality. The editors of *The Nation*
agreed on the Commission's lack of impartiality and indicated that

although Beals's imputations on the Commission's honesty were not necessarily true, they reinforced "the impression of bias." When the Commission returned a verdict of "not guilty," Bliven and Soule shifted the basis of the discussion. The Commission, they said, had been concerned with Trotsky's guilt or innocence, whereas the important question and the one that concerned "most Americans" was whether or not a conspiracy existed against the Soviet government. Less evasive than *The New Republic,* the editors of *The Nation* granted the Commission's discovery of "damaging discrepancies" in the government's case against Trotsky and its demonstration of the "improbability" of his guilt. But they viewed the investigation as a "waste of time" because it could not prove Trotsky's innocence or his guilt. The Commission's findings were inconclusive and should not be called a "verdict." It is significant that the editors of *The Nation* were calling for new evidence on the trials at the same time that they were belittling the evidence of the Dewey Commission. While Bliven and Soule refused to discuss the Commission's evidence, they seized on every scrap of evidence that might validate the verdicts.[14]

Although the editors of *The New Republic* and, to a lesser extent, the editors of *The Nation* were willing to accept the probability of the defendants' general guilt, and although they joined the Communists and fellow travelers in discrediting the Dewey Commission, they did not accept the Communists' view that the trials were strengthening the Soviet Union. As the trials and purges continued, they became more and more concerned with their disastrous effects on Russian industrial organization and Russian prestige. After the second major trial in January 1937, Bliven and Soule wrote that if the confessions proved false the harm done Russia would be "beyond calculation." If they were true, they indicated internal opposition that would encourage the Fascist nations. Continuing with this theme in the summer of 1937, Bliven and Soule criticized the whole entourage of secret police, espionage, plots, and counterplots, and said that the trials proved the new Constitution's promise of social democracy was far away. In August 1937 Bliven wrote that the trials had "altered and worsened" Russia's moral prestige, and by January 1938 the editors were convinced that, whatever the explanation, the trials were "a major disaster." In their attempt to understand the reasons for this major tragedy, Bliven and Soule said in February of 1937 that the trials revealed "the value of free political expression for opposition views . . . as a safeguard against plotting." In June they asserted that the inability to gain a hearing had turned men to treason. Agreeing with this view, the editors of *The Nation* wrote after the second major trial that the conspiracy had arisen from the lack of a legal opposition. This deprivation meant that Stalin's regime was not blameless. It was not simply the "wicked Trotskyites or faint-hearted liberals" who were responsible for the purges, Bliven and Soule declared in January of 1938. The events revealed "their own significance." The implication apparently was that political democracy or at least a legal opposition was needed in Russia.[15]

The spring of 1938 brought the third major trial. Maintaining their official "agnosticism," the editors of *The New Republic* and *The Nation* again insisted on the impossibility of judging the validity of the verdicts. Trying to get at the truth of the purges, wrote Bliven and Soule, was as futile as asking "Who won the San Francisco earthquakes?" Freda Kirchwey was willing to accept the existence of plotting, but felt the specific charges (which included pouring nails and broken glass in butter and infecting horses with cholera) were improbable. Bliven and Soule agreed that the specific charges were "incredible," but found it equally difficult to doubt the sincerity of the confessions. All one could do was guess; their guess was that neither the Stalinists nor the Trotskyists were right. Undoubtedly there had been opposition to the Stalin regime; it was possible that, deprived of the means of open opposition, "sincere Bolsheviks" had been forced to intrigue. But it seemed impossible to believe that all of the defendants had been "out-and-out conspirators" in behalf of Fascism and the return of capitalism, or that the defendants had plotted "so many murders, poisonings or massacres." Thus the defendants were probably "guilty of something," but not of "the extremes of treachery" charged against them. Freda Kirchwey did not even want to guess. "In the end," she wrote, "one abandons the attempt to render final judgment when the materials are so obviously out of reach."[16]

After the last trial the editors of both magazines placed increased emphasis on the purges' disastrous effects. Describing the trials as "one of the world's great tragedies" and reasserting the disaster to Soviet prestige, Bliven and Soule stated that, valid or fraudulent, the trials were incomprehensible to Western minds: "People who can behave like this are simply outside the realm of discourse." The editors of The Nation agreed that the trials were calamitous and feared they foreshadowed a collapse of anti-Fascist unity. Of particular importance to the editors of both periodicals were the flaws that the trials revealed in the Russian judicial and political systems: the absence of Western safeguards in judicial procedures and the absence of legal channels of opposition. The Nation felt that the trials made the whole idea of dictatorship suspect: the evolution of the Russian dictatorship necessitated a reexamination of the theory of dictatorship and of the Russian achievement. But The Nation was not prepared to make a wholesale condemnation of that achievement. "The solid material achievements of the revolution still stand," the editors wrote; "so do the need and desire of the Soviet government for peace, and its opposition to fascist aggression." The basis of The Nation's sympathy had survived the Moscow trials. Nor had the editors of The New Republic broken their emotional commitment to Russia. Bliven called on Stalin to publish the testimony of the preliminary investigations, to make future preliminary hearings open, to legalize the opposition, and even to go into temporary retirement. The appeal, however, could have been made only by one who accepted Stalin's good faith (Bliven assumed that Stalin's "heart" sank at the news of further purges). Although Bliven's suggestions were hardly made in a critical fashion, they did differ from the official Communist view that a legal opposition would mean the legalization of counterrevolution.[17]

It was this call for a legal opposition that particularly disturbed the Communists and fellow travelers. As the purges drew to a close, the question took on increased importance. In May 1938 the editors of *The New Republic* reported a Russian correspondent's interpretation of the trials which supported their belief that the defendants were "probably guilty, though not of everything charged," and had turned to treason only because open channels for opposing views had been denied them. They saw this position as more "credible" than the Communist view—that the defendants had been traitors from the beginning of the Revolution, that the trials and executions had strengthened Russia, and that friends of Russia should have no "regrets." Even Malcolm Cowley, who accepted the verdict of the final trial ("The real question is not why the conspirators pleaded guilty but why they conspired."), noted the significance of the phrase "the disappearance of avenues for legal work" in accounting for the activities of the conspirators. He believed the trials had taught "a new respect . . . for the political virtues of the old-fashioned liberals." It was these views against which Jessica Smith, editor of *Soviet Russia Today*, protested, reprimanding Cowley and denying the need for an "explanation." Undaunted, the editors of *The New Republic* replied that they still believed theirs to be "the best explanation of why revolutionaries become traitors." To this they added caustically: "Apparently the editors of *Soviet Russia Today* prefer the doctrine of original sin." On this theological note, the debate over the Moscow trials in *The New Republic* ended. But it is important to recognize *The New Republic's* and *Soviet Russia Today's* differences were not over the guilt or the treason of the defendants, but over why there had been treason and what effect it had had on Russia and her image and how such activities could be prevented in the future.[18]

Despite these divergences from the official Communist position, the editors of *The New Republic* and *The Nation* have often been charged with having been Stalinist apologists whitewashing the trials. Certainly they were not being truly "liberal" in insisting on the impossibility of judging without complete evidence. Had they been genuinely interested in discovering all possible evidence, they would have supported the Dewey-led investigation. Instead, despite their claim of "agnosticism," they actually sided with the Soviet government in their tendency to assume that the defendants were guilty of "something" and therefore punishable. But to accuse Bliven and Soule and Freda Kirchwey of merely whitewashing the trials is to underestimate their differences with the Communists and fellow travelers. Whereas the editors of *Soviet Russia Today* never publicly questioned any part of the evidence, the editors of *The Nation* and *The New Republic* saw the possibility that some of the charges might be false and that Trotsky might not be personally involved. Jessica Smith insisted that no explanation of the trials except the court record was required, but Bruce Bliven and Freda Kirchwey could not accept the official one of debased traitors as an adequate explanation. Corliss Lamont and Michael Gold maintained that the Soviet system and its achievements were "indivisible"; the editors of *The Nation* and *The New Republic* believed that the trials revealed weaknesses in the Soviet judicial system and in dictatorship as a form of government, particularly in its suppression of a legal opposition. Earl Browder and Maxwell Stewart felt that, by wiping out the traitors, the trials had strengthened the Soviet Union; Bliven and Soule and Freda Kirchwey felt that the whole tragic episode had seriously damaged the moral and diplomatic prestige of Russia. The Communists and fellow travelers "applauded" the trials; *The New Republic* and *The Nation* "regretted" them.

Nevertheless, the final effect was to prevent a basic questioning of the verdicts. By refusing to inquire seriously into the possibility of a barbarous hoax, the editors of *The New Republic* and *The Nation* gave credence to the verdicts just as they did to the Communist version of the Spanish Civil War. By couching their criticism in a multitude of qualifications, they rationalized the validity of the trials. Since they saw the trials threatening the unity of progressive forces, their object was, in part, to reduce controversy and partisanship, and even discussion of the trials and the issues that they raised. *The New Republic's* appeal to liberals to stop taking sides on the issue was based on the belief that if sides were taken, the domestic Popular Front would collapse. *The Nation's* emphasis on the damage of the trials to Russian prestige in foreign relations derived from the fears of disruption in the unity needed among democratic nations in their fight against Fascism. With partisanship quelled, all that remained was the official version or an agnosticism which doubted the parts but accepted the whole. In this sense they "apologized" for the trials.

Opposition and Debate

It should not be supposed that the defenders and rationalizers of the trials monopolized the liberal intellectual world of the thirties. Liberals like John Haynes Holmes, Oswald Garrison Villard, and John Dewey joined such anti-Stalinist radicals as Max Eastman, Sidney Hook, and James T. Farrell to denounce the ruthless terror of the Russian purges. Villard consistently criticized Stalin's "legal murder," and Dewey courageously and eloquently led the investigation of Trotsky. Holmes declared the trials had reduced the Soviet Union to the level of Nazi Germany; answering a Communist critic, he wrote: "In your devotion to Russia, you have made your mind a piece of mush, and such minds I am not interested in." Hook was especially devastating in his application of logic to the trials and to the arguments of the trials' defenders. However, it is true that some anti-Communist liberals who might have been expected to speak out clearly against the trials did not do so. Some of the reasons for this failure are apparent in the attitude of Alfred Bingham and Selden Rodman. At first, Bingham and Rodman did not appear to differ greatly from Bruce Bliven and Freda Kirchway in their evaluation of the trials. After the first trial they seemed to accept the confessions generally, but expressed doubt concerning Trotsky's role in the conspiracy and the link with the German Gestapo. In March of 1937, after the second trial, *Common Sense* published an article by the economist Harold Loeb supporting the trials' authenticity. In April 1937 the editors seemed to give equal weight to the Communists' explanation of discrepancies in the state's case and to Trotsky's and the Defense Committee's evidence seriously damaging that case. By September 1937, however, they were reviewing favorably an article by the English Socialist, H. N. Brailsford, which cast doubt on the validity of the Russian generals' confessions.[19]

Bingham's and Rodman's basic attitude toward the trials, however, had been established in an introduction to the Loeb article. Here they sided with neither Stalin nor Trotsky, but wanted to point both to Russia's great economic advances and to the continuation of her corrupt dictatorship. Whether valid or not, the trials resulted from regimentation which drove the opposition into plotting. The editors' conclusion was a reiteration of their position on Russia: the different traditions of the United States necessitated the maintenance of civil liberties and democratic procedures in any transition to a new social order. As the trials progressed, they pointed to terror and fear as an outcome of Marxist methods—methods to be shunned by believers in democracy and justice. The trials and executions, they said, indicated the "moral corruption" resulting from the doctrine that the end justifies the means, and were another reason for the United States to stay clear of Europe. They revealed the similarities between Fascist Germany and Communist Russia—clear proof that democracy versus Fascism was not the issue in the world. In December 1937 Selden Rodman reported on his interview with Trotsky in Mexico. He declared that Trotsky, definitely, and the Moscow defendants, probably, were not guilty either of terrorism or of plotting with foreign governments. While this was not a complete exoneration of the defendants, the statement clearly implied the trials' fraudulence. Rodman defended the liberals' giving Trotsky a hearing, but felt that the Dewey Commission, since it included two admirers of Trotsky, could prove nothing. His essential point, however, was the failure of the liberals demanding a hearing for Trotsky to recognize that the trials resulted directly from the

Marxist-Leninist philosophy of ends justifying the means. They could not be blamed on a "sinister latter-day sorcery known as Stalinism." It was therefore fair to assume that Trotsky and the opposition, had they been in power, would have "acted in the same way." The lesson of the trials, Rodman said, was for Americans to shun both Trotskyism and Stalinism, to stop "juggling with the comparative methods," and to see their common derivation in one basic philosophy and method. The implication was that America must find a better way.[20]

Bingham and Rodman cannot be said to have equivocated on the Moscow trials in order to preserve the Popular Front, of which they were critics. After the publication of the Loeb article and a pro-Communist comment on part of Trotsky's testimony, pro-Stalinist reactions to the trials disappeared from *Common Sense*. Rodman made it clear that he considered the trials fraudulent and the editors seemed to assume their fraudulence in reporting events in Russia. On the other hand, neither Bingham nor Rodman spoke out strongly against the trials. In fact, the striking phenomenon was that, except for the Loeb and Rodman articles and a symposium on the latter, *Common Sense* never printed a detailed discussion of the trials. The editors' opinions were contained in brief remarks or were expressed in relation to other issues. This failure to consider the trials adequately can be explained by Bingham's and Rodman's belief that the importance of the trials lay not in the question of Trotsky's and the defendants' guilt or innocence, but in the philosophical and political lessons to be drawn from them. As anti-Marxists, they used the trials to condemn both Marxism (as a philosophy) and Marxists—Trotsky and Stalin alike. The political lesson was that dictatorships were perpetuated and that terror was perpetuated with them. They believed both to be the result of the same general philosophy, and the particular lesson for the United States was that it must adhere to its nondictatorial, non-Marxist, democratic traditions. In this inference, they were largely motivated by their isolationism.

Certainly Bingham and Rodman were right in their contention

that much could be learned from the trials whether Trotsky was guilty of not. But ultimately the most important lessons depended on the answer to that question. By saying that Trotsky would have done the same as Stalin, Bingham and Rodman reduced the impact of the trials. The two having been equated, the horror perpetrated by Stalin was diminished. It became merely a matter of who got there first. By treating the trials as essentially a question of a single philosophy, the editors of *Common Sense* tempered the criticism of a particular totalitarian regime.[21] Bingham and Rodman were not apologists for Russia's political dictatorship, but neither did they add much to the voices challenging the verdicts of the trials. Nor did some other liberal opponents of the Russian dictatorship who, although they did not condone the trials, regarded the matter as a private quarrel between Trotskyists and Stalinists.* Carl Becker's biographer says that Beard and Becker both viewed the issue "as a family dispute" and did not want to take part in the quarrel.[22] But when the implications of the trials were set forth, more liberals were ready to take a stand. They received their chance with the formation of the Committee for Cultural Freedom.

In May of 1939 *The Nation* published a statement by the Committee for Cultural Freedom. The substance of the statement was the signers' opposition to all forms of totalitarianism. The controversial aspect was its association of the Russian regime with the Fascist nations. "Literally thousands of German, Italian, Russian, and other victims of cultural dictatorship have been silenced, imprisoned, tortured, or hounded into exile," it read in part. Signed by many prominent liberals, and challenging as it did the Popular Front distinction between Russia and the Fascist nations, the manifesto was bound to have a resounding effect.[23]

---

* Both the Communists and those who forthrightly condemned the trials disagreed with this interpretation. The Communists declared that the trials demonstrated the worldwide link between Fascism and Trotskyism and felt that the issue could not be treated as a personal squabble. They vilified as "isolationists" all those who professed that it was only that. The critics of the trials believed that they revealed more than a private feud. They saw in them a manifestation of Stalinist totalitarianism.

The Nation responded with a plea for unity. Freda Kirchwey urged liberals not to be influenced by bitterness over the Communists' past disruptive tactics. They were currently serving the cause of democracy, she said, and they shared the "larger hopes and fears" of all those on the Left. Thus the Popular Front distinction between Communism and Fascism was sound. Expressing hope for an end to sectarianism, she called for "an era of good will and decency" and "a little factional disarmament." In answer to a rebuttal by one of the Committee's founders, Sidney Hook, she renewed her appeal for unity. Spain had taught the lesson. Communists, non-Communists, and anti-Communists should "forget their mutual recriminations and concentrate on the major task of our generation"—to check the advance of Fascism.[24]

The New Republic reacted by refusing to print the statement. Misleading their readers into believing the Committee had contrasted perfect freedom in the United States with the lack of freedom in totalitarian countries, the editors went on to accuse the Committee of having had "a regrettable lack of historical perspective" when it linked Russia with the Fascist states. Whereas Fascism and individual freedom were incompatible, freedom and the theory of "a socialist commonwealth" were not. Socialism would further liberate humanity, they said; Fascism would further suppress it. Russia's absence of civil liberties resulted not from socialist theory but from her historical tradition. They found "unfortunate" the Committee's support of the doctrine of "neither fascism or communism" because Communism, unlike Fascism, was no threat to the United States. And they ended by slyly smearing the Committee with a Trotskyite label. The Committee had not spoken of America's perfect freedom nor of the incompatibility of socialist theory and individual freedom. Nor did it include any Trotskyists. A series of letters informed *The New Republic* of these matters. The end result was the editors' reaffirmation of the theory of the Popular Front: "We will work with anybody for objectives in which we believe—even though they may have other objectives in which we do not. This seems to us good democratic and liberal strategy." In the face of criticism by Ferdinand Lundberg, a member of the Committee, they defended their Russian record (neither complete praise or condemnation, but "freedom of judgment") and their Moscow trials record (no conclusive evidence of frame-ups). They concluded by applying the Red smear in reverse: they accused the Committee of being willing to apply the Red smear and of having as its "main preoccupation" the expression of anti-Soviet feelings.[25]

The fellow travelers reacted by issuing an Open Letter on August 14 in which they accused reactionaries of trying to split the anti-Fascist front by asserting "the fantastic falsehood" that Russia and the totalitarian states were alike. "Sincere" liberals had "fallen into this trap" by signing the Committee's manifesto. Listing differences between Russia and the Fascist nations, the Open Letter ended by affirming the shared values of Russia and the United States and the need for Americans to guard against efforts to disrupt cooperation between the two countries. The Open Letter had stated that the Soviet Union was "always . . . a consistent bulwark against war and aggression" and that it worked "unceasingly for the goal of a peaceful order." The irony was, as many have noted, that ten days later the Nazi-Soviet Pact was signed. In the issue before the Pact, the editors of *The New Republic* stated that the Open Letter was "less than candid" on the Russian dictatorship and civil liberties, but correct in its "general tendency." American and Russian friendship was "possible" and "desirable." It was clear they had more in common with the signers of the Open Letter than with the members of the Committee for Cultural Freedom. The editors of *The Nation* were unable to comment on the Open Letter before the Pact, and the news of the Pact rendered "lengthy discussion" unnecessary. But, the editors said, although two of their number had signed the statement, the majority of the board had opposed the letter. "Even when it was received it seemed uncritical." The debate over the manifesto of the Committee for Cultural Freedom had ended, though the issues raised remained alive.[26]

Although the Committee for Cultural Freedom was not concerned mainly with Red totalitarianism as *The New Republic* had charged, the Moscow trials were an important factor in its development. The trials had emphasized the parallels in terror and suppression between Russia and the Fascist nations. It was this that concerned the Committee. The issuance of the manifesto demonstrated that the trials had increased the awareness of many liberals (some of whom had previously been sympathetic to Russia) of the repressive aspects of Stalin's regime. Unlike the Spanish civil war and the rising labor movement, both of which helped to cement the Popular Front, the trials had a divisive effect. They hardened anti-Communist liberal opinion, caused a number of liberal sympathizers to become critics, drove members from the Party, and spurred the formation of an articulate group of anti-Stalinist radicals. Yet the general pattern of liberal thought remained intact; the basic divisions remained. Those who had been closest to Russia defended the trials in accordance with the official Communist position. Those liberals who, in varying degrees, had been sympathetic to the Russian system as a whole, despite certain tergiversations over the trials, remained basically pro-Russian. Even anti-Communist liberals like Alfred Bingham and Selden Rodman, who had admired Russia's economy while criticizing her political system, did not alter their appreciation of her economy when they recognized the fraudulence of the trials. But the trials did intensify their concern with the dangers of political dictatorship. Among the most prominent liberals signing the Committee's statement were John Chamberlain, George Counts, Elmer Davis, John Dewey, Horace Kallen, Carl Becker, and Oswald Garrison Villard. Of these men, all except Counts had been critical of many aspects of Russia since the early thirties and had condemned both Communism and Fascism. The Moscow trials reemphasized their previous opinions and dramatized the parallels between Fascism and Communism. But the trials had caused no massive shift in liberal opinion.

If the basic divisions in liberal thought survived the trials, it is necessary to inquire more deeply into the reasons why an issue which seemed to many radicals a monstrous perpetration of organized horror failed to shake the sympathy of many liberals. And it is the position of people like Bruce Bliven and Freda Kirchwey, not that of the unquestioning fellow travelers, that needs more explanation. First of all, a gigantic frame-up was simply hard to believe. The *New York Times* seems to have been confused by the first trials. Though the editors always used the trials as evidence to condemn the Communist system (they criticized the Trotskyists for failing to recognize the trials' source in Marxist philosophy), it was not until the subsequent trials that they seem to have clearly doubted the verdicts. If conservatives, traditionally hostile to Russia, had a hard time believing the trials were a fraud, it is understandable that liberals who were sympathetic to Russia would also find this difficult to believe. However, the Russian sympathizers continued to give credence to the verdicts after the *New York Times* had begun to imply doubt. Further explanations are required.[27]

There are certain psychological reasons why these liberals might have been unable to believe in the fraudulence of the trials. If one regards the liberal mind as congenitally unaware of the depths of human evil, then one can argue that the very monstrousness of a possible frame-up would be rejected as too horrible to imagine. If one accepts the liberal mind as ignorant of terror, then one can argue that mind's inability to understand the outpourings of the confessions. When the defendants at the second trial confessed, knowing that the defendants at the first trial had been executed, the liberal could not understand why they would confess unless they were guilty. This seemed the only "rational" explanation. The liberals were aware of legal injustice in the United States; they had been fighting it from Sacco-Vanzetti down to the Scottsboro boys. But being accustomed to Western concepts of law and jurisprudence, they found it hard to imagine wholesale frame-ups. Hence the tendency to feel that, even if some of the specific charges were incredible, the defendants must have been guilty of "something." These psychological explanations should not be overlooked completely. One has only to remember George Orwell's amazement at being wanted by the government in Spain when he had not done anything: "In spite of the innumerable arrests it was almost impossible for me to believe that I was in danger. . . . I kept saying, but why should anyone want to arrest me? What had I done? . . . It did not matter what I had done or not done. This was not a round-up of criminals; it was merely a reign of terror. I was not guilty of any definite act, but I was guilty of 'Trotskyism.' . . . It was no use hanging on to the English notion that you are safe as long as you keep the law."[28] Never having experienced this sort of terror, where all liberal notions of law were meaningless, the liberal found it hard to comprehend and therefore shied away from the realization to which Orwell was driven.

Such explanations are particularly helpful in arriving at an understanding of the liberals' inability to grasp the nature of the totalitarian state. But they do not provide a full understanding of why the trials did not destroy the sympathy for Russia of liberals like Bliven and Freda Kirchwey. Other liberals with the same general philosophy did understand the terror of the trials. Therefore, an inability to imagine terror or evil cannot be the sole explanation. Another possible explanation is suggested by a passage from *My America* (1938) by Louis Adamic. Adamic, an anti-Stalinist, had had his name placed on the Trotsky Defense Committee without permission by his friend Benjamin Stolberg, but he remained on the Committee when the Communists started to pressure him to withdraw. In recording his feelings toward the trials, Adamic said that, like most Americans, he believed the trials and executions were "the climax of . . . a horrible and stupid frame-up." But, since his knowledge of Russia was second-hand, he felt unqualified "to decide on the current Trotsky-Stalinist issue." And the key passage states: "Also to my view, Trotsky and his conspiratorial-revolutionary ideas, like Stalinism, had no close relation to the United States."[29] Adamic's attitude, common among certain anti-Communist liberals, should warn one against accusing Bliven of complete hypocrisy in urging American liberals not to take sides. There was a general belief among Americans that the Stalin-Trotsky feud was a private affair and, whether the defendants were guilty or not, the trials were none of America's business. But, in the last analysis, enmeshed as they were in all the issues of the Popular Front, the editors of *The New Republic* could not sincerely plead that it was not the American liberals' business. If the trials were not, then much else that they took a stand on was not. What Adamic's attitude does suggest is why people like Alfred Bingham and Selden Rodman did not take a stronger stand: the issues between the warring groups were not closely related to the United States except as a lesson. It also indicates why anti-Communist liberals like Carl Becker and Charles Beard were not inclined to join the defense of Trotsky. They were willing to go on record against both Fascism and Communism, but they were unwilling to take an active part in what appeared to them intra-Communist quarrels.

All of these explanations contribute toward an understanding of the liberal attitude toward the trials. However, there are several more basic reasons why the Russian sympathizers were relatively unaffected by the trials. One important consideration is the traditional liberal antipathy toward Trotsky and liberal sympathy for Stalin. In the twenties the editors of *The New Republic* had regarded Trotsky as a fanatical dogmatist and Stalin as a pragmatic and flexible leader, capable of adjusting his ideas to changing circumstances. This difference was reemphasized in the early thirties by the view of Stalin as an activist, the man who got things done. Trotsky remained, ironic as it may seem, the ineffectual intellectual trapped by his theoretical dogma. The attitude of *The New Republic* mirrored the resentment against Trotsky's theoretical brilliance found among many Russian sympathizers. On the other hand, many of these liberals sympathized with Stalin's theoretical ineptitude.[30] Therefore, on political grounds (because he was a fanatical revolutionary) and on psychological grounds (because his passion for theory stood in contrast to their admiration for achievement), Trotsky was already out of favor with liberals like the editors of *The New Republic*. They were predisposed to judge him severely. Similarly, because Stalin had been largely responsible for what they believed were the remarkable Russian achievements, they were predisposed to favor Stalin in any conflict between the two.

The all-important concept of unity—symbolized in the Popular Front—was also a vital reason for continued sympathy for Russia. Liberals like Bliven and Freda Kirchwey did not believe that all those who doubted the verdicts were "stooges" of Fascism. But they did feel that Fascism was the great danger and that anti-Fascist unity must be preserved at all costs. Recognizing that a basic questioning of the verdicts would only stir up controversy and partisanship, they lacked the will to believe in the fraudulence of the trials and sought to rationalize them.

Also of deep significance in rationalizing the trials was the double standard with respect to civil liberties. After the Kirov executions in February of 1935, in answer to a criticism by William Henry Chamberlin, the editors of *The New Republic* clearly stated their position: civil liberties were not the only standard, "or even the major standard," for judging countries. They justified their double standard in regard to Germany and Russia by the ends in view: whereas Germany aimed at a perpetual autocracy, Russia's goal was a classless society. Hence they were "more tolerant" of Russia. They justified their double standard in regard to Russia and the United States by the relativity of liberty: liberty depended on stability and was impossible during a period of social revolution. Since Russia was in such a period, and was threatened by outside enemies as well, she was an unstable state. The United States, however, was a stable country with a historic tradition of civil liberties. Therefore, suppression of civil liberties in the United States was inexcusable, while the hope for more civil liberties in Russia lay in increased stability. Meanwhile, Americans should suspend judgment against Soviet violations of civil liberty until "the facts of the specific case" were revealed. It was exactly this position that they adopted during the trials; the Russian sympathizers were simply not prepared to judge a country on what they took to be solely a question of civil liberties.[31]

By making civil liberties relative, the Russian sympathizers reduced their importance. A similar devaluation resulted from their bifurcation of economic and political democracy. In June 1936 *The New Republic* and *The Nation* enthusiastically greeted the announcement of the new Soviet constitution. The first trial seemed only a temporary diversion on the way to the new democracy. Even in December the editors of *The New Republic* were writing favorably of the constitution. But the subsequent trials forced them to retreat to their old position. By February 1937 they were repeating: "There are two broad aspects of democracy, political and economic. Russia has the second, but not the first. It nevertheless is a part, and an important part, of the anti-fascist front." Even without the constitution these Russian sympathizers would have leaned toward the government. Their division of democracy had assigned political and civil liberty a secondary role in Russia. It was relatively unimportant whether or not Russia had civil liberties. That was not what mattered about her system. What did matter was the Russian economy and her foreign policy. Liberals like Bliven and Miss Kirchwey based their sympathy for Russia on their belief in Russian economic democracy and in her consistent striving for peace in opposition to Fascism. Political and civil liberty did not play an important part. This was precisely why the trials were not a shattering blow. They did not challenge the two principal foundations of liberal sympathy. They only demonstrated Russia's lack of something these liberals did not look for in Russia. It was not until one of the pillars of their sympathy was attacked that the Russian sympathizers evinced a marked change in their alignment. The Nazi-Soviet Pact, which challenged the concept of Russia as a peace-loving and anti-Fascist power, established the necessary prerequisites for a realignment within the liberal community.[32]

A corollary question to consider is whether the trials and purges, if they had continued after 1938, could have caused a general abandonment of sympathy for Russia. There is some evidence for this possibility. *The New Republic* and *The Nation* were more critical of the third trial than they had been previously. The double standard of morality might eventually have been too much for them, the accumulation of terror too great, and they might have been pushed into a critical position. There is Freda Kirchwey's statement that a majority of *The Nation*'s editors had believed, even before the Pact, that the Open Letter to All Active Supporters of Democracy and Peace was too uncritical of Russia. Louis Fischer and the educator Goodwin Watson, both previously sympathetic to Russia, had refused to sign the Open Letter. There is also a passage written by Roger Baldwin in 1941 which reflects this decrease in sympathy: "For fifteen years I looked with hope on the Soviet Union as a pioneer in creating an ordered and planned economy in which compulsion would gradually disappear. My support of the combined factors represented by the Soviet Union varied from a high at one time of about eighty per cent to a low of little over fifty per cent until finally, after 1936 when the great purges began, it dropped to a point where the evidence against the promise of the Soviet Union outweighed my hopes." Although Baldwin went on to say that he had not ceased collaborating with the Communists in various organizations until the Nazi-Soviet Pact, his attitude does suggest that, given a continuation of the trials, other liberals' doubts would have outweighed their hopes and eventually their sympathy might have turned to criticism. However, while more disillusionment would certainly have come if the trials had continued, it is probable that the ingrained habits of rationalization needed a different kind of shock to destroy them.[33]

All this leads to the question of whether the Popular Front would have continued indefinitely if the Nazi-Soviet Pact had not occurred. Toward the end of the thirties a number of "anti-totalitarian" books by liberals appeared. George Counts's *The Prospect of American Democracy* (1938), Arthur Garfield Hays's *Democracy Works* (1939), and Alfred Bingham's *Man's Estate* (1939) all rejected both Communism and Fascism. Of the three, only Counts was a disillusioned Popular Front liberal. But such books indicated the increased pressure on the Popular Front liberal—with his double standard of morality where Russia was concerned. In addition, there was the formation of the Committee for Cultural Freedom, which dramatized the need for opposition to all forms of totalitarianism. Thus it is possible that under increased pressure, many liberals would have reexamined their premises and abandoned their double standard. To argue against this possibility over-estimates the chasm between the Popular Front liberal and his opponent. Both Bingham's *Man's Estate* and Max Lerner's *It Is Later Than You Think* (1938) advocated democratic collectivism and the continuance of democracy and civil liberty in the United States. The chief difference lay in the latter's excuses for Russian practices. However, the possibility must remain only a supposition. For it is also possible that under increased pressure from the opponents of all totalitarian systems, the Popular Front liberal would have grown more hysterical as his premises were challenged and would have allied himself more closely with the Communists. Most probably, he would simply have continued his rationalizations indefinitely and the Popular Front would have continued until some other cataclysm shook his beliefs.

10

THE COLLAPSE OF THE POPULAR FRONT

On August 24, 1939, the Nazi-Soviet Pact was announced. Pledging nonaggression and the development of economic cooperation, the Pact opened the East for Hitler's drive on Poland. On September 1 his armies invaded Poland; on September 3 England and France declared war on Germany. The Communist line immediately changed from a support of collective security to a call for strict isolationism in America. The slogan of dictatorship versus democracy was replaced by a denunciation of the imperialist war. The pro-New Deal policy was discarded for opposition—the New Deal was the "War Party" and the captive of the reactionaries. On September 17 Russia invaded Poland; on September 29 Poland was partitioned between Germany and Russia. Following the partition of Poland, Russia took control of the Baltic states through a series of pacts giving her strategic naval and air bases and allowing Soviet garrisons to be stationed in these countries. When Finland refused the terms offered by Russia, she was attacked on November 30. Finland's eventual defeat in March 1940 gave Russia certain strategic territories, and three months later Russia occupied the other Baltic countries under the pretense of treaty violations. The Communists presented all these Russian moves as necessary steps for peace and democracy in these countries; peace and democracy were literally on the march.

In May of 1939 Anna Louise Strong had written that under certain circumstances Germany and Russia might come together. But at present, she said, the rumors of a Nazi-Soviet agreement existed primarily in the consciences of the statesmen of France and England, who, having attempted to isolate Russia at Munich, now realized the predicament they would be in if Russia should join Germany.[1] When rumor and conscience became reality, the impact reverberated throughout the liberal and Communist world. Major "front" organizations either collapsed or were transformed into new isolationist vehicles. The Popular Front had ended.

Confirmation and a Few Surprises

The end of the Popular Front witnessed a convulsion in the traditional lines of liberalism in the thirties: fellow travelers, Russian sympathizers, and anti-Communist liberals. For most anti-Communist liberals, the Pact only confirmed previous beliefs. They agreed with Oswald Garrison Villard that "two conscience-less" men had joined together for "mutual advantage" (though they did not necessarily agree with Villard's isolationist conclusions). But even among previously anti-Communist liberals, the reaction to the Pact and its aftermath was not always what might have been expected. The reaction of Alfred Bingham and Selden Rodman, for example, was much milder than that of former Russian sympathizers. Throughout the spring and summer of 1939, *Common Sense* had been reporting the growing signs of a German-Russian rapprochement. Yet when the Pact was announced Bingham and Rodman were surprisingly temperate in their criticism. They admitted that it had precipitated the fighting, but saw no reason to believe in a new military alliance between Germany and Russia. The signing of the Pact did not automatically put " 'red' and 'brown' Bolshevism on the same side of the trenches." Bingham and Rodman considered it more likely that Stalin was attempting to protect himself from future German attack "by setting up a protectorate over Eastern Poland," perhaps even holding his army for "the knockout" blow if Germany showed signs of weakening. They viewed Russia as "an independent," capable of joining either side. Thus far she had generally supported Germany, but her aggression had also stopped Hitler's aggression in Poland. Moreover, the long-exploited White Russians and Ukrainians in Poland would welcome Russian rule, they said. In any event, although Hitler and Stalin might cooperate in dividing up countries, Stalin was "no friend of Hitler."[2]

Even their reaction to the invasion of Finland was relatively mild. They objected to a regime supposedly devoted to the common man killing the common man of Finland for military reasons. Yet they thought the invasion might prove "helpful" in stopping war. This reasoning was based on their desire for a negotiated peace leading to a federated western Europe: England and France would hesitate to crush Germany completely for fear of Russia's ambitions, while elements in Germany might exert pressure to end the war before Russia moved further westward. Yet, in the interim, it was at least "salutary" to have "the last democratic pretensions" stripped from totalitarianism. This might seem to indicate an intensified condemnation of totalitarianism. But, while they certainly did not defend it, they were fearful of the new bitterness toward Russia:

> Today accumulated venom is finding release in the direction of the Soviet Union and its loyal partisans here. Even many who consider themselves radicals have lost the ability to feel sympathy for the Red soldier blasted by a Finnish land mine or the Red propagandist persecuted for his faith in Stalin. Embittered ex-Communists are poisoning the atmosphere as much as the congenital patrioteers.[3]

The chief reason why Bingham and Rodman did not censure Russia more severely was their fear that aroused emotions might lead to American participation in the war. But another reason was their unwillingness to rule out Russia's economic techniques as a part of the large trend toward collectivism. Reviewing Corliss Lamont's *You Might Like Socialism* in November 1939, Alfred Bingham wrote: "For all his buoyant will-to-believe it is clear that as intelligent a person as Corliss Lamont could not paint such a glowing picture of Soviet democracy and progress purely out of his imagination. . . . His very uncriticalness enables us to get a picture of the positive dynamism of the revolution as it appears to the average believing Soviet citizen." According to Bingham, Russia was a land of many truths, and the economic progress portrayed by Lamont was one of the truths. While Russia's future was mixed, it was probably more hopeful than destructive. In fact, Bingham believed "the menace" of both Communism and Fascism was "probably exaggerated." If a long-range view were taken, it would not be surprising if "they promoted democracy more than destroyed it." And after Finland, the editors wrote: "The Soviet and Nazi rulers may be power-mad, but they have developed astonishingly effective new techniques of economic organization, which could conceivably be used for raising living standards."[4]

That the editors remained optimistic over the economic possibilities of the two totalitarian countries is indicative of the generally blasé attitude they adopted toward the cruel events on the international scene. In March 1940 they discussed the new American hatred of Russia. They were particularly afraid of Americans letting their emotions run away with them and becoming involved in Finland. "We have no more reason to fly to the defense of Finnish democracy than of Spanish democracy or Czech democracy," they declared. They were willing to admit the evils in the Russian regime, but they believed the necessary conditions had been created for future advance by her rapid industrialization, her economic planning, and her "ostensibly democratic constitution." There was an absolute dictator; there had been purges and economic disorganization. But there had also been progress and a sense of idealism in Russia. This was not "a threat to civilization." They warned of the least reliable commentators on Russia, the ex-Communists and disillusioned friends, who, unwilling to credit

Russia with anything, ignored the evidence of economic and cultural progress. In international affairs, the Russian excuse for the invasion of Finland was "flimsy": it had been purely a military move to strengthen her defense. But, they said, there had been no mass bombing of civilians for terroristic purposes, as asserted in the "inexcusable atrocity-mongering" of the American press. The editors concluded: "On the whole Soviet aggression cannot be justified, except by those in bondage to the Soviet myth. But it is no worse than many other instances of aggression by power-hungry national states, ancient and modern."[5]

However morally blind this mild attitude toward Finland might have been, it was not a justification of Russian action. Elsewhere Rodman wrote that the Pact and the "unprovoked" attack on democratic and progressive Finland had convinced all but the diehard Marxists of the need to reexamine their premises; it had demonstrated that, like the Nazis, the Communists used means both "corrupt and corrupting." The tepid attitude can best be explained by the editors' desire to prevent American involvement and their attempt to push the idea of a compromise peace. Peace did not come, of course, and as the war progressed, they began urging American aid to Great Britain; yet they continued to stand for a negotiated peace. Their temperate attitude toward both Germany and Russia stemmed from a traditional isolationism unrelated to the Communists' new isolationism. Proof of this lies in their continued support of negotiated peace after Russia's entry into the war and the Communists' reversal to an all-out American war effort and the crushing of Germany.[6]

Getting Off the Express

The greatest effect of the Pact and the invasions of Poland and Finland was not on the anti-Communist liberals like Bingham and Roman, but on the fellow travelers and Russan sympathizers. It split the former and drove the latter into varying degrees of criticism. Among the prominent fellow travelers renouncing the new

Communist line were Vincent Sheean, Ralph Bates, and Louis
Fischer. Sheean at first defended the Pact, but by November he
was writing in *The New Republic* that Stalin had embraced Fascism. He told of the horrors of collectivization and the terror of the
purges. It was not socialism that was being built, he said, but a
new slave state. After the invasion of Finland, Ralph Bates compared the Russian tactics with Hitler's, and disclosed his departure
from the Moscow Express: "I am getting off the train. . . . I had
thought the train was bound for a fertile place in the sun; but I have
found out that it is rushing toward the Arctic north, where it will
be buried beneath vast drifts of snow and be forever more silent."
Like many others who left the train, Bates believed in the essential
rightness of events up to the Pact. He was ready to admit that the
charges of Fascist collaboration against the P.O.U.M. in Spain were
"unscrupulous," but his break with the Communist line was accompanied by a general vindication of the Popular Front and the role
of the Communist Party in Spain and elsewhere.[7]

Perhaps the most noteworthy exit was made by *The Nation's*
Russian and Spanish correspondent, Louis Fischer. Before the
Pact, Fischer had believed Russia to be "the most effective—
perhaps the only—anti-fascist power." The Pact convinced him
that she was not. It was "a crime and a war stimulant" and "totally
indefensible" because Russia knew that England and France had
abandoned the policy of appeasement and would fight. Therefore,
the Pact contradicted the idea of collective security. In contrast to
those who, while criticizing the Pact, continued to emphasize
Russian-German conflict whenever possible (e.g., the editors of
The New Republic), Fischer treated Stalin and Hitler as full-
fledged partners: to help one was to help the other. Fischer believed the Pact resulted from the period of the purges, when the
promise of liberty under the new Constitution was increasingly replaced by arbitrary government. Each arbitrary move—the Pact,
Poland, Finland—was proof of Russian-German cooperation and
was symptomatic of the increasing similarity of their noneconomic
areas of life. Unlike some liberals who began to modify their criti-

cism when Hitler invaded Russia, Fischer continued to be critical of the Stalin regime. He accused it of a willingness to "sell out" to Hitler up until the end. And in a December 1941 review of Walter Duranty's *The Kremlin and the People*, Fischer declared that simply because Russia was battling Germany, it was not necessary "to paint Stalin as a lover of Jesus Christ and a sweet moderate who would never kill a fly."[8]

While many fellow travelers underwent this belated awakening, others could not abandon their faith in Russia and they tried, hysterically at times, to defend the Pact and the subsequent invasions of Poland and Finland. Corliss Lamont defended the Pact and placed the blame on England and France: they had refused "to cooperate with Soviet peace efforts." Anna Louise Strong declared that the Red army had marched into eastern Poland "for peace": it had stopped Hitler. Maxwell Stewart praised Soviet diplomatic triumphs and hailed the Soviet-Finnish peace for its prevention of war and of American intervention in that war (this from an old defender of collective security). *Soviet Russia Today,* having denounced the "lying rumors" and "cheap fabrications" of a Soviet-German rapprochement in March, celebrated that rapprochement in September: it was a *"pact for peace."* The editors insisted that there was no alliance between Germany and Russia— Germany had come to Russia. They glorified as "liberation" the subsequent Russian advances into Poland and Finland. The Polish people had hailed the onrushing Red army; Russia's action had stopped Hitler's advances and meant the beginnings of a new civilization. Finland had been a "dagger" aimed at Russia, they said, and behind her lay the imperialist powers. Once Russia had guaranteed her own security, then the people of Finland would achieve "independence." With a new concern for the Neutrality Act, the editors opposed loans to Finland as violations of the Act, and ironically buttressed their argument with a citation from the arch-conservative, David Lawrence.[9]

The defense of the Pact by the editors of *Soviet Russia Today* was highly emotional. Frederick L. Schuman, however, retained his usual coolness. To him the Pact was simply a master stroke of *Realpolitik*. Writing in *The New Republic* in November of 1939, Schuman declared that Russian foreign policy could be understood only in terms of power. Russia had always sought to defend herself against her enemies. The purges, he said, were aimed at Nazi "boring from within" tactics, and although innocent people had died, the purges, along with Western appeasement, had convinced Hitler of the danger in attacking Russia and had led him to see that his best chance was in the West. Collective security itself had been a policy of self-interest designed to protect Russia against Germany. But English and French appeasement in Spain and at Munich had killed collective security. Russia had then requested the use of the border states for her defense. But again England and France had gummed things up by refusing her reasonable terms. Thus they could blame only themselves if Russia looked elsewhere for protection. The result was the Pact: "a work of diplomatic genius worthy of a Medici, a Richelieu, or a Bismarck." By entangling Hitler in the West, Stalin had rendered him helpless. In Schuman's writings, it was always Stalin who was running the show. Unless either side won an immediate victory, he said, Russia would continue winning her own victories. On the other hand, if a compromise peace were arranged, it would be because France and England had come to Moscow for aid—to meet her terms or "face extinction." Finally, if both sides became exhausted, world revolution would become a distinct possibility. In any case Russia would triumph. Schuman justified all of these Russian maneuvers as *Realpolitik*. There was, of course, a built-in bias in favor of Russian *Realpolitik*. But Schuman pretended ethical objectivity. Discussing Russia's realistic strategy, he wrote: "That strategy is ethically indistinguishable from that of Hitler, Chamberlain, Mussolini and Daladier. It is merely more successful."[10]

Schuman had not issued a word of protest against the Russian invasion of Poland. Apparently Finland was different, for, following its invasion he wrote in *Events* that Russia was "for the first time . . . indulging in undisguised military aggression, ugly, naked, and unashamed." In *The New Republic* he still argued for the doctrine that the ends justify the means and for the logic of *Realpolitik*. But he regarded the invasion of Finland as "utterly indefensible." It had no legal, moral, or political justification. Russia's end—defense against Germany—was still the same, but the means were different. The means had been "shrewd and defensible" in Poland, Estonia, Latvia, and Lithuania, but with Finland they had become "indistinguishable" from the methods of the Fascist nations. The invasion of Finland was "worse than a crime"; it was "a blunder." Why a diplomatic blunder should be worse than a moral crime he did not explain. He remained morally blind until the end: Stalin had committed his first error in Finland, but it was only an error. Nor was Schuman breaking his pro-Russian orientation. After the invasion he denied the existence of a Stalin-Hitler military alliance and the death of socialism in Russia. After the peace treaty with Finland, his criticism of Russia decreased as he turned his attention to the need for American entrance into the war on the Allies' side. There was a strange contradiction here, for his support of the Allies was accompanied by no condemnation of Russia's aid to Hitler. Indeed, part of his reason for favoring American entrance was his hope of awakening Russia from her lethargy so that she too might help the Allies. Until Germany attacked Russia, he would continue this awkward straddling of the fence.[11]

The Pact and its aftermath split the fellow travelers, but the effect upon the Russian sympathizers was more one-sided: they turned critical, though not necessarily all at once. *The New Republic*'s course was hesitant and accompanied by backsliding. *The Nation*, however, moved quickly to a sharply critical position. Russia, the editors believed, had timed the Pact to give Hitler "the greatest possible benefit." The partition of Poland had been pre-arranged and the Russian explanations were "sickening." At the end of September they wrote that, although it appeared as if Stalin was presently leading Hitler, nevertheless the Pact had "enormously strengthened" Hitler's power to attack the West. In October Freda Kirchwey criticized the minimizers of the Pact's significance. "The long-range ambitions" of Stalin and Hitler would eventually clash, she said, but the present agreement was ominous for the Western democracies: "The Moscow-Berlin axis is a solid and menacing fact that cannot be figured out of existence." Even before the invasion of Finland, the editors criticized "Communist imperialism" in the Baltic states. As defensive measures, they could be understood, they said, but they should not be condoned. With the invasion of Finland, Freda Kirchwey wrote: "The horrors that fascism wreaked in Spain are being repeated, in the name of peace and socialism, in Finland. And the contemptible pretenses that have accompanied fascist aggression . . . are . . . being revived. . . . The Finns . . . are fighting to resist a concept of revolution that threatens every ideal that the working-class movement has stood for." In June of 1940 she wrote that Russia's appeasement had made her "a captive of Hitler." This remained *The Nation's* point of view until Germany invaded Russia in June of 1941.[12]

In domestic affairs, *The Nation* was afraid of a new Red scare resulting from post-Pact anti-Communism. Nevertheless, it did not hesitate to criticize the Communists. The editors ridiculed the new Communist line. They supported the American Federation of Teachers' ouster of the Communist-controlled locals. They urged the Newspaper Guild to free itself from Communist domination. They spoke of the "dupes" who defended Morris Schappes, a Communist teacher accused of perjury, on the grounds of academic freedom. The major issue dividing them from the Communists was, of course, foreign policy. *The Nation* supported all-out aid to England and France, whereas the Communists interfered with the war effort. Even after the German invasion of Russia, it distrusted the Communists and in August of 1941 the editors praised the U.A.W. leadership for continuing to be wary of the Communists.[13]

To follow the tortured reaction of *The New Republic* to the Pact and the succeeding events is to see the agonizing effort involved in the painful recognition that an idealized hero had feet of clay. In October of 1938 Bruce Bliven wrote of a possibility of a German-

Russian alliance. However, the matter was dropped and *The New Republic* denied such rumors in January 1939.[14] Yet if the editors had been able to see the implications of their logic, their writing in the months preceding the Pact might have prepared them to accept it. For they viewed England and France as attempting to isolate Russia at Munich, and felt that, after Munich, Russia was preparing to remain neutral in the event of a war between Germany and the democracies. They had been skeptical of Chamberlain's post-Munich tough line and had supported Russia during the negotiations for an Anglo-Soviet alliance. They had doubted England's good faith in bargaining and had treated Russia's demands as just and her suspicions as wise. But while they were prepared to see Russia go her own way, they were not prepared to see her come to terms with her supposed arch-enemy.

The New Republic's immediate reaction to the Pact was that it was another example of disastrous appeasement. It separated the democracies from Russia, strengthened Hitler, and lowered the prestige of the Soviet government and of the Communist Party. But the next week the editors backtracked: the Communist claim for the Pact as "a great stroke for peace and democracy" was nonsense, but they rationalized it on the grounds of Russia's defensive needs. Russia had never lied about "treaty commitments," as had the Western nations; she had never been imperialistic. Therefore, she was entitled to the benefit of the doubt in regard to rumors of a Russian and German partition of Poland. The only thing wrong with the Pact, they said, was in its being negotiated in secret by the principal supporter of collective security while she was also negotiating with England and France. Its timing had helped Germany. The implication seemed to be that if Stalin had publicly announced the negotiations and concluded them at a less inopportune time, the Pact would have been all right.[15]

Before the invasion of Poland, the editors continued to give Russia the benefit of the doubt: the Pact was in her interest and she might still aid both sides. But the invasion of Poland forced them into a more critical position. They acknowledged Poland's reactionary government and her misgoverned minorities, but felt these were no excuse. Russia had broken her nonaggression agreement and her technique of liberation resembled Hitler's. She was no longer "a bulwark of honesty and humanity in a treacherous world." Though her aims might be pacific and she might only intend the erection of a buffer state, she had nevertheless become "a member of the Fascist bloc." This was going far, and, characteristically, the editors retreated the next week. They found no evidence that Stalin, holding the balance of power in Europe, would support Hitler. The Pact and the invasion of Poland had not guaranteed a victory for Hitler, but they had removed the threat of a German invasion of the Russian Ukraine. In fact, the editors seemed to celebrate the forced "bolshevization" of Poland: a new society, for which Russia was responsible, would emerge. "Thus far," they concluded, "events would seem to justify the statement . . . that by signing the nonaggression pact, Hitler made himself second man in Europe and Stalin first."[16]

The editorials continued to reveal doubt and confusion; Bliven and Soule were men trying desperately to keep their faith while one of the main props of that faith was fast crumbling. Hence they equivocated, praising elections in Poland one week, ridiculing them the next. Criticism of Russia's "armed conquest . . . for 'socialist liberation'" was accompanied by a defense of her actions in the Baltic states. These countries had never been free; they were bases of counterrevolution, and Russia was defending them without destroying the people's liberty. The editors criticized the hypocrisy of the Soviet attack on the American repeal of the arms embargo ("If it is immoral to sell war necessities to an imperialist combatant, just how moral is it to sell them to Hitler?"). But generally they placed Russia in the best possible light. They rationalized Stalin's invasion of Poland: it was realistic power politics. Stalin, an excellent practitioner, had made Hitler "virtually his prisoner." They believed Stalin was aiding neither Hitler nor England and France. And they treated his imperialism gently: "He is extending the boundaries of Russia a little, increasing the area where Soviet communism holds sway and reentering European politics in the role of arbiter."[17]

On November 15, two weeks before the invasion of Finland, the editors summarized their views on Russia. The occasion was Vincent Sheean's attack on Russia in *The New Republic*. The editors asserted that, because of their opposition to collective security and their traditionally mixed attitude toward Russia, they were better able to understand the Soviet Union than were disillusioned enthusiasts like Sheean. Admitting the repressive features of the Soviet dictatorship, they nevertheless insisted that the great economic and cultural reforms made Sheean's remarks about a new slave state "extreme." Moreover, they argued for the need to understand Russian foreign policy in terms of *Realpolitik:* England and France had defeated collective security and forced Stalin into isolation. But, like a good politician, Stalin struck a bargain with the other side. He had brilliantly outmaneuvered Hitler and had established himself in eastern Europe. He had strengthened Russia's defense—his aim in the game of power politics. In fact, it was all power politics: the Soviet Foreign Office was neither "more altruistic" nor "more villainous" than any other foreign office. But this wasn't editorial neutrality; imperialism that they condemned in others became in Russia "pressure discreetly applied."[18]

The attitude here expressed was very similar to Schuman's. But such a perspective did not satisfy the editors of *The New Republic,* and at the end of November they tried to distinguish between the two outlooks. They agreed with Schuman that power politics explained Russian foreign policy, but disagreed when he seemed to justify "unmitigated power politics à la Stalin" and when he urged liberals to adopt similar tactics. "Ordinary people," they said, needed to believe in something more than "raw power." Russia had previously satisfied that need, but her change in policy revealed her abdication of leadership of "a world movement"; she was acting nationalistically. The liberal required more sincerity and consistency, they argued, than the practitioners of Machiavellian methods provided. Russia had issued "insincere propaganda for collective security and the popular front." Thus, they concluded, "though, in any given case, the end may justify the means, we still cannot conclude that the means adopted need not be appropriate to the ends in view."[19]

These differences in theory were reflected in differences in practice: Schuman did not utter a word of criticism until the invasion of Finland; *The New Republic*, to the degree that it refused to accept pure power politics as a norm, was critical of the Pact and of the invasion of Poland. But it accepted power politics as a partial norm and therefore these events were rationalized and Russia was placed in a relatively good light. Then came Finland. The editors accused Russia of using "Hitler's techniques" to provoke war. Part of their criticism was that Stalin had overplayed his hand at power politics and thus made Communism vulnerable to attack by the reactionaries. But there was a new directness to their criticism: "There never has been a clearer case of calculated and unprovoked aggression by a large power against a small neighbor than the invasion of Finland by the Soviet Union." It could be compared only to Czechoslovakia, the editors said, and Hitler had "better excuses" (the German minorities in the Sudetenland) than Stalin.[20]

At the same time that it was moving toward this outright criticism of Russia, *The New Republic* was slowly progressing toward a more open criticism of the American Communists. Before Finland, the editors opposed the Communists' ordered-from-above isolationist policy. The new line was unacceptable to American liberals: "Moscow is not playing our tune; it is playing its own tune." But the editors were also very sensitive to any criticism of the Communists. They were fearful of a new Red scare, they thought attacks on the various Popular Front organizations were unfair, and they dismissed charges of Communism in the C.I.O. They spoke of the continued need for "progressive unity," and they maintained that the American Labor Party's attempt to purge itself of Communists and Communist sympathizers was breaking that unity. Finland, however, made them more critical of the domestic Communists. They agreed with the necessity (though they regretted that it would be misinterpreted as Red-baiting) of the American Civil Liberties Union's barring Communists as well as Fascists from office. Neither, they said, shared "the democratic belief in individual freedom." They singled out as hypocrisy the Communist charges of brutality against the Mannerheim government in Finland: if Mannerheim was cruel toward Communists, Hitler had been worse and the Communists were silent on Hitler's crimes. They also supported the American Federation of Teachers' expulsion of Communist locals. What is remarkable here is that they wrote: "The editors of *The New Republic* have no decisive evidence that the charge of Communist control was true; but certainly, the leaders of these suspended locals have acted as if it were true." Not only would they not have reasoned this way during the Popular Front period, but even after the Pact they had criticized the American Labor Party's move to oust Michael Quill on grounds that there was no definite evidence of his being a Communist and that he had consistently denied being one. Even when Quill's record was pointed out to them, they persisted in their attitude. It took Finland and the continued disruptive tactics of the Communists in supporting their isolationist policy to effect a change in reasoning.[21]

Although the editors of *The New Republic* had torn themselves from the outer web of Russian and Communist sympathy, they were still caught in the inner fiber; they continued to misunderstand the nature of the Communist Party. In June 1940 they wrote: "Most American Communists are acting in what they conceive to be the best interests of the international working class; this fact need not be questioned." Thus, although the editors did question "the good faith and good sense" of the policies the Communists were advocating for America, they continued to assume a relation between Communism and genuine working-class movements. Moreover, although Bliven and Soule realized that the American Communists were thinking in terms of Russia's undemocratic interests, they continued to treat the American Communists as if they were not directly and integrally connected with Russia, as if they could be censured separately. The desire to treat the American Communists as semi-independent indicates another tendency: the editors criticized the American Communists more harshly than Russia. They were not, of course, uncritical of Russia. At the close of the Finnish war, George Soule spoke of the "cruel cynicism" of Russia and described Hitler and Stalin as partners. In May of 1941 the editors said that Stalin was almost in full partnership with Hitler, that he wished to see England defeated, and that he did not intend to fight Germany in the near future. The accord with Germany, they said, had reduced the differences between Communism and Nazism until they were indistinguishable in their actions. Yet despite these criticisms, they did not reexamine their basic attitudes toward Russia, and they continued to regard her as a mixture of good and evil.[22]

In January 1940 the editors made an attempt at such a reexamination. They criticized the Stalin-haters—those who kept repeating that Stalin was a tyrant. But they admitted that a machine "90-per cent socialism and 10-per cent despotic tyranny" in the beginning had directly reversed these proportions. That some Americans remained loyal to Russia, they wrote, should be "an occasion . . . for searching our hearts." But the result of their reexamination of their basic premises was hardly "heart-searching." In answer to the Stalin-haters, they asserted that, though Stalin was indeed a tyrant, Russia had made great economic and cultural advances. It was "absurd to identify 170,000,000 people with one man." Stalin would not live forever. Americans were urged to focus on American problems and not to think primarily of what was happening in Russia.[23] The editors' attitude reveals the continuation of a certain attachment to Russian achievement: Stalin might be bad, but the economic achievements remained. The point is not that the Russian people were guilty of Stalin's crimes, or that Russia had not advanced industrially. The point is that *The New Republic's* reasoning demonstrated an emotional need to salvage *something* from the Russian dream. The effect of the editors' views was to show that they had not freed themselves from Russia; what they had done was to separate Stalin from the whole totalitarian bureaucracy. Stalin was responsible for the crimes—and he would die some day; one could still believe in the 170,000,000 people.

The Aftermath

It is clear that, except for the die-hard fellow travelers, the majority of liberals between August 24, 1939, and June 22, 1941, were moving in an opposite direction from the Communists. The influence of Russia during this period was less than at any time during the thirties. This decline in influence should not be attributed solely to the Pact. It took the cumulative effect of Poland and, even more, of Finland to induce the editors of *The New Republic* to free their criticism of most of its qualifications and rationalizations. But it is clear that the Communists and most liberals could unite on very little. *The Nation* and *The New Republic* were supporting Roosevelt's third term; the Communists viewed him as a "warmonger." Freda Kirchwey was calling for all-out aid to England and France; Bruce Bliven and George Soule were moving slowly toward the same position. In turn, both periodicals were labeled "idealistic whitewashers of the imperialist war" by Earl Browder.[24] Even Alfred Bingham was advocating some aid to England. The strongest isolationists among the liberals—people like Charles Beard, Oswald Garrison Villard, and John Chamberlain—were careful to dissociate their opposition to the war from that of the Communists.

This is why statements like the following by Eugene Lyons have no perspective. After pointing out that former friends of Russia were now beginning to tell some of the truth, Lyons wrote in April 1941: "Nevertheless, the towering myth of a free, happy, democratic, equalitarian and peace-loving Russia under the benign smile of Stalin still stands in our midst—if anything more glittering than ever. Neither pacts with Hitler nor attacks on Finland, neither purges nor mounting privations, can dim its artificial effulgence."[25]

Actually the myth of Russia was severely tarnished. Only the Communists (minus some prominent members) and the staunchest fellow travelers continued to look to Russia for deep sources of inspiration. That Russia continued to hold an appeal for such men is remarkable; to argue that the myth was "if anything more glittering" is to perpetuate another kind of myth. But to say that the myth had been completely destroyed among the post-Pact liberal critics of Russia would not be true either. It had been severely damaged but not irremediably destroyed. After June 22, 1941, it was to rehabilitate itself, although the terms on which it was re-formed were somewhat different. But its re-emergence had been latent within the post-Pact period. In July of 1941 Max Lerner criticized those liberals who were saying that there was nothing to choose between Communist Russia and Nazi Germany:

> The invasion of Russia is in itself . . . no proof of the difference. Yet historic events are not pulled out of a hat. From the very start there was a desperate opportunism about the Nazi-Soviet pact that gave it a febrile quality. Hitler's policy could be summed up in the line from Racine: "I embrace my enemy in order the better to strangle him." And Stalin's was born of appeasement and sired by resentment of England. Despite the pact, the hostility reaches . . . beyond power politics. It is true that Russia and Germany are both totalitarian and both despotisms. But the deeper truth is that social systems remain somehow moored to their ideological origins. The Nazi origins were in the anti-humanist and life-denying doctrines of war as an end, of racial exclusiveness, of contempt for the common man. The origins of the Soviet system, for all the perversions that Stalinism has been guilty of, were in the humanist and life-affirming doctrines of mass progress and human worth.[26]

Lerner's reaffirmation of the root differences between Communism and Fascism was not the only aspect of the myth to reappear. In September 1941 Bruce Bliven compared Russian and American morale: "The Russians, in spite of everything, have found in their miserable and backward land, so lacking in pink and blue tiled bathrooms, something for which they are willing to fight to the end." By 1943 George Soule was applying the Popular Front argument to those who criticized any compromise with the Communists: "We need only recall the factional struggles on the left which occurred in the years immediately preceding the war. And we need only remember the eagerness of some orthodox Socialists and followers of Trotsky to apply the Red Smear to any progressive or liberal who ever had a good word to say for the Soviet Union—an eagerness which gave substantial support to Fascism before the war and does so even to this day." Here, then, was the reemergence of many beliefs of the thirties: Russia and Germany were morally distinguishable; Russians had a purpose in life lacking in Americans; and the anti-Communist liberals and Socialists were aiding the Dies Committee and Fascism.[27]

The reaffirmation of these beliefs belies the complete destruction of the myth. The immediate question, then, is "why?" Why had not the "new" critics of Russia completely divested themselves of their previous sympathies? An important part of the answer lies in the failure of these liberals, while abandoning the Popular Front, to challenge its interpretations of events. Nor had they challenged its premises. They kept the habit of mind minus its Russian layer. This was going far, but when history took another turn, the layer re-formed. Some liberals, of course, were willing to admit the errors in the Popular Front facts, but there was certainly no wholesale reappraisal of the period, such as one would have expected if these liberals were really intent upon freeing themselves of old emotional ties. After the Pact, Malcolm Cowley could speak of the perversion of the Revolution, but most of the Popular Front beliefs stayed in place. He continued to accept the Communist explanation of Spanish events, and his view of the purges did not change drastically. Reviewing General Krivitsky's *In Stalin's Secret Service* in January 1941, Cowley wrote: "He wants us to believe something that seems highly improbable—namely, that there was never any plot against Stalin and that all the victims of the purge were wantonly executed." Reviewing Arthur Koestler's *Darkness at Noon* in June 1941, he seemed less certain, but held to the same position: "He fails to consider a possibility for which there is at least circumstantial evidence, that an actual plot against Stalin came close to being successful." Nor was there any attempt to re-examine the role of the Communist Front organization. When he resigned from the League of American Writers, Cowley made it clear that his resignation was over matters of policy and not over control of the organization: "The League is not a Communist or-ganization." In writing of the League for Peace and Democracy in November 1939, Freda Kirchwey said: "The Communist Party at times backed the league and even gave some money to it. The league has supported a program of resistance to fascism here at home as well as in Europe to which almost any liberal person would subscribe; if it has been 'controlled' by its Communist members, their influence has been singularly moderate." *The New Republic,* writing of the same organization, declared that it was formed by Communists and non-Communists alike and that there was no evidence that the Communists had "used it for any purpose except that for which it was ostensibly formed." That purpose was to fight Fascism and avoid war. It was a policy supported by the Commu-nists during the Popular Front period, it said, and the policy had caused non-Communists desiring the same objectives as the Com-munists to accept them as allies.[28]

The general tendency, then, was to minimize the Communist role in the Popular Front period. In April 1940 Bruce Bliven wrote: "Practicing their United Front tactics, the Communists joined every liberal and progressive organization in sight. Naturally, in reporting back to Moscow and in boasting of their successes at their own pep-meetings, they greatly exaggerated their influence in these organizations. They seemed to the public far more numer-ous and more powerful than they actually were. The non-Com-munist individuals, forced into often unwilling collaboration, would emphasize the fact that they themselves did not adhere to Marxian theory."[29] Perhaps more needs to be said about the various Popular Front organizations and how far the Communists did dominate them. But these liberals did not frankly reexamine their relationship with the Communists in these organizations. Like

Bliven, they minimized it and even distorted it. And this is indicative of the lack of a reexamination of the Russian myth and their whole relationship with the Communists during the thirties.

That they did not attempt to make this necessary reappraisal of their former attitudes is evidenced by two revealing exchanges. Noting the hesitation of the former Communists and fellow travelers to admit their mistake, Max Eastman suggested in a letter to *The New Republic* in October 1939, that *The New Republic, The Nation,* and the various deserters of the line would be better off if they would say: "We were wrong. YOU CANNOT SERVE DEMOCRACY AND TOTALITARIANISM." *The New Republic* replied: "The editors . . . have never said or believed that totalitarianism and democracy are compatible. We have repeatedly criticized the lack of civil and political liberties in Soviet Russia. We doubt, however, whether Mr. Eastman and his friends would have been satisfied except by a treatment of that country as violent in one direction as that of the unswerving Community Party members is in the other." Here the editors hid behind their old argument that their "mixed" reporting of Russia was "objective," while the anti-Communist view was necessarily distorted. Moreover, they had not "repeatedly criticized" Russia for her lack of civil and political liberties. And it was disingenuous to say that they had never said that totalitarianism and democracy were compatible. They may not have said that the theories could be reconciled, but they believed that democratic and totalitarian states could cooperate actively. Thus instead of making a frank acknowledgment of error, and thus gaining a chance at a brand new perspective, the editors clung to old beliefs about themselves.[30]

In a similar letter in September 1939, James T. Farrell accused *The Nation* of having agreed with the foreign policy of the Stalinists during their collective security period, of not having taken a clear stand on the Moscow trials, and of not having helped those fighting them. He accused Max Lerner of publicly defending the trials and Freda Kirchwey of having advocated collaboration with the Stalinists and of having attacked the non-Stalinists of the Left who refused to collaborate. After condemning *The Nation*'s refusal to listen to the anti-Stalinists' revelations of the Stalinists' conduct in Spain, he concluded: "It is insufficient for *The Nation* now to remove itself from the Stalinist orbit by showing a sudden moral indignation. It is necessary now to explain and to assimilate any change of orientation which you may adopt. . . . Also it is more than appropriate to reopen questions which you have closed or ignored. Now is the time to reopen the question of the Moscow trials. Now is the time to reopen and to study anew questions connected with the Spanish War."

The editors replied: "Without agreeing to undertake the multiplicity of jobs Mr. Farrell offers us, we are glad to accept his main challenge. . . . We agreed with Stalin . . . as long as he agreed with us. When he shifted sides, we stayed put. This does not represent any 'change of orientation' but the contrary. We have therefore nothing to 'explain'; but Stalin must explain, in more intelligible terms that his followers have yet discovered, his repudiation of a policy upheld by his government from the time Russia joined the League of Nations until Litvinov was dismissed from his post of Foreign Minister. We shall only add that *The Nation* strongly and clearly attacked the Soviet trials." The last remark cannot be substantiated, but there is some truth in the editors' reply. *The Nation*'s support of collective security was not simply a result of following the Communist line. In a sense it was true that when the Communists abandoned collective security the editors continued in their own beliefs. Yet the idea implied in the statement—that any relationship was superficial and involved only a particular issue—was an oversimplification. In not accepting Farrell's challenge, *The Nation* also missed its chance to gain a completely new perspective.[31]

This refusal to reconsider the issues of the Popular Front, not to mention those of the entire decade of the thirties, entailed more than a failure to set the record straight. It tended to perpetuate myths that later prevented the realism and skepticism necessary for a close scrutiny of Russia's professed aims. If the trials were not monstrous frame-ups and Spain remained a simple issue of democracy versus Fascism, then there seemed little wrong in regarding Russia as one of the democratic allies in war and peace. It further prevented any reexamination of the premises of the Popular Front. The Popular Front had been built on the concept of society and the world as a struggle between progressive and retrogressive forces. After the Pact, Russia had joined the latter. But, if the world view remained basically the same, there was nothing to prevent her from returning to the progressive side if she abandoned her retrogressive behavior.

Thus many liberals did not learn from their Popular Front experience when critical support must give way to critical non-support. Finally, there remained the old view of Left and Right. To aid Russia is to aid Germany, Louis Fischer had declared after the Pact, and most liberals agreed. But too many continued to believe that the association between Russia and Germany was only a case of parallel action, and failed to see the symbolic union of Red and brown totalitarianism—the enemies of democracy. In these liberals' minds, perverted, besmirched, corrupted Russia nevertheless remained at heart on the Left, although she had been misguided to the Right. Because the Nazi-Soviet Pact and its aftermath shook one of the basic foundations of the liberals' sympathy for Russia (the conception of Russian foreign policy as peace-loving and anti-Fascist), they shook that sympathy loose. They destroyed the Popular Front, made fellow travelers ex-fellow travelers, and made sympathizers critics. But because many liberals did not undertake a reexamination of the Popular Front after the Pact (although some did), there was nothing to prevent their reorientation toward Russia in the months following Hitler's crossing of the Niemen.

11

PERSPECTIVES—PAST AND PRESENT

The Myth of the Red Decade

The image of the thirties as the "Red decade" derived largely from the work of Eugene Lyons. According to Lyons, the Communists had denied the obviously man-made famine of 1932-33 in Russia and the "duped" liberals in America had blindly seconded their denials; the Communists had covered up their political terrorism in Spain in 1937 and the "duped" liberals had helped them to cover it up; the Communists had shouted "hurrah" for the murder of the "Old Bolsheviks" from 1936 to 1938 and the "duped" liberals had echoed their hurrahs. In fact, the Communists had conducted their own intellectual reign of terror in the United States from 1930 to 1940, according to Lyons, and only a few hardy souls among the American liberals had had the courage to speak out against it.

Writing in *Harper's Magazine* twelve years later, Granville Hicks, who had been a Communist during the thirties, asked, "How Red Was the Red Decade?" Using Lyons' book and an article by Irving Kristol as a starting point, Hicks answered that it was not as Red as they had portrayed it. In an article in *Commentary* in 1952 Kristol, at that time one of the editors of the magazine, had written: "Did not the major segment of American liberalism, as a

216

result of joining hands with the Communists in a Popular Front, go on record as denying the existence of Soviet concentration camps? Did it not give its blessing to the 'liquidation' of millions of Soviet 'kulaks'? Did it not apologize for the mass purges of 1936-38, and did it not solemnly approve the grotesque trials of the Old Bolsheviks? Did it not applaud the massacre of the non-Communist left by the GPU during the Spanish Civil War?" To these questions, Hicks answered "No." While some liberals did these things, he said, "the major segment of American liberalism" did not. To Lyons' picture of Stalinist penetration, he answered that while true in some respects, it exaggerated the influence of the Communists in the intellectual world of the thirties.[1]

There seems little doubt that a complete study of all varieties of liberalism—the conservative liberals, the "New Dealers," the left-wing liberal intellectuals under examination here—would tend to support Hicks's position. But even as regards the left-wingers, the picture is more complex and subtle than either Lyons or Kristol made it. Although Lyons did distinguish between conscious fellow travelers and liberal "innocents" and "dupes," the net effect of the book was to portray a monolithic liberal capitulation to Stalinism. And Kristol, by his choice of language, perpetuated this picture. But without belittling the moral damage wreaked by the fellow travelers and the Russian sympathizers, there were differences—and even tensions—between these two groups. *The New Republic* and *The Nation* did not "applaud," "bless," or even "approve" the murders and liquidations in the same way as *Soviet Russia Today*. They rationalized them, apologized for them, and showed an amazing default of the moral imagination. But their attitude was different from the categorical support of the fellow travelers.

Where Lyons and Kristol go wrong is not in their justifiable outrage, but in their basic approach to the material. Except for a few "honor rolls," Lyons views Communist and liberal culture—from the Communist inner core to the concentric rings of "innocent dupes"—as a monolithic totality. It is always the Stalinists that set the tone; their opponents are always few and far between. Kristol focuses on the capitulation of the "major segment" of American liberalism to the Communists. Such pictures are misleading because they propound the myth that American liberalism can best be studied in terms of "major segments" or as one group, whereas, in reality, American liberalism, even left-wing liberalism, in the thirties must be understood in terms of conflicts, tensions, and a variety of trends and groups. In a brilliant refutation of the theory of communal guilt as applied to liberals and radicals for the Communist sins of the thirties, Harold Rosenberg, writing in *Dissent* in 1954, gave a possible clue to a better understanding of the thirties: "Instead of Communists, fellow travelers, liberals, and radicals in one lump, the reality of the period lay in its battles."[2] As applied to the Left generally, this is clearly the correct approach; applied to the liberals with whom this study has dealt, the battles were not as fierce, the polemics were not as lacerating, but the variety of opinions suggested by the world "battles" was present.

On every major issue of the thirties, there were at least two and usually three different attitudes. The fellow travelers believed planning to be impossible under a capitalist system, but liberals from Beard on the right to Bingham on the left and including Stuart Chase and George Soule thought that planning could start before a revolution. Fellow travelers wrote uncritically on Communism, but a large number of liberals like John Dewey, Oswald Garrison Villard, and Carl Becker criticized it severely, while still others like Bruce Bliven and George Soule rejected it as a solution to America's ills, although their rejection was not unfriendly. Discussion of Russia followed similar lines, uncritical fellow travelers and indulgent Russian sympathizers, with a few reservations, being deeply impressed by Russian achievements, while men like Beard, Kallen, and Villard were highly critical. Liberals also split on Fascism, polarizing around Bingham's middle-class interpretation or the Communist extension-of-capitalism interpretation, but some liberals like Bliven and Soule showed tendencies toward both. The Communists criticized the New Deal before 1936 as the dictator-

ship of finance capitalism, but few liberals accepted this definition. Some, like Stuart Chase, gave critical support to the New
Deal throughout the thirties; others, like Beard and Villard, became increasingly disenchanted with it after initial enthusiasm;
still others, like Bliven and Soule, focused on its inadequacies, but
came to support it after 1936.

During the Popular Front period fellow travelers and Russian
sympathizers united on ideology. But anti-Communist liberals like
Alfred Bingham and John Chamberlain continued to criticize that
ideology. Spain presented the clearest example of unanimity in
liberal opinion, but even here Bingham and Chamberlain questioned the Popular Front interpretation of events. Many liberals
joined the Communists in support of collective security, although
not all were motivated primarily by the change in the Communist
line. Many other liberals, some like Bliven and Soule highly sympathetic to Russia, rejected this central part of the Communist
Popular Front line. On the Moscow trials the fellow travelers supported the verdicts uncritically; anti-Communist liberals like
Dewey and Villard questioned them. A third group of liberals like
Bruce Bliven and Freda Kirchwey rationalized the verdicts, but
did not believe they strengthened Russia or resulted from diaboli-
cal traitors—the lack of a legal opposition, they thought, had played
a role. The Nazi-Soviet Pact destroyed the Popular Front, splitting
the fellow travelers, confirming the anti-Communist liberals' views,
and driving the Russian sympathizers, some quickly, some slowly,
toward criticism of Russia.

Placing these differences in perspective, one can distinguish
between the fellow travelers, the Russian sympathizers, and the
anti-Communist liberals. These groupings were not fixed, of course.
A man like Alfred Bingham admired Russian planning in much
the same manner as Bruce Bliven. But his vocal criticism of Communism and the Russian political system was similar to Cohen's
or Kallen's or Dewey's. Somebody like Bliven could participate
deeply on the side of the Popular Front, but clearly oppose its
program of collective security. While these groupings were fluid,

they do suggest that Lyons'—and I feel Kristol's—picture of the Red decade needs modification. For even the differences and divisions among the liberals treated in this book suggest that the proper way to approach the relation of liberalism and Communism is not through blanket condemnation of a culture with a few interspersed "honor rolls," nor even through studies of "the major segments." Liberalism in the thirties cannot be approached adequately by nose-counting or by parading petitions whitewashing Stalin's crimes; it must be studied through the dialectic of debate and argument.

If Lyons' and Kristol's views suffer from an inadequate approach to the liberal culture of the thirties, are they completely unjustified in all their assumptions? The answer is that there was a large body of liberal opinion extremely indulgent where Russia was concerned, very susceptible to Communist arguments, and unwilling to apply the same critical standards to Russia as it did to the United States. Much of the reason for this indulgence lay in the liberal Left-Right world view. To place Russia on the Left was to endow her actions with a progressive character. Her ends were taken to be progressive; one did not have to worry about the means. Even liberals opposed to Russia did not necessarily reject the Left-Right world concept. They simply rejected all dictators, Left and Right. This is an important point, for it indicates that more liberals than those sympathetic to Russia did not understand the peculiar characteristic of Stalinist totalitarianism. They opposed it for the very good reason that Stalin was a dictator who practiced terror. But they too did not wholly grasp the fact that the Left-Right division of the world meant nothing when applied to Stalinist totalitarianism; nor did they necessarily grasp the bureaucratization of terror.

As the thirties progressed, the total nature of totalitarianism—that the ruling class dominated every facet of social life—began to be realized. But the concept was new; speaking in "Leftist," and later "progressive," terms, the Stalinist brand of totalitarianism presented itself as a forward-looking movement. It was easy to recognize that Fascist totalitarianism was retrogressive and "backward-looking," but people like Freda Kirchwey and Bruce Bliven were not able thoroughly to understand that the ideology of Stalinism was irrelevant to its ends; that, indeed, it was practically useless to speak about ends where it was concerned. They squirmed uneasily at its repressive character, but failed to grasp the impossibility of separating the economic and political culture of a totalitarian state. They never capitulated wholly to that totalitarianism as fellow travelers did (*The Nation* and *The New Republic* were not duplicates of *Soviet Russia Today*), but in their ambiguous and evasive relationship to it, they lent a certain amount of credence to the Lyons myth of the Red decade.

The "Innocent Dupe"

One of Lyons' favorite expressions in *The Red Decade* was "innocent dupe"; the term was primarily used to refer to those "idealistic" and "naive" liberals who were sucked into the "concentric rings" of front organizations that spread outward from the vortex of the conspiratorial base. Lyons' stress on liberal collaboration with the Communists in various front organizations was probably necessary because of the tendency of former Popular Front liberals to diminish the role of the Communists in these organizations. In an article on Lyons' book in *The New Republic*, Bruce Bliven wrote: "The degree of collaboration was rarely so complete as Mr. Lyons . . . would have you suppose. The liberals were well aware that, in many cases, the Communists did more harm than good to the cause they were supposedly trying to help, by arousing anti-red hysteria, by helping the tories to claim that everybody who wanted minimum wages or collective bargaining was a minion of Moscow. There were some instances where the liberals rudely told the Communists to go away." It is possible that a separate investigation of the various front organizations would bear out Bliven's statement that the degree of collaboration was not as great as Lyons makes it. But I have found no evidence that, in the realm of attitudes and ideas, the liberals cooperating in the Popular Front ever told the Communists "rudely . . . to go away." This, like the earlier remark of Bliven's about "unwilling cooperation," seems to me to be an attempt to picture the liberals as more "independent" than they were. Undoubtedly some liberals in the various organizations fought Communists for control, but many did not. In his review of Lyons' book, Reinhold Niebuhr made what seems to me a fairer statement: "Some of us spent considerable time trying to prevent the Communists from gaining control of these organizations, though it must be admitted that this was a pretty difficult task."[3]

To focus almost exclusively on the liberal as a "duped innocent" —implying that the liberal did not know who was who and what was what—is to propound the myth that the main influence of Communism lay in its manipulative skills and strategically located cells. However, when Communism was most influential during the Popular Front, its influence did not result primarily from this type of manipulation. It resulted from an ideological and emotional appeal attuned to the liberals' need for ideological explanation and emotional assurance. In responding to this appeal, the liberals did not respond simply as "innocent dupes." It was part of their creed that various groups, differing in methods, but agreeing in general principles, could work together. One can call this a "naive" or an "innocent" creed, but the liberals were not duped into believing it. They had always believed it and they consciously accepted the Communists as partners and leaders.

In the last analysis, the Popular Front philosophy was itself "innocent," in the sense of being simplistic and rudimentary. Not only did many liberals not understand the nature of totalitarianism, but they believed a good cause would not be corrupted by Communist participation. In the same review of Lyons' book, Bliven wrote of progressive causes: "The liberals were working for these things, and winning a reasonable percentage of them, long before the Communists, under orders from the Third International, tried to get aboard the bandwagon; and they have gone on fighting during the years when the eccentricities of the party line have caused the CP members to hop on and off like boys stealing rides on a bobsled. Would Mr. Lyons have had us abandon all our principles merely because the Communists said, 'Me, too'?"[4] The obvious answer is that Bliven was not being asked to abandon his humanitarian principles, but to think twice about his principle of cooperation with those who subscribed neither to his ends nor to his means and, in fact, endorsed means that would pervert the very progressive causes he believed in. To him a good cause remained a good cause as long as it was on the progressive side. One marvels at the lack of political sophistication. But this was not the result of any deliberate Communist trickery; it was part of the liberals' own social philosophy.

Ideals, Idealism, and Values

The thirties are often pictured as a period of social idealism. No one would deny the concern for economic and social justice that underlay much of the thinking of the period. What is often forgotten is the Machiavellianism in regard to power politics and the deep cynicism in regard to truth and evidence that often existed side by side with it. Dwight MacDonald once compared *The New Republic* and *The Nation* in the later forties: "*The Nation* is more fuzzy minded, naive, and 'idealistic' than its colleague."[5] The same tended to be true in the thirties: Bliven and Soule, though not without idealistic motivation, were more drawn to power—they were "harder"—than Freda Kirchwey with her desire for all forward-looking people to work together. Here a distinction needs to be made between the editors of *The New Republic* and such regular contributors as Frederick L. Schuman, on the one hand, and many of its readers, on the other. What came through to many of the readers was not the cynicism, the calculated tone in which these men applied the Trotskyist smear, or their refusal to meet criticism squarely. To the reader who was unsophisticated in left-wing politics, whose community experience demonstrated that the reactionaries were the main enemy, who might even oppose the Communists on a local level, but who, on the other hand, desired the Russian experiment to succeed, and who, above all, wanted all men of good will to work together against Fascism—what came through to these people was the progressive verbiage characteristic of *The New Republic*'s writing. If one understands the special terminology of liberalism in the thirties, one can better understand why people who in their daily lives would never condone anything like the Moscow trials could accept *The New Republic*'s account as objective and liberal.

The question of the liberal's idealism is ultimately related to the liberal's values. This question is particularly important in a consideration of the liberals who were sympathetic toward Russia. In an essay on the American writers who were sympathetic to Communism during the thirties, Norman Holmes Pearson has written:

> The error of American writers in the 1930's had not been so much that their method or values were fallacious as that putting them into effect had been only partial. Examining the abstract terms that had clouded the realities on one side, they had not pursued their method sufficiently to examine them on the other. They had for the moment drifted into a position where they were themselves properly suspect in thoroughness. . . . What was importantly true . . . was not that any of their values had been proved wrong, but only the disheartening correlation of facts to them. To the values, they . . . had stuck. It was not that being educated to truth . . . was incorrect, but only that their education had been incomplete."[6]

Pearson's statement indicates the abstract quality of the Russian sympathizers' adherence to the liberal values of truth, free inquiry, and political liberty. They believed in these values for the United States, and in the abstract for everyone. But they failed to apply these values concretely to the other side—to Russia. But there was another reason for this double standard of morality. It lies in the values themselves: they were often wrong. The Russian sympathizers were not wrong in believing in economic democracy, though they were in error in thinking that it existed in Russia. But in stressing economic democracy they minimized the liberal values of political and civil liberties. They did not believe in these values deeply enough to use them as criteria in judging the facts of life in Russia.

"Red Fever" or "Russian Enchantment"?

Any complete understanding of the relation of liberalism and Communism during the thirties must recognize that it was not orthodox Marxist doctrine that appealed to liberals: a class struggle leading to violent revolution, a dictatorship of the proletariat, and elimination of private property. When the Communist program was most revolutionary, during the early thirties, it was least influential among liberals. People like Bliven, Soule, and Freda Kirchwey, who were sympathetic to Russia, did not accept the Communist Party's revolutionary program. When Communism was least revolutionary, in the late thirties, it was most influential among these liberals. In fact, throughout the thirties, it was not the Communist Party or Communism as a philosophy that had the greatest impact on liberals. It was the existence of Russia.

Liberals who were vaguely sympathetic toward socialism were influenced by Russia because they believed she was a socialist state. But for such liberals the precise theory of Communism mattered less than Russia's "planned" economy—planned, of course, for the people and not for the capitalists. This, in addition to her foreign policy, gave Russia her prestige among people like Bliven and Soule. During the Popular Front period Communist theory was deemphasized; liberals respected and cooperated with the Communist Party but, without Russian prestige behind it, it would have been far less influential than it was. It could not have influenced these liberals on theory alone. The fact that, after the Nazi-Soviet Pact, the editors of *The New Republic* were more severe on the American Communists than on Russia shows that they had always been more sympathetic to Russia than to the American Communists. In a revealing passage, following the Pact, the editors of *The New Republic* wrote: "People must have something in which to repose hope and confidence; it is more likely that with the eclipse of Russia's moral prestige they will turn more and more to this country—the last great nation to remain at peace under democratic institutions."[7] I do not mean to suggest that the Russian sympathizers were not trying to serve American interests. But to a man such as Bliven, Russia was an emotional bulwark in which one could rest "hope and confidence." It was not necessarily a perfect bulwark, for people like Bliven were not utopians. But it was moving in the right direction and thus its errors could be excused. If one understands the emotional prop that Russia offered to the liberal living during the depression, then one has part of the reason for many liberals' refusal to face the reality of Russia, for their tortured, agonizing, evasive rationalizations and justifications. To surrender Russia was to be thrown back on oneself.

This enchantment with a foreign country was a unique phenomenon in American history. Americans in the late eighteenth century had rejoiced when the French Revolution seemed to usher in a period of political liberty. But France did not serve as an anchor for their beliefs as Russia did for many liberals in the 1930's. Many American social reformers saw late nineteenth-century Germany as a model for welfare legislation, but few had deep emotional ties with her total experience. It was understandable that in the 1930's radicals would turn emotionally toward Russia; many hoped for a repeat performance in the United States. That liberals like Bliven and Soule, with no desire for violent revolution, and with no particular concern for Communism as a theory, should have found spiritual support in Russia can be understood only in terms of the disintegrating effects of the depression on the prestige of the United States. Ironically, Eugene Lyons realized this himself when he wrote: "The Depression, the moral disintegration of the intelligentsia and the middle classes as the economic debacle developed, these were more potent in shaping the Red Decade than any of the masterminds on New York's Union Square." Unfortunately, later in his book Lyons forgot all about the historical setting and portrayed a kind of Red Fever that was induced in Union Square.

If the historical imagination can recall the havoc of the depression, the enchantment can become more understandable. The depression quickened the liberal's awareness of economic injustice, made him skeptical of contemporary political democracy, and dulled his suspicion of dictatorial solutions. Russia held out for the liberal an end to economic injustice, a future political democracy based on the solid foundation of economic democracy, and it softened any latent fears of dictatorship with pledges that it was a dictatorship of the majority and promises that it was preparing its own dissolution. Given the depression, it is small wonder that many liberals should have found in Russia an emotional bulwark for their hopes and desires. The bulwark was a delusion; and Russia and a depression-ridden United States were not the only possible alternatives. Many liberals, in fact, with their traditional belief in civil liberties and political freedom, were quick to point out that the social imagination was not exhausted by the current Russian and American systems. Dewey knew it; Morris Cohen knew it; Villard knew it. Because of them, and others like them, the historian is justified in faulting Bliven and Soule and Freda Kirchwey for their lack of social and political imagination. Even Bliven, Soule, and Miss Kirchwey realized that there were more than two alternatives: Russian planning was an inspiration, not a model, for them. But too often liberals, seeking a basis for their faith and hopes for mankind, fixed on Russia as the leading contemporary and viable alternative to a defunct capitalism. They were neither "radical" enough nor "utopian" enough to create alternative visions of human life; thus they served to narrow the range of liberal choice. They had forgotten the eloquent words of Randolph Bourne, written in 1917 in deep disillusionment over the moral posture of the American intellectuals in relation to World War I:

> To those of us who have taken Dewey's philosophy almost as our American religion, it never occurred that values could be subordinated to technique. We were instrumentalists, but we had our private utopias so clearly before our minds that the means fell always into its place as contributory. And Dewey, of course, always meant his philosophy, when taken as a philosophy of life, to start

with values. But there was always that unhappy ambiguity in his doctrine as to just how values were created, and it became easier and easier to assume that just any growth was justified and almost any activity valuable so long as it achieved ends. The American, in living out this philosophy, has habitually confused results with product, and been content with getting somewhere without asking too closely whether it was the desirable place to get. It is now becoming plain that unless you start with the vividest kind of poetic vision, your instrumentalism is likely to land you just where it has landed this younger intelligentsia which is so happily and busily engaged in the national enterprise of war. You must have your vision and you must have your technique. The practical effect of Dewey's philosophy has evidently been to develop the sense of the latter at the expense of the former.[8]

Dewey, I think, came to realize something of what Bourne was saying when he later wrote: "While the solution has to be reached by action based on personal choice, theory can enlighten and guide choice and action by revealing alternatives, and by bringing to light what is entailed when we choose one alternative rather than another." Too many liberals in the thirties suffered from lack of a "poetic vision" and absence of a theory—and came to accept the images of "growth" and "process" in Russia without questioning what was being created. Breaking with the sodden vision of normalcy on one hand, and the inadequate vision of superficial reform on the other, they had not the imagination to replace them with new democratic vistas. They too frequently accepted the "given" in Russia, as the conservatives accepted the "given" in American system. The ultimate source of their failure lay within their social philosophy, and in the social system which produced them.

The Lessons for Liberalism

The concept of cooperation among diverse groups—the ethos of the Popular Front—was not new in 1936. Liberals had been asserting it for years, especially in the early thirties, when sectarianism seemed to be the curse of the Left. It was the ingredients that were new—the totalitarian Communists were to be included in the "democratic" unity. This has led recent commentators to marvel at the naiveté of the liberals caught up in the Popular Front, to point out how little true cooperation there was and how much manipulation, and to draw back aghast at what liberals often rationalized and submerged under the rhetoric of unity. This retrospective judgment would indicate that liberalism today has advanced beyond that of the thirties. Though a few voices still mourn the Popular Front, the mode of thought peculiar to that period is not typical of contemporary liberals. To some, the thirties were a brief interlude that taught liberals the dangers of cooperation with the Communists. But there is more to be learned from the thirties than this, for in many ways contemporary liberalism can be defined as a reaction to the Popular Front mind.

Following the collapse of the cordial World War II relations between the United States and Russia (which may, with historical perspective and a few modifications, be seen as a kind of national Popular Front), liberals found themselves undergoing an agonizing reappraisal; for some the process had started earlier. The Popular Front ideology was no longer adequate, but no new ideology had arisen to take its place. The social forces at work in the world could no longer be contained within the progressive and reactionary categories of the Popular Front, and a redefinition of that world view was in order. The old labor-liberal alliance of the New Deal was under severe attack at home and either a drastic re-formation of the alliance or a broader definition of liberalism was necessary. The conservative attack on civil liberties was getting under way—it had started with the Smith Act—and it was necessary to look again at the problem of civil liberties in a democratic society. The optimism that many liberals associated with the Popular Front mind now seemed inadequate to comprehend the horrors of either Hitler's Germany or Stalin's Russia.

The broad outlines of the new turn in liberalism can only be charted briefly here, and it would be wrong to assume that the victory of the trend to be charted has been complete. However, certain tendencies are apparent. In revolt against the ideology of the Popular Front, liberalism has eschewed ideological thinking. It has proclaimed the "end of ideology." This, which has sometimes seemed an ideology in itself, has necessitated a more complex world view. The old Left-Right division of the world has been displaced by a view in which totalitarianism of any sort is a new third force, added to the traditional liberal and conservative divisions. Totalitarianism, in this view, is neither Left nor Right, but is a self-perpetuating and self-serving elite bureaucracy. Since ideology is no longer viewed as a proper weapon, liberalism, it is held, cannot meet totalitarianism with an opposing ideology; it must be dealt with on an ad hoc, "pragmatic," "realistic" basis.

The result has been that liberalism has often committed itself to defensive action and narrowly conceived containment. In domestic reaction against what was taken to be a dogmatic alliance with labor, liberalism has made constant efforts to broaden its base. Arthur Schlesinger, Jr., has viewed the Democratic Party as a multi-interest party, in clear contrast to liberals who, in the thirties, wished to turn the Democratic Party into a Popular Front party. Schlesinger has also spoken of the need for a new "qualitative" liberalism to distinguish it from the "quantitative" liberalism of the New Deal. There are many ways of viewing this demand, but it is clearly an attempt to extend the base of liberalism to include other interest groups besides labor. This trend in Schlesinger's thought is clearly revealed in the comparisons he has made between the New Frontier of John F. Kennedy and the New Nationalism of Theodore Roosevelt, a comparison that is meant to indicate both men's placement of "national interest" and the "public good" above the interests of any single social or economic class. Finally, the broad movement toward "consensus" liberalism, culminating in the election of Lyndon Johnson, can be seen in historical perspective as a reaction to the liberal-labor alliance.

Awareness of Communist aims also has caused a reexamination of the problem of civil liberties. Although the response has varied from reassertion of the absolute concept of civil liberties to a new type of relativism, one trend has emerged: the rejection of the double standard of civil liberties as formulated by a number of liberals during the thirties. The new type of relativism is the most noteworthy trend because it is in some ways in clearest reaction against the naive assumptions of the Popular Front concerning Communism. But strangely enough, it has rested its case for the restrictive granting of civil liberties to antidemocratic groups on grounds that are philosophically similar to those of the Popular Front. Sidney Hook, in particular, has developed the argument that because freedom is not absolute, restrictions on civil liberties of Communists are permissible under certain circumstances.

Finally, in reaction against the optimism of the Popular Front, the pessimistic theology of Reinhold Niebuhr has become influential among secular liberals. The fallibility of man, his proneness to evil, have become liberal, as well as conservative, clichés since the war, just as man's cooperative tendencies and good will were the liberal clichés of the Popular Front. This shift in the view of human nature has served to justify the "end of ideology" and the narrowly conceived pragmatic politics of contemporary liberalism. It has reemphasized the impossibility of man's total reconstruction of society around ideological concepts.

Is the new liberalism resulting from a reaction against Popular Front thinking an improvement over that of the thirties? "Those who have forgotten the past are doomed to repeat it," George Santayana once wrote. A part of the new "radical" younger generation in the United States, impatient with old ideologies and thinking that the history of contemporary man began at Hiroshima, has turned its back on the thirties, denying that there are any lessons to be learned. "Granted that the issue of Stalinism will never be dead as long as there is a Left, that it was 'the good fight'; it is nonetheless so far from primary at this time as to be virtually an irrelevant trap for men of good will," one of the young radicals has written.[9] But the contemporary liberal has not written off the thirties as irrelevant; he has taken from them the lessons of Communist subterfuge and has rejected the sentimental, hazy view of unity that masked the horrors of Stalinism. The young radicals are wrong in thinking there is nothing to learn from the thirties, and many contemporary liberals are wrong in feeling they have learned everything worth learning. For there are other lessons to be learned besides the dangers of liberal-Communist cooperation. For example, the Popular Front was accepted because it provided a rudimentary ideology; today liberals scorn ideology. But they have placed themselves again in the predicament of liberals in the pre-Popular Front period: how to comprehend world developments without at least the rudiments of ideology? The first lesson to be learned, then, would seem to be that there are not two alternatives—ideology or no ideology. That is a dichotomy typical of the Popular Front mind; actually there can be many kinds and degrees of ideology. Nor can the liberals rest content with their new knowledge of totalitarianism, which has often paralyzed them in terms of positive political action. In short, the abandonment of ideology plus the knowledge of Communist totalitarianism leads to support of the status quo. This is not an optimistic outlook for liberalism. Nor has the new tough-minded, pessimistic pragmatism helped either: it has too often become an excuse for retreating before conservative opposition. Like the liberals of the thirties, the contemporary pragmatic liberalism has also failed to heed Bourne's words: "Vision must constantly outshoot technique, opportunist efforts usually achieve less even than what seemed obviously possible. An impossibilist élan that appeals to desire will often carry further. A philosophy of adjustment will not even make for adjustment. If you try merely to 'meet' situations as they come, you will not even meet them."[10]

Besides the dangers of a loss of creativity, there are even deeper lessons for liberalism to be gained from the thirties. These lessons revolve around power, the role of the intellectual, and the moral callousness of modern man. Many liberals in the thirties, sensing that the "Left-progressive" side was the wave of the future, chose to side with history, and therefore, ultimately, with power. It would seem, at first glance, that the contemporary liberal has transcended this. But what has actually happened is not a lessening of the lure of power, but a shifting of terms: to be on the right side of history is equated with being on the right side of the Democratic administration in power.

This thirst for the sources of influence and power is directly related to the role of the intellectual. Many liberal intellectuals of the Popular Front and the war years revealed an atrophy of the critical function. Only Fascism received its deserved condemnation. In dealing with Russia and even with the New Deal, many liberals restrained their criticism of those whom they regarded as their friends. During the Eisenhower years there was, of course, much discontent, impatience, and criticism among liberals. But one suspects now that their objections were more to the superficial style than to the substance. The Kennedy administration pursued basically the same foreign policy; its economic philosophy was only slightly less conservative; its support of civil rights was stronger, but often ambiguous. Yet the Kennedy policies were hailed by liberals as a rebirth of liberalism—the new "multi-interest," "national interest" style, of course. Of course there were exceptions; some liberals objected to the Bay of Pigs adventure (though no leading liberal resigned from the administration); there was criticism on South Vietnam; the inadequacies of this or that domestic reform were pointed out. During the thirties many liberal intellectuals, in their desire to be on the right side of history, too often became uncritical cheerleaders for the self-styled "progressive forces." In their desire to be on the right side of the present sources of power, many liberal intellectuals have again too often abdicated their role of critic and become equally unthinking backslappers.

In the end, this liberal greediness to be "in" would be no worse—and perhaps better—than other forms of sycophancy if it had not so often revealed the moral callousness of modern man. The Popular Front liberals, with their simplistic ideology and sentimental unity of "progressives," betrayed a moral callousness toward those who suffered under Stalin's crimes. But the contemporary liberal, with his new-found knowledge of totalitarianism, his hard-headed, realistic, tough-minded pragmatism, has temporized with social ills, avoided conflicts with conservatives in the name of consensus, suggested and justified outrageous actions in the name of the "free world." The old shibboleths of the Popular Front have vanished. But the Popular Front and the whole intellectual history of the thirties is in need of reexamination today not because, in rejecting them, liberals have progressed so much; they force our attention because, in coming so far, liberals have learned so little.

A NOTE ON SOURCES
NOTES
INDEX

A NOTE ON SOURCES

Since the principal sources for this work were the books and periodicals of the 1930's, it seems unnecessary to list separately the relatively few secondary works that I have consulted. They can be found in the notes. I would, however, like to call attention to Irving Howe's and Lewis Coser's *The American Communist Party* (1957), which was particularly helpful to me. Because the periodical literature from which I have drawn is so vast, a list of every article and editorial that I have read would be needlessly prolonged. Let me say only that I have read the editorials, book reviews, and letters to the editor columns in *Common Sense, The Nation, The New Masses, The New Republic*, the *New York Times, The Social Frontier*, and *Soviet Russia Today* between 1929 and 1940. Also in these periodicals, and in the others that are included in the list at the beginning of the notes, I have read the articles by the following people: Roger Baldwin, Ernest Sutherland Bates, Ralph Bates, Theodore Bayer, Carleton Beals, Charles Beard, Carl Becker, Alfred Bingham, Paul Blanshard, Bruce Bliven, H. N. Brailsford, Van Wyck Brooks, Heywood Broun, Earl Browder, Raymond Leslie Buell, Alan Calmer, V. F. Calverton, Robert Cantwell, John Chamberlain, William Henry Chamberlin, Stuart Chase, John Childs, Eunice Clark, Morris Cohen, Dudley Collard, Lewis Corey, John Cornford, George S. Counts, Malcolm Cowley, Elmer Davis, Jerome Davis, John Dewey, John Dos Passos, Theodore Draper, Pete Drucker, Robert Dunn, William Dunne, Walter Duranty, Max Eastman, Sherwood Eddy, Robert Evans, James T. Farrell, Leon Feuchtwanger, Louis Fischer, John T. Flynn, Robert Forsythe, Waldo Frank, Joseph Freeman, John Garnett, Michael Gold, C. Hartley Grattan, Harold Groves, Samuel Harper, George Hartmann, Arthur Garfield Hays, Maurice Hindus, John Haynes Holmes, Sidney Hook, Quincy Howe, Matthew Josephson, Horace

Kallen, Freda Kirchwey, Corliss Lamont, Jack Lebrome, Max Lerner, Frederick J. Libby, Walter Lippmann, Harold Loeb, Robert Morss Lovett, Ferdinand Lundberg, Eugene Lyons, Archibald MacLeish, A. B. Magil, Carey McWilliams, Agnes Meyer, Bruce Minton, Lewis Mumford, Reinhold Niebuhr, Liston Oak, David Ramsay, Selden Rodman, Edwin Rolfe, James Rorty, Anne Ross, Paul Salter, Frederick L. Schuman, Vincent Sheean, Upton Sinclair, Jessica Smith, George Soule, S. C. Spitzer, John Stevens, Maxwell S. Stewart, Allen Stiller, Benjamin Stolberg, I. F. Stone, Leland Stowe, John Strachey, Anna Louise Strong, Lillian Symes, Norman Thomas, Abraham Unger, Mary Van Kleeck, Oswald Garrison Villard, Harry F. Ward, Goodwin Watson, Otto Werner, Edmund Wilson, Ella Winter, Bertram D. Wolfe.

In addition to the periodical literature of the thirties, I have used the following books.

Adamic, Louis. *My America*. New York, 1938.

Baldwin, Roger, *Liberty Under the Soviets*. New York, 1928.

Beard, Charles A. *America in Midpassage*, New York, 1939.

————. *The Devil Theory of War*. New York, 1936.

————. *Giddy Minds and Foreign Quarrels*. New York, 1939.

————. *The Open Door at Home*. New York, 1934.

————, ed. *America Faces the Future*. Boston, 1932.

————, and William Beard. *The American Leviathan*. New York, 1930.

————, and George H. E. Smith. *The Future Comes: A Study of the New Deal*. New York, 1934.

Bingham, Alfred. *Insurgent America*. New York, 1935.

————. *Man's Estate*. New York, 1939.

————. *The United States of Europe*. New York, 1940.

————, and Selden Rodman, eds. *Challenge to the New Deal*. New York, 1934.

Bittelman, Alex. *The Communist Party in Action*. New York, 1932.

————. *Fifteen Years of the Communist Party*. New York, 1934.

————. *Milestones in the History of the Communist Party*. New York, 1937.

Browder, Earl. *Fighting for Peace*. New York, 1939.

————. *New Steps in the United Front*. New York, 1935.

————. *The People's Front*. New York, 1938.

————. *The People's Road to Peace*. New York, 1940.

————. *Reports to the Ninth Convention of the Communist Party*. New York, 1936.

————. *Talks to America*. New York, 1937.

————. *Trotskyism Against World Peace*. New York, 1937.

————. *The Way Out*. New York, 1941.

————. *What Is Communism?* New York, 1936.

Chamberlain, John. *Farewell to Reform*. New York, 1932.

Chamberlin, William Henry. *Russia's Iron Age*. Boston, 1934.

Chase, Stuart. *The Economy of Abundance*. New York, 1934.

————. *Government in Business*. New York, 1935.

————. *The Nemesis of American Business*. New York, 1931.

————. *A New Deal*. New York, 1932.

————. *The New Western Frontier*. New York, 1939.

————. *Out of the Depression—and After*. New York, 1931.

————. *Poor Old Competition*. New York, 1931.

————. *The Promise of Power*. New York, 1933.

Counts, George S. *Dare the School Build A New Social Order?* New York, 1932.

————. *A Ford Crosses Russia*. Boston, 1935.

————. *The Prospects of American Democracy*. New York, 1938.

————. *The Soviet Challenge to America*. New York, 1931.

————, Luigi Villari, Malcolm Rorty, and Newton D. Baker. *Bolshevism, Fascism, and Capitalism*. New Haven, 1932.

Davis, Jerome. *Capitalism and Its Culture*. New York, 1935.

————, ed. *The New Russia*. New York, 1933.

Dewey, John. *Impressions of Soviet Russia*. New York, 1929.

————. *Individualism Old and New*. New York, 1930.

————. *Liberalism and Social Action*. New York, 1935.

————. *Truth Is on The March*. New York, 1937.

————, et al. *The Case of Leon Trotsky*. Report of Hearings on the Charges Against Him in the Moscow Trials. New York, 1937.

————, et al. *Not Guilty*. Report of the Commission of Inquiry into the Charges Made Against Leon Trotsky in the Moscow Trials. New York, 1938.

Duranty, Walter. *Duranty Reports Russia*. New York, 1934.

————. *I Write as I Please*. New York, 1935.

Dutt, R. Palme. *Fascism and the Social Revolution*. New York, 1934.

Eddy, Sherwood. *The Challenge of Europe*. New York, 1933.

————. *The Challenge of Russia*. New York, 1931.

————. *Europe Today*. New York, 1937.

————. *Russia Today*. New York, 1934.

Fischer, Louis. *Machines and Men in Russia*. New York, 1932.

————. *Men and Politics*. New York, 1941.

————. *Soviet Journey*. New York, 1935.

————. *Stalin and Hitler.* New York, 1940.

Frank, Waldo. *Dawn in Russia.* New York, 1932.

Grattan, C. Hartley. *The Deadly Parallel.* New York, 1939.

Hallgren, Mauritz. *The Tragic Fallacy.* New York, 1937.

Hays, Arthur Garfield. *Democracy Works.* New York, 1939.

————. *Trial by Prejudice.* New York, 1933.

Hindus, Maurice. *The Great Offensive.* New York, 1933.

————. *Humanity Uprooted.* New York, 1929.

————. *Red Bread.* London, 1931.

Howe, Quincy. *Blood Is Cheaper Than Water.* New York, 1939.

————. *England Expects Every American to Do His Duty.* New York, 1939.

————. *The News and How to Understand It.* New York, 1940.

Kallen, Horace. *A Free Society.* New York, 1934.

————. *Individualism: An American Way of Life.* New York, 1933.

Lamont, Corliss. *Russia Day by Day.* New York, 1933.

————. *You Might Like Socialism.* New York, 1939.

League of American Writers. *Writers Take Sides.* New York, 1938.

Lerner, Max. *It Is Later Than You Think.* New York, 1938.

Lyons, Eugene. *Assignment in Utopia.* New York, 1937.

————. *Moscow Carrousel.* New York, 1935.

Matthews, Herbert L. *Two Wars and More to Come.* New York, 1938.

Mumford, Lewis. *Men Must Act.* New York, 1939.

Russell, Bertrand, John Dewey, Morris Cohen, Sidney Hook, and Sherwood Eddy. *The Meaning of Marx: A Symposium.* New York, 1934.

Schuman, Frederick L. *Europe on the Eve.* New York, 1939.

————. *The Nazi Dictatorship.* New York, 1936.

————. *Night Over Europe.* New York, 1941.

Sheean, Vincent. *Personal History.* New York, 1937.

Sinclair, Upton, and Eugene Lyons. *Terror in Russia?* New York, 1938.

Soule, George. *The Coming American Revolution.* New York, 1934.

————. *An Economic Constitution for Democracy.* New Haven, 1939.

————. *The Future of Liberty.* New York, 1936.

————. *The Planned Society.* New York, 1932.

Stolberg, Benjamin, and Warren Jay Vinton. *The Economic Consequences of the New Deal.* New York, 1935.

Stowe, Leland. *Nazi Means War.* New York, 1934.

Strachey, John. *The Coming Struggle for Power.* London, 1932.

————. *The Menace of Fascism.* New York, 1933.

Strong, Anna Louise. *I Change Worlds.* New York, 1935.

————. *The New Soviet Constitution.* New York, 1937.

————. *The Soviets Conquer Wheat*. New York, 1931.

————. *Spain in Arms: 1937*. New York, 1937.

Swing, Raymond Gram. *Forerunners of American Fascism*. New York, 1935.

Thomas, Norman. *America's Way Out: A Program for Democracy*. New York, 1931.

————. *As I See It*. New York, 1932.

————. *The Choice Before Us*. New York, 1934.

————. *Democracy versus Dictatorship*. New York, 1937.

————. *Socialism on the Defensive*. New York, 1938.

————. *A Socialist Looks at the New Deal*. New York, 1933.

Ward, Harry F. *Democracy and Social Change*. New York, 1940.

————. *In Place of Profit*. New York, 1933.

————. *Our Economic Morality*. New York, 1929.

Wattenberg, William C. *On the Educational Frontier*. New York, 1936.

Williams, Albert Rhys. *The Soviets*. New York, 1937.

NOTES

The following abbreviations are used in the notes:

A, *Atlantic Monthly*
AA, *Annals of the American Academy of Political and Social Science*
AM, *American Mercury*
AS, *American Scholar*
C, *Contemporary Review*
CC, *Christian Century*
CH, *Current History*
CM, *Century Magazine*
CS, *Common Sense*
E, *Events*
F, *Forum*
H, *Harper's Magazine*
IW, *Independent Woman*
MM, *Modern Monthly*
N, *Nation*

NAR, *North American Review*
NM, *New Masses*
NR, *New Republic*
NS, *New Statesman and Nation*
PQ, *Political Quarterly*
S, *Scribner's Magazine*
SEP, *Saturday Evening Post*
SF, *Social Frontier*
SG, *Survey Graphic*
SR, *Southern Review*
SRL, *Saturday Review of Literature*
SRT, *Soviet Russia Today*
VQ, *Virginia Quarterly*
WT, *World Tomorrow*
YR, *Yale Review*

2. *Liberalism Reconsidered: 1930-1935*

1. N (March 28, 1934), p.345.
2. George Soule, "Hard-Boiled Radicalism," NR (January 21, 1931), pp.262-63.
3. Quoted in William Leuchtenberg, *The Perils of Prosperity 1914-32* (Chicago, 1958), p.124.
4. Allan Nevins, "A General Evaluation," in *John D. Rockefeller: Robber Baron or Industrial Statesman?*, ed. Earl Latham (Boston, 1949), pp.77-82.

5. Quoted in Leuchtenberg, p.122.

6. Michael Gold, "Notes of the Month," *NM* (October, 1930), p.4; Paul Salter and Jack Lebrome, "Dewey, Russell and Cohen: Why They Are Anti-Communist," *NM* (July 24, 1934), p.23; *NM* (June 5, 1934), p.6; Gold, "Notes of the Month," *NM* (April, 1930), pp.3-5; S. C. Spitzer, "A Liberal Has an Open Mind," *NM* (June, 1931), p.11; Gold, "Mr. Steffens Liked Everybody," *NM* (June, 1931), p.5.

7. Reinhold Niebuhr, "After Capitalism—What?," *WT* (March, 1933), p.203; Lewis Mumford, "What I Believe," *F* (November, 1930), p.263; C. Hartley Grattan, "What Is Liberalism," *CS* (September, 1933), pp.15-17.

8. Louis Fischer, "America Revisited—1935," *NS* (May 4, 1935), p.612.

9. Elmer Davis, "Interregnum," *SRL* (May 16, 1931), p.831; Horace Kallen, *A Free Society* (New York, 1934), pp.43-44; Morris Cohen, "Why I Am Not a Communist," *MM* (April, 1934), pp.135-36, 141; John Dewey, "Why I Am Not a Communist," *MM* (April, 1934), pp.136-37; Alfred Bingham, *Insurgent America* (New York, 1935), pp.29, 179; Alfred Bingham and Selden Rodman, "Radical Parties (II), The Communist Party of America," *CS* (November, 1934), p.120 ff; Elmer Davis, "Confidence in Whom?" *F* (January, 1933), p.33; Archibald MacLeish, "Technocracy Speaks," *SRL* (January 28, 1933), p.400.

10. Oswald Garrison Villard, "Issues and Men," *N* (January 23, 1935), p.91; Carl Becker, "Liberalism—A Way Station," *SRL* (December 3, 1932), p.282; Charles A. Beard and William Beard, *The American Leviathan* (New York, 1930), pp.11-19; Archibald MacLeish, "To the Young Men of Wall St.," *SRL* (January 16, 1932), p.454; Kallen, *A Free Society*, pp.2-10, 38-40; Charles Beard, "Congress under Fire," *YR* (September, 1932), pp.44-45; Cohen, "Why I Am Not a Communist," p.138; John Chamberlain, "Democracy and Capitalism," *CS* (December, 1934), pp.6-8.

11. *CS* (April, 1934), p.3; Alfred Bingham, *CS* (September, 1935), p.28.

12. Cohen, "Why I Am Not a Communist," pp.141-42.

13. Edmund Wilson, "What Do the Liberals Hope For?," *NR* (February 10, 1932), pp.345-48; Stuart Chase, "Mr. Chase Replies," *NR* (February 10, 1932), pp.348-49.

14. Stuart Chase, *A New Deal* (New York, 1932), pp.153-73.

15. *N* (March 12, 1930), pp.284-85; *N* (July 26, 1933), p.86.

16. *NM* (June 5, 1934), p.6; *N* (December 12, 1934), p.660; *N* (July 3, 1935), p.3.

17. *NR* (August 9, 1933), pp.329-30.

18. Bruce Bliven, "The Second World War," *NR* (March 9, 1932), p.94; George Soule, "William Z. Foster," *NR* (October 5, 1932), p.199; Soule, "U.S.S.A.," *NR* (September 28, 1932), p.186.

19. *NR* (August 17, 1932), pp.4-6; *NR* (October 26, 1932), pp.272-74; Matthew Josephson, "Norman Thomas: The Enraptured Socialist," *NR* (August 10, 1932), pp.352-55.

20. *NR* (August 19, 1931), pp.4-5; *NR* (October 7, 1931), p.210.

21. *NR* (May 10, 1933), p.349.

22. *NR* (October 5, 1932), p.194; *NR* (February 28, 1934), pp.58-59; *NR* (March 7, 1934), p.87.

23. George Soule, *The Coming American Revolution* (New York, 1934), pp.10-22, 66-71.

24. Ibid., pp.10, 146-49, 183-201.

25. Ibid., pp.207-209, 217-18, 258-61, 281-83, 302-304.

26. Ibid., pp.283-89.

27. John Dewey, *Liberalism and Social Action* (New York, 1935), p.88.

28. Edmund Wilson, "An Appeal to Progressivism," *NR* (January 14, 1931), pp.234-38.

29. George Soule, "Hard Boiled Radicalism," *NR* (January 21, 1931), pp.261-65; *NR* (May 27, 1931), pp.31-32.

30. Edmund Wilson, "What Do the Liberals Hope For?," *NR* (February 10, 1932), p.348; *NR* (February 10, 1932), pp.336-37.

31. *NR* (January 23, 1935), pp.290-91; *NR* (February 10, 1932), p.337.

32. *NR* (January 23, 1935), pp.291-92.

33. *NR* (January 23, 1935), p.292.

34. Alfred Bingham, *CS* (September, 1935), p.28; John Dewey, *CS* (December, 1935), p.23.

35. Dewey, *Liberalism and Social Action*, pp.32-34, 38, 47-48, 54-55, 57, 62-63, 86-87, 91.

36. Bingham, *Insurgent America*, pp.16-17, 21-29, 42-43, 55-56, 60-63, 65-66, 78-87, 97, 179, 196-206, 237-246.

37. Ibid., p.85.

3. Crisis of Capitalism

1. George S. Counts, "Education—for What?," *NR* (May 25, 1932), p.40.

2. Daniel Bell, "The Background and Development of Marxian Socialism in the United States," in *Socialism and American Life,* ed.

Donald Egbert and Stow Persons (Princeton, 1952), I, 351n; William Z. Foster, *Toward Soviet America* (New York, 1932), p.69; Earl Browder, *Communism in the United States* (New York, 1935), p.27; Irving Howe and Lewis Coser, *The American Communist Party* (Boston, 1957), p.189.

3. Alfred Bingham, *Man's Estate* (New York, 1939), p.37.

4. Oswald Garrison Villard, *N* (July 26, 1932), pp.52-53; Charles A. Beard, "A 'Five-Year Plan' for America," in *America Faces the Future*, ed. Charles A. Beard (Boston, 1932), p.120; Foster, *Toward Soviet America*, p.69; *NR* (June 24, 1931), pp.138-39.

5. "Manifesto of the Communist Party of the United States," in Earl Browder, *What Is Communism?* (New York, 1936), pp.239-40; "Report of the Central Committee to the Eighth Convention of the Communist Party in April, 1934," in Browder, *Communism in the United States*, pp.28-29, 31, 35-36; Browder, "What Every Worker Should Know About the N.R.A.," in *Communism in the United States*, pp.166, 171-72; "Excerpts from Report to the Extraordinary Party Conference in July, 1933" in Browder, *Communism in the United States*, pp.114-19; *NM* (March 19, 1935), p.8; William F. Dunne, "Three Months of the New Deal," *NM* (June, 1933), p.15.

6. Bell, "Marxian Socialism in the United States," p.353; Howe and Coser, *The American Communist Party*, pp.233, 329; A. B. Magil, "Roosevelt's Record," *NM* (June 9, 1936), pp.13-15; Browder, *The People's Front* (New York, 1938), pp.25-26, 29-30, 81, 129-30, 322, 332; A. B. Magil, "The New Deal: 1933-1938," *NM* (July 5, 1938), p.6; Browder, *Fighting for Peace* (New York, 1939), pp.144-45.

7. Harry F. Ward, "The Development of Fascism in the United States," *AA* (July, 1935), pp.56-61. Also Stuart Chase, *The Economy of Abundance* (New York, 1934), p.316; "Government in Business," *CH* (March, 1935), pp.641-42; "The Consumer's Tomorrow," *S* (December, 1933), pp.335-36; "If Roosevelt Fails," *S* (July, 1934), p.11; "How Can the State Do Business?," *CH* (May, 1935), p.128; "The Trend Toward Collectivism," *Fortnightly* (April, 1935), p.431; *Government in Business* (New York, 1935), pp.40-45; "Elegy for the Elite," *N* (November 21, 1936), p.600.

8. Oswald Garrison Villard, "America's National Recovery in the Balance," *PQ* (January, 1934), p.54; Villard et al., "A Statement to the President," *N* (May 30, 1934), pp.617-19; "President Roosevelt in Mid-Channel," *C* (May, 1935), pp.531-32; "Issues and Men," *N* (February 6, 1935), p.147; "Issues and Men," *N* (December 25, 1935), p.731; "Issues and Men," *N* (October 10, 1936), p.420; "Issues and Men," *N*

(May 14, 1938), p.561. Also Charles A. Beard and George H. E. Smith, *The Future Comes: A Study of the New Deal* (New York, 1934), pp. 161-170. Also Charles A. Beard, "Behind the New Deal," *SRL* (December 22, 1934), p.382; "National Politics and War," *S* (February, 1935), p.70; *America in Midpassage* (New York, 1939), pp.947-48.

9. Bruce Bliven, "Franklin D. Roosevelt," *NR* (June 1, 1932), pp. 63-64; *N* (July 13, 1932), p.22; *N* (January 20, 1932), p.58.

10. *N* (March 9, 1933), p.251; *NR* (January 17, 1934), p.263; George Soule, "Destination Unknown," *NR* (May 2, 1934), p.341; *N* (March 7, 1934), p.263; *N* (February 13, 1935), p.172; *N* (January 3, 1934), p.4; *N* (December 20, 1933), p.696; *NR* (June 7, 1933), pp.85-86; William Dunne, "Three Months of the New Deal," *NM* (June, 1933), p.15; *NR* (November 9, 1932), p.341; Bruce Bliven, "Roosevelt and the Radicals," *NR* (July 12, 1933), p.230; George Soule, "Roosevelt Confronts Capitalism," *NR* (October 18, 1933), p.271; *NR* (December 27, 1933), p.182; *NR* (June 20, 1934), p.141; *NR* (August 14, 1935), p.6; *CS* (April 27, 1933), p.2; *CS* (March, 1934), pp.2-3; *CS* (September, 1934), pp.2-3.

11. *CS* (February, 1934), pp.2-3; *CS* (September, 1934), pp.2-3; *N* (July 5, 1933), p.1; *N* (September 27, 1933), p.337; *NR* (August 23, 1933), pp.33-34; *NR* (August 30, 1933), pp.59-60; *NR* (August 30, 1933), p.56; George Soule, "The New Deal in Practice," *NR* (July 5, 1933), p.199; *NR* (July 12, 1933), p.222; *N* (June 27, 1934), p.716; *NR* (August 1, 1934), pp.305-306; *N* (June 12, 1935), pp.669, 672-73; *NR* (June 5, 1935), p.86.

12. Bruce Bliven, "Not Kerensky: Lloyd George," *NR* (April 11, 1934), p.232.

13. Norman Thomas, "Will Fascism Come to America?," *MM* (September, 1934), p.463; Reinhold Niebuhr, "Notes from a Berlin Diary," *CC* (July 5, 1933), p.872; Niebuhr, "The Germans: Unhappy Philosophers in Politics," *AS* (October, 1933), p.409.

14. *NR* (January 16, 1935), pp.279-80.

15. *NR* (October 16, 1935), pp.257-58; Max Lerner, "What Is Usable in Veblen?," *NR* (May 15, 1935), p.10; *CS* (June, 1936), p.4.

16. *CS* (April 13, 1932), p.2; *CS* (August, 1936), pp.3-4; *CS* (December, 1936), pp.3-5; *CS* (August, 1937), pp.3-5; *CS* (June, 1936), p.3; *CS* (October, 1936), pp.3-4 ff.; *CS* (November, 1936), pp.3-4.

17. *CS* (July, 1937), pp.3-4; *CS* (September, 1937), pp.3-5.

18. *N* (September 4, 1937), p.230; *N* (June 12, 1937), p.666; *N* (November 20, 1937), p.545; *NR* (September 29, 1937), pp.201-202.

19. *N* (August 21, 1935), p.202.

20. John Dewey, *Individualism Old and New* (New York, 1930), p.118; *NR* (February 10, 1932), p.337; *N* (May 27, 1931), p.573.

21. Browder, *Communism in the United States*, p.105; Browder, "Why Capitalism Can't Plan," *NM* (December 25, 1934), pp.17-19; Michael Gold, "Notes of the Month," *NM* (October, 1930), p.4; Gold, "The Intellectual Road to Fascism," *NM* (November, 1931), pp.10-11; Granville Hicks, "How I Came to Communism," *NM* (September, 1932), p.8; Louis Fischer, George Soule, Edward A. Filene, "Can We Have National Planning Without a Revolution?" *Foreign Policy Association Pamphlets*, No. 81 (April 2, 1932), pp.3-9.

22. *CS* (March 2, 1933), p.15.

23. Quoted from the Chamber of Commerce Report, May 1, 1931, in Charles A. Beard, "The Rationality of Planned Economy," in *America Faces the Future*, ed. Charles A. Beard (Boston, 1932), p.402.

24. Stuart Chase, *Out of the Depression—and After* (New York, 1931), pp.6-7; Chase, "If Roosevelt Fails," *S* (July, 1934), p.7; Chase, *The Economy of Abundance* (New York, 1934), pp.309-10; Chase, "How Can the State Do Business?," *CH* (May, 1935), p.133; Chase, *Government in Business* (New York, 1935), pp.216-57; Chase, "The Age of Distribution," *N* (July 25, 1934), p.94.

25. J. M. Clark, George Soule et al., "Long-Range Planning," *NR* (January 13, 1932), p.7; *NR* (January 13, 1932), p.225; *NR* (February 10, 1932), p.337; George Soule, *The Planned Society* (New York, 1932), pp.277-79; Soule, "Planning—for Profit," *CS* (March 2, 1933), p.15; Fischer, Soule, et al., "Can We Have National Planning Without a Revolution?" pp.11-13.

26. Beard, "A 'Five-Year Plan' for America," pp.124-135; Beard, "The Rationality of Planned Economy," p.408.

27. "A Plan of Transition to an Economy of Abundance through Production for Use," *CS* (May, 1935), pp.6, 9-10; *CS* (July, 1935), p.25.

28. "A Plan of Transition . . . ," pp.9-10.

29. Stuart Chase, "Harnessing the Wild Horses of Industry," *A* (June, 1931), pp.784-785; Michael Gold, "Hunger March," *NM* (December, 1931), pp.7-8; Robert Evans, "Pilgrims of Confusion," *NM* (February, 1932), p.8; David Ramsey and Alan Calmer, "The Marxism of V. F. Calverton," *NM* (January, 1933), p.25; Chase, "A Ten Year Plan for America," *H* (June, 1931), p.7; Chase, *Government in Business*, pp.280-81.

30. George Soule, "Mr. Keynes' Recipe for Stabilization," *NR* (May 13, 1931), p.361; Soule, *The Planned Society*, pp.182, 252-263, 276-77.

31. Beard, "A 'Five-Year Plan' for America," pp.118, 122, 134, 139; Beard, "The Rationality of Planned Economy," pp.403-404.

32. Soule, *The Planned Society*, pp.205, 216, 228-29; Stuart Chase, *A New Deal* (New York, 1932) pp.48-49; Chase, *Government in Business* (New York, 1935), pp.74-75, 246, 260-61; Chase, "Harnessing the Wild Horses of Industry," p.781.

33. Chase, *A New Deal*, p.252. Eugene Lyons seized on this sentence to demonstrate the self-delusion of liberals who mistook "heaped-up horror and multiple catastrophe for 'fun.' " See Eugene Lyons, *The Red Decade* (Indianapolis, 1941), p.102. It was necessary for someone to point out the horror of what was going on in Russia and the liberal's picture of Russian planning. But there is a certain literalness in Lyons' view that is slightly unfair to Chase. In the context of Chase's thought, the passage shows more of a desire and impatience to "get moving" in America than to imitate the Russian experiment.

34. Soule, *The Planned Society*, pp.152-53; Chase, *The Economy of Abundance*, pp.287-96; Chase, *The Promise of Power* (New York, 1933), p.15.

35. Soule, *The Planned Society*, pp.210-11; Chase, "The Consumer's Tomorrow," S (December, 1933), p.336; Chase, *The Nemesis of American Business* (New York, 1931), pp.95-96; Chase, "Column Left," S (March, 1932), p.142.

36. Chase, *Out of the Depression—and After*, p.11.

37. Chase, "Column Left," p.141.

4. Soviet Russia: Lodestone of the American Liberal

1. Roger Baldwin, *Liberty Under the Soviets* (New York, 1928), pp.2-3; John Dewey, *Impressions of Soviet Russia* (New York, 1929), pp.114-16.

2. Baldwin, *Liberty Under the Soviets*, pp.2-7, 270-72; Dewey, *Impressions of Soviet Russia*, pp.24, 31-32, 52-58, 61, 109, 114-16, 120-23, 130-32.

3. George Soule, "Will the 'Five-Year Plan' Succeed?," NR (December 3, 1930), pp.61, 64; NR (August 12, 1931), pp.327-29; NR (November 16, 1932), p.3; N (February 22, 1933), p.190; Alfred Bingham, "What Is Production for Use?" CS (May, 1936), pp.21-24; CS (December, 1935), p.5; Sherwood Eddy, *Russia Today* (New York, 1934), pp. 45-66; Stuart Chase, "The Engineer as Poet," NR (May 20, 1931), p.24.

4. Charles A. Beard, "Congress Under Fire," *YR* (September, 1932), pp.35-51; Carl Becker, "Liberalism—A Way Station," *SRL* (December 3, 1932), p.282; Becker, "Freedom of Speech," *N* (January 24, 1934), p.96; Elmer Davis, "Can Business Manage Itself?," *H* (March, 1931), p.388; Davis, "Interregnum," *SRL* (May 16, 1931), p.831; John Dewey, "Surpassing America," *NR* (April 15, 1931), pp.241-43; Dewey, "Making Soviet Citizens," *NR* (June 8, 1932), p.104; Dewey, "Why I Am Not a Communist," *MM* (April, 1934), pp.135-37.

5. Horace Kallen, "Arts Under a Dictatorship," *SRL* (December 29, 1928), pp.550-51; Kallen, "Consumers' Economy—and Its Rivals," *CC* (January 9, 1935), pp.46-47; Oswald Garrison Villard, "The Observer's Problem," *N* (November 6, 1929), p.517; Villard, "Russia from a Car Window: V. The Soviets and the Human Being," *N* (December 4, 1929), p.654; Villard, "Russia from a Car Window: VI. The Soviets and the Future," *N* (December 11, 1929), p.714; Villard, "Our Attitude Toward Russia," *N* (August 3, 1930), p.173; Villard, "Issues and Men," *N* (December 26, 1934), p.729; Villard, "Issues and Men," *N* (January 23, 1935), p.91.

6. Sherwood Eddy, *The Challenge of Russia* (New York, 1931), p.7; Bruce Bliven, "Russia in Hope," *NR* (December 2, 1931), p.60; *New York Times,* January 26, 1930, Sec. 3, p.4; Chase, "The Engineer as Poet," *NR* (May 20, 1931), pp.24-25.

7. Louis Fischer, "The Russian Revolution Comes of Age," *N* (November 13, 1935), p.557; Fischer, "The Russian Giant," *N* (October 23, 1935), p.466; Eddy, *The Challenge of Russia,* p.21; Anna Rochester, *NM* (April, 1931), p.18; Corliss Lamont, "What Sherwood Eddy Failed to Learn," *SRT* (March, 1934), p.16; Liston Oak, *NM* (March 6, 1934), p.24.

8. *NR* (April 11, 1934), pp.229-230; *NR* (September 14, 1932), pp.111-112; *NR* (August 30, 1933), p.57; Bliven, "Russia in Hope," p.61; Anna Louise Strong, *The Soviets Conquer Wheat* (New York, 1931), passim; Michael Gold, "Is the Small Farmer Dying?" *NR* (October 7, 1931), p.211.

9. Maurice Hindus, *The Great Offensive* (New York, 1933), pp. 28-29; Hindus, *Humanity Uprooted* (New York, 1939), p.173; Hindus, *Red Bread* (London, 1931), pp.73-74, 334-35; William C. White, Maurice Hindus, et al., "Social Conditions in Soviet Russia," *Foreign Policy Association Pamphlets,* No. 72 (New York, January 31, 1931), p.10.

10. Louis Fischer, *Soviet Journey* (New York, 1935), pp.93, 172; Walter Duranty, *I Write As I Please,* pp.274, 302; Lamont, "What Sher-

wood Eddy Failed to Learn," p.16; Harry F. Ward, *In Place of Profit* (New York, 1933), p.221.

11. George S. Counts, *The Soviet Challenge to America* (New York, 1931), p.337; Hindus, *The Great Offensive*, pp.60, 189, 204, 235, 326; Eddy, *Russia Today*, pp.117-29; Maxwell S. Stewart, "Why Do Russians Work So Hard?" *CC* (September 16, 1931), p.1144; Ward, *In Place of Profit*, pp.93, 96-97, 389-90, 429-58; Ward, *NR* (March 29, 1933), pp.188-89.

12. Frederick L. Schuman, "Intervention—Myth or Menace?," *SRT* (August, 1932), p.12.

13. Schuman, "Soviet Foreign Policy: An Interpretation," *SRT* (November, 1932), pp.4-5 ff; Eddy, *The Challenge of Russia*, pp.198-205; Hindus, *The Great Offensive*, pp.349-68; Louis Fischer, *Men and Machines in Russia* (New York, 1932), pp.70, 80; Corliss Lamont, "Peace, Business and Recognition of Soviet Russia," *SRT* (September, 1932), p.3; *NR* (February 17, 1932), p.2; *NR* (May 27, 1931), p.28; Bliven, "Russia in Hope," p.61.

14. *New York Times*, December 1, 1931, p.26; Lamont, "Peace, Business and Recognition of Soviet Russia," p.3; Louis Fischer, "Bolshevik Foreign Policy," *YR* (March, 1930), p.517; *NR* (August 2, 1933), p.304; *NR* (December 28, 1932), p.175.

15. Louis Fischer, "What Is Soviet Russia?" *N* (July 6, 1932), p.6; Eddy, *The Challenge of Russia*, pp.198-217; *CS* (September, 1935), p.6; *NR* (July 23, 1930), p.276; *NR* (December 31, 1930), p.176.

16. Jerome Davis, "The Communist Party and the Government," in *The New Russia*, ed. Jerome Davis (New York, 1933), p.130; Davis, "Capitalism and Communism," *AA* (July, 1931), pp.62-75; Louis Fischer, "Russia Moves Toward Democracy," *CH* (September, 1935), p.609; Bliven, "Russia in Hope," p.60; Lamont, "What Sherwood Eddy Failed to Learn," p.16; Davis, "The Challenge of Dictatorship," *CM* (Spring, 1930), p.174; Davis, "Joseph Stalin—Russia's Ruler Today," *CH* (March, 1929), p.966; *NR* (October 26, 1932), p.271; Counts, *The Soviet Challenge to America*, pp. 41-42; Eddy, *The Challenge of Russia*, p.187; Fischer, "Russia Moves Toward Democracy," *CH* (September, 1935), pp.602-609; Fischer, "Behind the Kirov Executions II," *N* (May 15, 1935), pp.566-68; Roger Baldwin, "Freedom in the U.S.A. and the U.S.S.R.," *SRT* (September, 1934), p.11; Ward, *In Place of Profit*, p. 225.

17. Baldwin, "Freedom in the U.S.A. and the U.S.S.R.," p.11; Walter Duranty, *Duranty Reports Russia* (New York, 1934), p. 253; Davis, "The Communist Party and the Government," p.131.

18. Davis, "Joseph Stalin—Russia's Ruler Today," p.966; Ward, *In Place of Profit*, pp.224-25; Anna Louise Strong, "Stalin in Action," *Asia* (January, 1934), pp.19-21; Strong, "The Soviet Dictatorship," *AM* (October, 1934), pp.170-71, 177, 179.

19. Anna Louise Strong, "Searching Out the Soviets," *NR* (August 7, 1935), p.357; Louis Fischer, "Servants of the State," *N* (November 26, 1930), p.577; Walter Duranty, "A Letter from Moscow," *Spectator* (December 20, 1930), p.976; Duranty, *I Write As I Please*, p.188.

20. *CS* (January, 1935), p.5; Eddy, *The Challenge of Russia*, pp. 198-217; *N* (April 26, 1933), p. 457; *N* (May 3, 1933), p.490; *N* (December 19, 1934), p. 696.

21. *NR* (November 26, 1930), pp.28-29; *NR* (December 10, 1930), p.84; *NR* (December 17, 1930), pp.121-22; *NR* (December 12, 1934), p.115; *NR* (December 19, 1934), p.151; *NR* (January 9, 1935), p.233; *NR* (January 16, 1935), p.259.

22. *NM* (December 25, 1934), p.10; *NM* (January 8, 1935), p.5; *NM* (January 29, 1935), p.5; *NM* (March 5, 1935), pp.4-5.

23. *NR* (January 23, 1935), pp.292-93; *NR* (January 30, 1935), p. 316.

24. Maxwell S. Stewart, *CC* (December 24, 1930), pp.1597-1598.

25. See Irving Howe and Lewis Coser, "Authoritarians of the 'Left,' " in *Voices of Dissent* (New York, 1954), pp.89-99. Howe and Coser write: "An essential element of 'left' authoritarianism is the idea that expansion of productive forces is 'progressive' or at least potentially progressive.' " (p.92.)

26. See e.g., Bruce Bliven, "Russia Marches Up a Mountain," *NR* (May 27, 1931), p.43.

5. The Fascist Tiger at the Gates

1. Bruce Bliven, "Germany in Fear," *NR* (November 18, 1931), p.8.

2. *NR* (June 13, 1934), p.113; *NR* (August 15, 1934), pp.5-7.

3. R. Palme Dutt, *Fascism and the Social Revolution* (New York, 1934), p.80; John Strachey, *The Menace of Fascism* (New York, 1933), p.125; *NM* (October 15, 1935), p.8; "Report of the Central Committee of the Eighth Convention of the Communist Party in April, 1934;" in Earl Browder, *Communism in the United States* (New York, 1935), p.27; Alfred Bingham, *Insurgent America* (New York, 1935), pp.104, 122-23, 134-35.

4. Bingham, *Insurgent America*, pp.104-105, 111, 134-35; "Report

of the Central Committee . . .," p.29; Strachey, *The Menace of Fascism,* pp.126-27; Dutt, *Fascism and the Social Revolution,* pp.77, 81.

5. Strachey, *The Menace of Fascism,* p.77; Bingham, *Insurgent America,* p.142.

6. "Report of the Central Committee . . ., p.28; Strachey, *The Menace of Fascism,* pp.142, 266-67; Bingham, *Insurgent America,* pp. 154-71; *CS* (August, 1933), pp.2-3; *CS* (September, 1935), pp.2-3; *CS* (August, 1937), pp. 3-5.

7. Max Lerner, "The Patterns of Fascism," *YR* (December, 1934), pp.301-302; A. B. Magil, "On the Right We Have," *NM* (September 24, 1935), p.24.

8. Frederick L. Schuman, *The Nazi Dictatorship* (New York, 1936), pp.87-91, 388, 396, 501, 503; Schuman, "Fascism: Nemesis of Civilization," *SR* (Summer, 1936), pp.126-33.

9. Stuart Chase, "Will Fascism Come to America?" *MM* (September, 1934), pp.456-57; John Chamberlain, "Capitalism by Violence," *SRL* (October 7, 1933), pp.157-58.

10. *NR* (August 31, 1932), p. 60; *NR* (July 4, 1934), pp.196-97; *N* (February 15, 1933), p. 164; *N* (October 11, 1933), p. 397; *NR* (July 18, 1934), pp. 251-52; *NR* (July 25, 1934), pp. 278-79; *NR* (August 15, 1934), p. 6.

11. *NR* (December 5, 1934), pp.87-89; *N* (February 27, 1935), p.334.

12. *NR* (March 20, 1935), pp.146-47.

13. Sidney Hook, "Against the Fascist Terror in Germany," *NM* (April, 1933), pp.11-12.

14. "Report of the Central Committee . . .," p.28.

15. *NR* (November 10, 1932), p.6; *NR* (February 8, 1933), p.337; *NR* (November 7, 1934), p.355; Reinhold Niebuhr, "Why German Socialism Crashed," *CC* (April 5, 1933), p.451.

6. Behind the Popular Front

1. Earl Browder, *The People's Front* (New York, 1938), p.25.

2. Browder, *The People's Front,* pp.31-33, 112, 153-281; Browder, *Fighting for Peace* (New York, 1939), p.157.

3. Corliss Lamont, "The March to Socialist Victory," *SRT* (November, 1937), pp.8-9; Mary van Kleeck, "Soviet Planning," *SRT* November, 1937), p. 17 ff; Anna Louise Strong, "I Watched the Soviets Grow," *SRT* (November, 1937), pp.14-15 ff; Jerome Davis, "The Soviet Union in 1938," *SRT* (November, 1938), pp. 38-39; George Soule, "Does Socialism Work? I. How People Live in the Soviet Union,"

NR (February 5, 1936), pp.358-59; Soule, "Does Socialism Work? II. Materialism and Culture in the Soviet Union," *NR* (February 12, 1936), pp.9-13; Soule, "Does Socialism Work? III. Judging the Soviet Union," *NR* (February 19, 1936), pp.37-41; Harry F. Ward et al., "Leaders of Labor, Science, Religion, Letters—Hail Soviet Peace Effort," *SRT* (November, 1936), pp.18-19; Corliss Lamont et al., "The Soviet Union: Defender of Democracy and Peace," *SRT* (November, 1938), pp.8-9; Lamont, "Champion of World Peace," *SRT* (May, 1937), p.48; Louis Fischer, "The New Soviet Constitution," *N* (June 17, 1936), p.772; *N* (June 17, 1936), p.761; *NR* (June 24, 1936), pp. 192-93; Anna Louise Strong, "100 Million Voters," *SRT* (December, 1937), p.7 ff; Strong, *The New Soviet Constitution* (New York, 1937), passim; Fischer, "The First True Democracy," *SRT* (May, 1937), p.9.

4. In denying that the success of the Popular Front and the influence of Stalinism were due to a "machiavellian conspiracy," Irving Howe and Lewis Coser have written: "The influence of Stalinism grew in the intellectual or quasi-intellectual world mainly because it was best able to provide the rudimentary ideology, the few threadbare slogans that corresponded to the yearnings of men of good will and not much political sophistication." See Irving Howe and Lewis Coser, *The American Communist Party* (Boston, 1957), p.314.

5. *NR* (April 18, 1934), p.274.

6. Harry F. Ward, "Liberalism at the Crisis," *CC* (March 25, 1936), p.464; *SF* (January, 1936), p.104; *NR* (January 8, 1936), p.241.

7. Frederick L. Schuman, "Liberalism and Communism Reconsidered," *SR* (Autumn, 1936), pp.326-28.

8. Schuman, "Liberalism and Communism Reconsidered," pp.328-32, 336-38; Schuman, "Give Me Liberty," *NR* (June 23, 1937), p.201.

9. Max Lerner, *It Is Later Than You Think* (New York, 1938), pp. x, 46-47, 66-72, 139-42, 235-38.

10. Lerner, *It Is Later Than You Think*, pp.73-74, 77-78.

11. Ernest Sutherland Bates, "Walter Lippmann: The Career of 'Comrade Fool,' " *MM* (June, 1933), p.270; Harry F. Ward, "Christians and Communists," *CC* (December 25, 1935) pp.1651-1652; Maurice Hindus, "A Russian-German Kinship? Fundamentally Opposed," *Christian Science Monitor Weekly Magazine*, August 5, 1939, p.5 ff; I. F. Stone, "Max Lerner's Capitalist Collectivism," *SR* (Spring, 1939) p. 658; *NR* (September 7, 1938), p.115; *N* (April 10, 1937), p.396.

12. *NR* (December 12, 1934), p.114; *NR* (July 8, 1931), pp. 189-90.

13. *NR* (May 15, 1935), p.3; Roger Baldwin, "Forces that Hamper

the School from Without," *SF* (March, 1936), pp.183-84; Baldwin, "Personal Liberty," *AA* (May, 1936), pp.162-69; Max Lerner, "The Task for Progressives," *N* (November 14, 1936), pp.569-70; Frederick L. Schuman, "The Nazi International," *NR* (July 8, 1936), p.275; *CS* (February, 1935), pp.2-3; *CS* (June 8, 1933), p.3; John Dewey, *Liberalism and Social Action* (New York, 1935), p.91; Dewey, "United, We Shall Stand," *SF* (April, 1935), p.12; Norman Thomas, *The Choice Before Us* (New York, 1934), p.81.

14. Freda Kirchwey, "Fable for Our Time," *N* (April 29, 1939), p.486; Heywood Broun, "Shoot the Works: Shades of Thomas Jefferson," *NR* (July 20, 1938), p.305; *N* (June 4, 1938), pp.632-33; Malcolm Cowley, "Notes on a Writers' Congress," *NR* (June 21, 1939), pp. 192-93.

15. Heywood Broun, "Shoot the Works: Only a Boy," *NR* (August 17, 1938), p.45.

16. Upton Sinclair and Eugene Lyons, *Terror in Russia?* (New York, 1938), pp.25-26; Quincy Howe, "The Liquidation of the Liberal Tradition," *NA* (Autumn, 1939), p.65.

17. *NR* (December 22, 1937), p.202; *N* (August 7, 1935), p.145.

18. Browder, *The People's Front,* p.347; Ward, "Christians and Communists," pp.1651-1652; Bruce Bliven, "Twilight of Capitalism," *AM* (September, 1938), p.85; Archibald MacLeish, "Liberalism and the Anti-Fascist Front," *SG* (May, 1939), pp.321-22; A. B. Magil, "Mr. MacLeish Hesitates," *NM* (May 30, 1939), pp.21-24.

19. Max Lerner, "Do Free Markets Make Free Men?" *SR* (Spring, 1938), p.638; George Soule, "Capitalism Without Capital," *H* (June, 1938), p.27; *N* (June 4, 1938), p.632; Van Wyck Brooks, "The League of American Writers: A Personal Statement," *NR* (February 22, 1939), p.66; A. B. Magil, "Max Lerner's Credo," *NM* (February 21, 1939), p.25.

20. Heywood Broun, "Shoot the Works: Foray into the Past," *NR* (August 10, 1938), p.15; Broun, "Shoot the Works: Vermont Granite," *NR* (September 28, 1938), p.211; *NR* (June 15, 1938), p.144; MacLeish, "Liberalism and the Anti-Fascist Front," pp.321-23; MacLeish, "Freedom to End Freedom," *SG* (February, 1939), p.117; Magil, "Mr. MacLeish Hesitates," pp.21-24; John Garnett, "Calling the *Survey Graphic,*" *SRT* (May, 1939), pp.26-28.

21. George S. Counts and Reinhold Niebuhr, Letter to Mrs. Florence C. Hanson, Secretary of the American Federation of Teachers, August 16, 1935, in William Wattenberg, *On the Educational Frontier* (New York, 1936), pp.146-47; Max Lerner, "Democracy with a Union

Card," *VQ* (April, 1938), p.224; John Chamberlain, "Browder," *NR* (April 13, 1938), p.310; *N* (February 12, 1938), p.171.

22. *NR* (July 27, 1938), p.321; *NR* (August 17, 1938), p.33; *NR* (January 26, 1938), p.324; Heywood Broun, "Shoot the Works," *NR* (January 26, 1938), p.335; Robert Cantwell, "The Communists and the C.I.O.," *NR* (February 23, 1938), pp.65-66; *N* (January 29, 1938), p.114.

23. Browder, *The People's Front*, pp.279-80; Malcolm Cowley, "Adamic Omnibus," *NR* (June 8, 1938), p. 135; Cowley, Partisan Review," *NR* (October 19, 1938), pp.311-12; Heywood Broun, "Shoot the Works: How Not to Get Tough About It," *NR* (March 30, 1938), p.219; Broun, "Shoot the Works: Trotskyism at Home and Abroad," *NR* (March 23, 1938), p. 191; Broun, "Shoot the Works: Phil La-Follette Sounds Off," *NR* (May 11, 1938), p.16.

24. Heywood Broun, "Is There a *Nation?*" *N* (April 17, 1937), p.437; Broun, "Shoot the Works: Free Speech with Reservations," *NR* (July 13, 1938), p.278; Arthur Garfield Hays, *NR* (July 27, 1938), p.337; *NR* (August 3, 1938), p.348; Roger Baldwin, *NR* (August 31, 1938), p. 105; *NR* (August 31, 1938), p.106.

25. See, e.g., MacLeish, "Freedom to End Freedom," pp.117-19.

26. *CS* (September, 1935), p.3; *CS* (December, 1935), pp. 2-3; *CS* (September, 1938), p.5; John Chamberlain, "It's Your State!" *CS* (October, 1938), pp.9-10.

27. Charles A. Beard, "The Rise of the Democratic Idea in the United States," *SG* (April, 1937), p.203; John Dewey, "Education, Democracy, and Socialized Economy," *SF* (December, 1938), p.71; John Chamberlain, "Can Democracy Survive?" *MM* (Summer, 1939), p.69; John Dewey, "Democracy Is Radical," *CS* (January, 1937), p.11; *CS* (October, 1937), pp.3-5; *CS* (May, 1937), p.22.

28. *CS* (July, 1938), p.28; *CS* (October, 1938), p.4; *CS* (March, 1938), pp.4-5.

29. Elmer Davis, "On the American Way of Life," *H* (February, 1937), p.331; John Dewey, "Liberalism in a Vacuum: A Critique of Walter Lippman's Social Philosophy," *CS* (December, 1937), p.11; George S. Counts, *The Prospects of American Democracy* (New York, 1938), pp.3-4; Arthur Garfield Hays, *Democracy Works* (New York, 1939), p.27; John Chamberlain, "Ten Points for Democrats," *NR* (September 28, 1938), p.219; Chamberlain, "Mathematics of Domination," *NR* (October 12, 1938), pp.275-76; Alfred Bingham, "War Mongering on the Left: II. A Religious War in the Making," *CS* (June, 1937), pp.16-18; *CS* (July, 1937), pp.3-4.

7. Liberalism Fights the "Little World War"

1. League of American Writers, *Writers Take Sides* (New York, 1938), passim; Alfred Bingham, "War Mongering on the Left: III. Spain and American Progressivism," *CS* (July, 1937), p.14; George Orwell, *Homage to Catalonia* (New York, 1952), passim.

2. Earl Browder, *The People's Front* (New York, 1938), p.97; *NR* (August 12, 1936), p.5; *N* (August 1, 1936), p.116; *N* August 29, 1936), p.229; Malcolm Cowley, "To Madrid I," *NR* (August 25, 1937), p.64; *NR* (August 12, 1936), p.2; Archibald MacLeish, "Spain and the American Writers," in *The Writer in a Changing World,* ed. Henry Hart (New York, 1937), p.62.

3. John Chamberlain, "*Was* it a Congress of American Writers?" *CS* (July, 1937), p.15; *New York Times*, August 6, 1936, p.18; Bingham, "War Mongering on the Left: III. Spain and American Progressivism," p.12.

4. *New York Times*, January 3, 1937, Sec. 4, p.8; Browder, *The People's Front*, p.285; Max Lerner, "Behind Hull's Embargo," *N* (May 28, 1938), p.607; Frederick L. Schuman, "Pogroms and Power Politics," *E* (January, 1939), p.5; Louis Fischer, "Peace on Earth," *N* (December 24, 1938), p.688; Lewis Mumford, *Men Must Act* (New York, 1939), p.104; *N* (January 9, 1937), p.34.

5. *NR* (January 13, 1937), pp. 315-16; *NR* (January 4, 1939), p.244; Charles Beard, "Will Roosevelt Keep Us Out of War?" *E* (July, 1937), p.2; Beard, *Giddy Minds and Foreign Quarrels* (New York, 1939), pp.48-49.

6. Chamberlain, "*Was* It a Congress of American Writers?" p.15; Chamberlain, "Pluperfidious Albion," *NR* (August 31, 1938), p.108; *CS* (April, 1937), p.6; Bingham, "War Mongering on the Left: III. Spain and American Progressivism," pp.11-15.

7. Anita Brenner, "Class War in Republican Spain," *MM* (September, 1937), p.9.

8. Sherwood Eddy, "The Tragedy of Spain," *CC* (September 22, 1937), p.1165.

9. Louis Fischer, "Under Fire in Madrid," *N* (December 12, 1936), p. 693; *N* (January 2, 1937), p. 7; John Cornford, "On the Catalonia Front," *NR* (December 2, 1937), p.137; Ralph Bates, "Castilian Drama: An Army Is Born," *NR* (October 20, 1937), p.287; Malcolm Cowley, "To Madrid: V. International Brigade," *NR* (October 6, 1937), p. 235; Cowley, "Abyssinia and Spain," *NR* (February 16,

1938), pp.50-51; Herbert L. Matthews, *Two Wars and More to Come* (New York, 1938), pp. 294-95; 311-12.

10. *NM* (May 18, 1937), p.9; Browder, *The People's Front*, p.324; James Hawthorne, "Trotsky's Agents in Spain," *NW* (July 13, 1937), pp.15-17.

11. *NR* (May 19, 1937), pp.29-30; *N* (May 15, 1937), p.552.

12. *N* (June 5, 1937), pp.657-58 ff.

13. Malcolm Cowley, "To Madrid: I," *NR* (August 25, 1937), p.65; Matthews, *Two Wars and More to Come*, p.288.

14. Ralph Bates, "Castilian Drama: The Emergence of the Unified Command," *NR* (October 27, 1937), pp.336-37; Matthews, *Two Wars and More to Come*, p.288; Louis Fischer, "Loyalist Spain Gathers Its Strength," *N* (July 3, 1937), p.8.

15. Edwin Rolfe, "Trotskyites on Trial," *NM* (October 25, 1938), p.7; Louis Fischer, "Loyalist Spain Gathers Its Strength," *N* (July 3, 1937), p.8; *NR* (November 10, 1937), pp.5, 18-19.

16. *N* (August 21, 1937), pp.185-86; Louis Fischer, "Loyalist Spain Takes the Offensive," *N* (July 17, 1937), p.145.

17. John Dos Passos, "Farewell to Europe," *CS* (July, 1937), pp.9-11; Dos Passos, "The Communist Party and the War," *CS* (December, 1937), pp.11-14; *CS* (June, 1937), pp.6-7; *CS* (September, 1937), p.7.

18. Waldo Frank, "Spain in War: II. Parties and Leaders," *NR* (July 20, 1938), pp.298-99; Louis Fischer, "Hitler's New Threat," *N* (March 18, 1939), p.313; *NR* (April 12, 1939), p.265.

19. W. G. Krivitsky, "Stalin's Hand in Spain," *SEP* (April 15, 1939), p.5-6 ff; *NR* (May 10, 1939), p.2; *NR* (June 7, 1939), p.114.

20. Ralph Bates, "Disaster in Finland," *NR* (December 13, 1939), p.224; Malcolm Cowley, "Lost Battalion," *NR* (October 25, 1939), p.346; Cowley, "Krivitsky," *NR* (January 22, 1940), pp.121-22.

21. Oswald Garrison Villard, "Issues and Men: Stage Set for Massacre," *N* (April 1, 1939), p.378.

22. Ibid., p.378; Norman Thomas, "Spain: A Socialist View," *N* (June 19, 1937), p.700.

23. Ibid., pp.699-700.

8. Collective Security: Peace Policy or War Policy?

1. Earl Browder, *The People's Front* (New York, 1938), pp.73, 185, 243, 332-33; John Garnett, "Calling the *Survey Graphic*," *SRT* (May, 1939), p.26; Harry F. Ward et al., "Leaders of Labor, Science, Religion, Letters Hail Soviet Peace Efforts," *SRT* (November, 1936),

p.18; Corliss Lamont, "Champions of World Peace," *SRT* (May, 1937), p.20; *SRT* (November, 1937), p.4; *SRT* (February, 1938), p.4.

2. Frederick L. Schuman, "The Dismal Science: World Politics," *AS* (Spring, 1937), p.175; Schuman, "American Neutrality: What Type Shall It Be?" *IW* (February, 1937), pp. 39-40 ff; Schuman, *NR* (December, 1935), p.200; Schuman, "Peace by Surrender," *E* (January, 1938), pp.1-8; Schuman, "Fascist Diplomacy Wins Again," *E* (February, 1938), pp.86-89; Schuman, "America in That Giant Game World Politics," *IW* (June, 1938), p.163; Schuman, *NR* (March 8, 1939), p.133; Schuman, "The Great Conspiracy," *NR* (October 26, 1938), pp.325-26; Schuman, "The Perfidy of Albion," *NR* (April 20, 1938), pp.321-23; Schuman, "Fascism Marches Westward," *E* (March, 1939), pp.172-73; Schuman, "Towards the New Munich," *NR* (May 31, 1939), pp.92-93.

3. Louis Fischer, "Keeping America Out of War," *N* (March 27, 1937), pp.347, 349; Fischer, "Chamberlain's Choice," *N* (April 29, 1939), p.491; John Childs, *NR* (December 22, 1937), pp.200-201; Reinhold Niebuhr, "America and the War in China," *CC* (September 29, 1937), pp.1195-1196; Niebuhr, "Synthetic Barbarism," *NS* (September 9, 1939), pp. 368-69; Archibald MacLeish, "The Young Can Choose," *CS* (May, 1939), pp.13-14.

4. Lewis Mumford, "Call to Arms," *NR* (May 18, 1938), pp.39-42; Mumford, *Men Must Act* (New York, 1939), passim; Mumford, "When America Goes to War," *MM* (June, 1935), p.204; Theodore Draper, "How Safe Is America?" *NM* (March 21, 1939), p.22.

5. Eugene Lyons, "War Mongering on the Left," *AM* (November, 1938), p.296.

6. Lewis Mumford, *NR* (June 1, 1938), p.103.

7. Charles A. Beard, *Giddy Minds and Foreign Quarrels* (New York, 1939), pp.63-65, 73; John T. Flynn, "U.S. Neutrality," *CS* (October, 1937), p.8; Alfred Bingham, "War Mongering on the Left: II. A Religious War in the Making," *CS* (June, 1937), p.18; Beard, "Collective Security—a Debate: II. A Reply to Mr. Browder," *NR* (February 2, 1938), p.359; John Chamberlain, "The House that Hitler Built," *NR* (March 2, 1938), p.107; *NR* (November 13, 1935), p.5; Beard, *The Open Door at Home* (New York, 1934), passim; Stuart Chase, *The New Western Frontier*, New York, 1939, passim; Bingham, *CS* (April, 1939), pp.25-26; Oswald Garrison Villard, *N* (February 18, 1939), p.215; John T. Flynn, "America Plays a Risky Game," *Asia* (April, 1938), p.230; John Chamberlain, "The Politics of Thomas Mann," *NR* (August 3, 1938), p.367.

8. Alfred Bingham, "War Mongering on the Left: I," *CS* (May, 1937), p.8; Charles A. Beard, *The Devil Theory of War* (New York, 1936), passim; Beard, "Five Pages from Newton D. Baker," *NR* (October 7, 1936), pp.247-48; Beard, *Giddy Minds and Foreign Quarrels*, pp.85-86; *NR* (May 13, 1936), p.6; *NR* (April 14, 1937), pp.279-80; Bruce Bliven, "Pacifism: Its Rise and Fall," *NR* (November 18, 1936), p.68; C. Hartley Grattan, "No More Excursions," *H* (April, 1939), p. 465.

9. Beard, *Giddy Minds and Foreign Quarrels*, p.95; *NR* (February 5, 1936), p.354; *NR* (April 3, 1935), p.202; *CS* (August, 1938), p.4; Grattan, "No More Excursions," pp.460, 464; *NR* (February 5, 1936), p.354; *CS* (May, 1938), p.5; Bingham, "War Mongering on the Left: I," p.10; Oswald Garrison Villard, "Issues and Men," *N* (July 10, 1937), p.46; John Haynes Holmes, "How America Entered the Next War," *CC* (February 23, 1938), pp.236-37; Norman Thomas, "Toward the American Commonwealth," *SF* (January, 1938), p.128; Elmer Davis, *H* (March, 1938), pp.345-47; John Chamberlain, "Browder," *NR* (April 13, 1938), p.310; Chase, *The New Western Frontier*, p.173; John Dewey, " 'No Matter What Happens—Stay Out,' " *CS* (March, 1939), p.11; Sidney Hook, "Radicals and War: Against Sanctions," *MM* (April, 1936), p.15.

10. Charles A. Beard, "America's 'Duty' to England," *E* (November, 1937), pp.327-31; Beard, "We're Blundering Into War," *AM* (April, 1939), pp.388-90; Oswald Garrison Villard, "Issues and Men," *N* (April 30, 1938), p.505; John T. Flynn, "U.S. Neutrality," *CS* (October, 1937), p.8; Elmer Davis, "We Lose the Next War," *H* (March, 1938), p.344; Quincy Howe, *England Expects Every American to Do His Duty* (New York, 1937), passim; Bruce Bliven, "Collective Insecurity," *NR* (December 1, 1937), p.94; Villard, "Issues and Men," *N* (June 10, 1939), p.673; Stuart Chase, "Word Trouble Among the Statesmen," *H* (January, 1938), p.153; Chamberlain, "Browder," p.310; Selden Rodman, *CS* (October, 1937), p.29; Bingham, "War Mongering on the Left: I," pp.9-10; Bingham, "War Mongering on the Left: II. A Religious War in the Making," pp.15, 18.

11. *CS* (September, 1938), p.5; *NR* (February 5, 1936), p.154; Earl Browder, *Fighting for Peace* (New York, 1939), pp.51-52.

12. John Dewey, "Are Sanctions Necessary to International Organization? No," *Foreign Policy Association Pamphlets*, No. 83 (June, 1932), pp.26-28; Beard, "Collective Security—A Debate: II. A Reply to Mr. Browder," p.357; *NR* (March 2, 1932), p.76; *NR* (January 15, 1936), p.266; *N* (December 25, 1937), p.704; *NR* (December 25,

1935), p.185; Bruce Bliven, "Collective Insecurity," *NR* (December 1, 1937), p.95.

13. Beard, *Giddy Minds and Foreign Quarrels*, passim; Beard, "Will Roosevelt Keep Us Out of War?," *E* (July, 1937), p.6; Beard, "Rough Seas for the Super-Navy," *NR* (March 30, 1938), p.210; *NR* (October 13, 1937), p.253; *NR* (March 22, 1939), p.181; *CS* (January, 1939), pp.3-5; Beard, *The Devil Theory of War*, pp.122-24; Oswald Garrison Villard, "How to Stay Out of War: Neutrality," *F* (April, 1937), pp.92-93; John T. Flynn, "U.S. Neutrality," *CS* (October, 1937), p.10; Chase, *The New Western Frontier*, pp.133-42; *NR* (February 10, 1937), pp.3-5; Howe, *England Expects Every American To Do His Duty*, pp. 216-17; Bingham, "War Mongering on the Left: I," p.10.

14. *NR* (December 25, 1935), p.186; *NR* (October 5, 1938), pp. 229-230; *NR* (July 28, 1937), p.320.

15. W. H. Chamberlin, "Soviet Russia's Wars of Conquest," *AM* (April, 1938), pp.385-96; John Chamberlain, "Mathematics of Domination," *NR* (October 12, 1938), p.275; Elmer Davis, "The Road to Munich," *H* (December, 1938), pp.40-48; Oswald Garrison Villard, "Issues and Men: The Disaster in Europe," *N* (September 24, 1938), p.299; Villard, "Issues and Men," *N* (October 1, 1938), p.325; *NR* (September 28, 1938), pp.200-201; *CS* (November, 1938), p.5; William Henry Chamberlin, *N* (December 3, 1938), p.603; Bingham, "War Mongering on the Left: I," pp.9-10; Bingham, "War Mongering on the Left: II," pp.15, 18; *CS* (October, 1938), p.4; *CS* (May, 1938), pp.4-5.

16. *CS* (March, 1939), pp.3-5; *CS* (August, 1938), pp.4-5; *CS* (May, 1938), pp.4-5; *CS* (October, 1938), pp.4-5; *CS* (May, 1939), p.17.

17. *NR* (May 18, 1938), pp.32-33; *NR* (March 30, 1938), pp.253-56; Bruce Bliven, "Just Before Zero," *NR* (July 19, 1939), pp.299-300; *NR* (November 4, 1936), p.6; Bliven, "Pacifism: Its Rise and Fall," *NR* (November 18, 1936), p.68; Bliven, "This Is Where I Came In," *NR* (January 5, 1938), p.246.

18. Bliven, "Collective Insecurity," pp.93-95; *NR* (February 5, 1936), p.354.

19. Theodore Draper, "The Case Against Isolation," *NM* (November 23, 1937), p.6; Earl Browder, "Collective Security—A Debate: I. For Collective Security," *NR* (February 2, 1938), p.354; Browder, *Fighting for Peace*, pp.33-34; *NR* (April 20, 1938), p.318; Bruce Bliven, "They Cry 'Peace': III Neutrality Is Not Enough," *NR* (November 20, 1935), p.39; *NR* (March 9, 1938), p.114; Bruce Bliven, *AM* (March, 1938), p.374.

20. James Rorty, "Mobilizing the Innocents," *F* (January, 1938), p.47.

9. *The Moscow Trials on Trial*

1. Edmund Wilson, *Travels in Two Democracies* (New York, 1936), p.321.

2. Earl Browder, *The People's Front* (New York, 1938), p.212; *NM* (September 1, 1936), p.4; Mauritz Hallgren, "Letter to the American Committee for the Defense of Leon Trotsky," *NM* (September 1, 1936), p.4.

3. Frederick L. Schuman, "Leon Trotsky: Martyr or Renegade?" *SR* (Summer, 1937), pp.53, 64-68, 71-74.

4. Dudley Collard, "A Lawyer Views the Radek Trial," *SRT* (March, 1937), p.6; Abraham Unger, More Light on the Moscow Trial," *SRT* (February, 1937), p.22 ff; Leon Feuchtwanger, "Leon Feuchtwanger on the Trial," *SRT* (March, 1937), p.12; Sherwood Eddy, "The Guilt of Leon Trotsky," *SRT* (June, 1937) p. 15 ff; Upton Sinclair, "American-Soviet Friendship," *SRT* (May, 1938), p.24; Newton D. Baker, *SRT* (April, 1937), p.8; Theodore Bayer, *SRT* (March, 1937), pp.32-33.

5. Earl Browder, *Fighting for Peace* (New York, 1939), pp.110-35; Browder, *The People's Front*, pp.227-28; Jerome Davis, "The Soviet Union in 1938," *SRT* (November, 1938), p.39; Corliss Lamont, "Moscow Cable from Corliss Lamont," *SRT* (June, 1938), p.9; *NM* (June 22, 1937), p.13; Joshua Kunitz, "The Moscow Trial: II," *NM* (March 22, 1938), pp. 13-14 ff; Maxwell S. Stewart, "Progress and the Purges in Soviet Russia," *N* (September 17, 1938), pp.266-67.

6. Sam Darcy, "What's Going On in the Soviet Union?" *NM* (July 13, 1937), p.6; *NM* (November 10, 1936), pp.11-13.

7. *SRT* (January, 1937), p.7; Corliss Lamont et al., "An Open Letter to American Liberals," *SRT* (March, 1937), pp.14-15; *NM* (April 20, 1937), p.28; Carlton Beals, "Mr. Beals Resigns from Trotsky Commission," *SRT* (May, 1937), p.38; Schuman, "Leon Trotsky: Martyr or Renegade," p.70; Corliss Lamont, "Faith in the Soviet Union," *SRT* (August, 1937), pp.6-7; *SRT* (January, 1938), p.3; Robert Forsythe, "Is John Dewey Honest?" *NM* (January 4, 1938), p.16; Michael Gold, "Notes on the Cultural Front," *NM* (December 7, 1937), p.3; Lamont, "The Moscow Trials," *SRT* (January, 1938), p.14 ff; *SRT* (February, 1938), p.8.

8. *SRT* (April, 1938), p.9; Morris Schappes, "An Open Letter to John Haynes Holmes," *NM* (April 13, 1937), p.19; Schappes, *NM* (April 20, 1937), p.29; *NM* (May 18, 1937), pp.10-11; *NM* (May 25,

1937), p.20; John Garnett, "A Trial of Traitors," *SRT* (April, 1938), p.9; *SRT* (July, 1938), p.6; *NM* (March 22, 1938), p. 10.

9. Malcolm Cowley et al., "American Progressives on the Moscow Trials," *SRT* (May, 1938), p.5; *SRT* (August-September, 1938), p.28.

10. *NR* (September 12, 1936), pp.88-89; *N* (August 29, 1936), p.226; *N* (August 22, 1936), p.201; *N* (October 10, 1936), p.409.

11. *NR* (February 3, 1937), p.400; *N* (January 30, 1937), p.114; *N* (February 6, 1937), pp.143-45; Suzanne LaFollette, *N* (February 13, 1937), p.196; Franz Hoellering, *N* (February 20, 1937), p.224; James Rorty, *N* (February 27, 1937), p.252.

12. Malcolm Cowley, "The Record of the Trial," *NR* (April 7, 1937), pp.267-70; *NR* (February 17, 1937), pp.33-34; *N* (November 13, 1937), p.521.

13. *NR* (February 17, 1937), pp.33-34; *NR* (May 19, 1937), pp.33-34; *NR* (June 23, 1937), p.174; *NR* (January 5, 1938), pp.240-41.

14. *NR* (June 23, 1937), p.174; *NR* (April 26, 1937), p.343; *NR* (December 22, 1937), pp.181-82; *NR* (January 12, 1938), p.266; *N* (May 22, 1937), p.578; *N* (May 1, 1937), pp.496-97; *N* (December 25, 1937), p. 703.

15. *NR* (February 3, 1937), p.400; *NR* (June 23, 1937), p.174; Bruce Bliven, "Birthday Balance Sheet," *NR* (August 4, 1937), p.260; *NR* (January 5, 1938), p.241; *N* (February 6, 1937), p.145.

16. *NR* (March 16, 1938), pp.151-52; *N* (March 12, 1938), pp.287-88.

17. *N* (March 12, 1938), pp.287-88; Bruce Bliven, "A Letter to Stalin," *NR* (March 30, 1938), pp.216-17.

18. *NR* (May 4, 1938), pp.383-84; Malcolm Cowley, "Moscow Trial: 1938," *NR* (May 18, 1938), p.51; Cowley, "Moscow Trial: II," *NR* (May 25, 1938), p.80; *NR* (July 6, 1938), p.252.

19. Oswald Garrison Villard, "Issues and Men," *N* (May 15, 1937), p.564; John Haynes Holmes, *NM* (April 20, 1937), p.29; Sidney Hook, "Liberalism and the Case of Leon Trotsky," *SR* (Autumn, 1937), pp.267-87; *CS* (October, 1936), p.7; Harold Loeb, "Science vs. Faith at the Moscow Trials," *CS* (March, 1937), p.19; *CS* (April, 1937), pp. 7, 24-25; *CS* (September, 1937), p.25.

20. *CS* (March, 1937), p.20; *CS* (July, 1937), p.6; *CS* (October, 1937), pp.4-5; *CS* (December, 1937), p.8; Alfred Bingham, *CS* (December, 1937), p.28; Selden Rodman, "Trotsky in the Kremlin: An Interview," *CS* (December, 1937), p.19.

21. For a somewhat similar point, see Sidney Hook, "As a (Marxist) Professor Sees It," *CS* (January, 1938), p.22.

22. Burleigh Taylor Wilkins, *Carl Becker* (Cambridge, Mass., 1961), p.171.

23. Louis Adamic et al., *N* (May 27, 1939), p.626.

24. Freda Kirchwey, "Red Totalitarianism," *N* (May 27, 1939), p. 605; Kirchwey, *N* (June 17, 1939), pp.710-11.

25. *NR* (May 31, 1939), pp.88-89; John Dewey, *NR* (June 14, 1939), pp.161-62; *NR* (June 14, 1939), p.144; Ferdinand Lundberg, *NR* (June 28, 1939), pp.216-18; *NR* (June 28, 1939), p.202.

26. Dr. Thomas Addis et al., "To All Active Supporters of Democracy and Peace," *SRT* (September, 1939), pp.24-25 ff; *NR* (August 23, 1939), p. 63; *N* (September 2, 1939), p.231.

27. *New York Times*, August 23, 1936, Sec. 4, p.8; *New York Times*, February 14, 1937, Sec. 4, p.8; *New York Times*, September 20, 1937, p.20.

28. George Orwell, *Homage to Catalonia* (New York, 1952), p.82.

29. Louis Adamic, *My America* (New York, 1938), p.82.

30. In 1937 Malcolm Cowley wrote: "But without paying allegiance to Stalin I am certainly against Trotsky. My opposition is partly a question of temperament: I have never liked the big-city intellectuals of his type, with their reduction of every human question to a bald syllogism in which they are always right at every point, miraculously right, and their opponents always stupid and beneath contempt." On Stalin, he wrote: "Cromwell, a dictator in spite of himself, or partly in spite of himself—a conscientious, lonely, suspicious man trying to do his best for England and the revolutionary classes while living in daily fear of assassination—a man of integrity rather than genius whom Stalin resembles at so many points that I am surprised to find the comparison had never been made." See Malcolm Cowley, "The Record of a Trial," *NR* (April 7, 1937), pp.267, 269.

31. *N* (March 27, 1937), p.339; William Henry Chamberlin, *NR* (February 27, 1935), pp.76-77; *NR* (February 27, 1935), pp.60-62.

32. *N* (June 17, 1936), p.761; *NR* (June 24, 1936), pp.192-93; *NR* (December 9, 1936), pp.160-61; *NR* (February 17, 1937), p.51.

33. Louis Fischer, *Men and Politics* (New York, 1941), pp. 600-601; *N* (August 26, 1939), p.228; Roger Baldwin, "A Liberal Looks at Life," *SF* (May 15, 1941), p.236.

10. *The Collapse of the Popular Front*

1. Anna Louise Strong, "Is Moscow Out of the World?" *Asia* (May, 1939), p.276.

2. Oswald Garrison Villard, "Issues and Men," *N* (September 2,

1939), p.247; Peter Drucker, "That Coming Nazi-Soviet Pact," *CS* (March, 1939), pp.16-17; *CS* (August, 1939), pp.6, 19; *CS* (October, 1939), p.18; *CS* (November, 1939), pp. 16, 18; *CS* (December, 1939), p.18.

3. *CS* (January, 1940), p.17.

4. Alfred Bingham, "Progress Without Freedom," *CS* (November, 1939), pp.24-25; *CS* (January, 1940), pp.16-17.

5. *CS* (March, 1940), pp.16-17.

6. Seldon Rodman, "Poetry and Democracy," *SRL* (August 10, 1940), p.14; *CS* (April, 1940), pp.16-18; *CS* (August, 1941), pp.240-41.

7. Vincent Sheean, "What People Are Saying," *SRT* (October, 1939), pp.36-37; Sheean, "Brumaire," *NR* (November 8, 1939), pp. 7-9; Sheean, "Brumaire II," *NR* (November 15, 1939), pp.104-106; Ralph Bates, "Disaster in Finland," *NR* (December 13, 1939), pp.221-25.

8. Louis Fischer, "America and Europe," *N* (July 22, 1939), p.100; Fischer, "Europe Goes to War," *N* (September 9, 1939), p.262; Fischer, "Two Views of the Russian Pact: II. An Inexcusable Treaty," *NR* (September 13, 1939), pp.150-51; Fischer, *Stalin and Hitler* (New York, 1940), pp.4-5, 38, 45-50, 61; Fischer, "Russia—Twenty-Two Years After," *N* (February 10, 1940), p.183; Fischer, "Did Stalin Want War?" *N* (July 5, 1941), p.6; Fischer, "Still the Enigma," *SRL* (December 6, 1941), p.14.

9. Corliss Lamont, "The Soviet Union and the World Crisis," *SRT* (October, 1939), p.18; Lamont, "Moral Indignation Versus Facts," *SRT* (November, 1939), p.18; Anna Louise Strong, "The Red Army Marches for Peace," *SRT* (October, 1939), pp.13-15 ff; Maxwell Stewart, "The Month in Soviet Foreign Policy," *SRT* (November, 1939), p.13 ff; Stewart, "The Soviet-Finnish Treaty and World Peace," *SRT* (April, 1940), p.9; *SRT* (March, 1939), p.6; *SRT* (September, 1939), p.6; *SRT* (October, 1939), p.6; *SRT* (February, 1940), p.5; *SRT* (December, 1939), p.6; *SRT* (March, 1940), p.6.

10. Frederick L. Schuman, "Machiavelli in Moscow," *NR* (November, 1939), pp.158-160.

11. Frederick L. Schuman, "Design for Chaos," *E* (January, 1940), p.6; Schuman, *New York Times*, December 10, 1939, Sec. 4, p.8; Schuman, *NR* (December 27, 1939), p.290; Schuman, "America's Stake in Britain's War," *N* (January 6, 1940), pp.11-13; Schuman, *NR* (July 8, 1940), pp.55-57; Schuman, "Flight from Apocalypse," *E* (October, 1940), p.262; Schuman, "Two Variations of a Russian Theme," *SRL* (April 6, 1940), p.10.

12. *N* (August 26, 1939), p.212; *N* (September 23, 1939), p.309; *N* (September 30, 1939), pp.337-38; Freda Kirchwey, "Moscow-Berlin Axis," *N* (October 7, 1939), pp.365-66; *N* (October 21, 1939), pp.427-28; *N* (November 11, 1939), pp.511-12; Freda Kirchwey, "By Fire and Sword," *N* (December 9, 1939), pp.639-40; Kirchwey, "Escape and Appeasement," *N* (June 29, 1940), p.773.

13. Freda Kirchwey, "Communists and Democracy," *N* (October 14, 1939), p.400; *N* (October 21, 1939), pp.429-30; *N* (March 1, 1940), pp.228-29; *N* (June 28, 1941), p.742; *N* (March 29, 1941), pp.367-68; *N* (August 9, 1941), pp.102-103.

14. Bruce Bliven, "Picking Up the Pieces," *NR* (October 19, 1938), p.294; *NR* (January 4, 1939), p.243.

15. *NR* (August 30, 1939), pp.88-89), *NR* (September 6, 1939), p.118.

16. *NR* (September 13, 1939), p.143; *NR* (September 20, 1939), p.175; *NR* (September 27, 1939), p.201; *NR* (October 4, 1939), pp.227, 230-31.

17. *NR* (November 1, 1939), p.352; *NR* (November 8, 1939), p.2; *NR* (October 11, 1939), pp.254, 257-58; *NR* (October 18, 1939), p.281.

18. *NR* (November 15, 1939), pp.98-99.

19. *NR* (November 29, 1939), p.155.

20. *NR* (December 13, 1939), pp.218-19.

21. *NR* (November 15, 1939), pp.97, 99-100; *NR* (November 22, 1939), p.124; *NR* (September 6, 1939), p.114; *NR* (September 20, 1939), p.171; *NR* (November 1, 1939), p.356; *NR* (October 18, 1939), p.286; *NR* (February 22, 1940), p.197; *NR* (January 29, 1940), p.135; *NR* (June 16, 1941), p.809; *NR* (November 1, 1939), p.356; Norman Thomas, *NR* (December 13, 1939), pp.232-233; *NR* (December 13, 1939), p.233.

22. *NR* (June 24, 1940), p.841; George Soule, "The War Nobody Won," *NR* (March 25, 1940), pp.396-97; *NR* (May 26, 1941), pp. 715-16.

23. *NR* (January 15, 1940), pp.70-72.

24. Earl Browder, *The Way Out* (New York, 1941), p.202.

25. Eugene Lyons, "The Myth of a Happy Russia," *AM* (April, 1941), p.498.

26. Max Lerner, "Russia and the War of Ideas," *NR* (July 7, 1941), p.18.

27. Bruce Bliven, "Russia's Morale—and Ours," *NR* (September 1, 1941), p.275; George Soule, "Russia, Germany and the Peace," *NR* (March 22, 1943), pp.372-73.

28. Malcolm Cowley, "From the Finland Station," *NR* (October 7, 1940), p.480; Cowley, "Krivitsky," *NR* (January 22, 1940), pp.122-23; Cowley, "Punishment and Crime," *NR* (June 2, 1941), pp.766-67; Cowley, "In Memoriam," *NR* (August 12, 1940), pp.219-220; Freda Kirchwey, "The Law and Mr. Dies," *N* (November 4, 1939), p.487; *NR* (November 8, 1939), p.4.

29. Bruce Bliven, "The Road to Hysteria," *VQ* (April, 1940), p.195.

30. Max Eastman, *NR* (October 25, 1939), p.344.

31. James Farrell, *N* (September 30, 1939), p.359.

11. Perspectives—Past and Present

1. Granville Hicks, "How Red Was the Red Decade?" *H* (July, 1953), pp.53-61; Irving Kristol, "'Civil Liberties,' 1952—A Study in Confusion," *Commentary* (March, 1952), p.233.

2. Harold Rosenberg, "Couch Liberalism and the Guilty Past," in *Voices of Dissent* (New York, 1954), p.235.

3. Bruce Bliven, "The Scotch Plaid Decade," *NR* (October, 1941), p.433; Reinhold Niebuhr, "The Red Thirties," *N* (September 20, 1941), p.257.

4. Bliven, "The Scotch Plaid Decade," p.433.

5. Dwight MacDonald, *Memoirs of a Revolutionist* (New York, 1957), p.292n.

6. Norman Holmes Pearson, "The Nazi-Soviet Pact and the End of a Dream," in *America in Crisis*, ed. Daniel Aaron (New York, 1952), p.347.

7. *NR* (September 27, 1939), p.198.

8. Randolph Bourne, "Twilight of Idols," *The Seven Arts* (October, 1917), pp.697-98.

9. Roger Hagan et al., "The Younger Radicals: A Symposium," *Dissent* (April, 1962), p.135.

10. Bourne, "Twilight of Idols," pp.698-99.

INDEX

Aaron, Daniel, 4
Adamic, Louis, 121, 187, 188
Agricultural Adjustment Act (A.A.A.), 42
American Civil Liberties Union, 63, 121-122, 207
American Committee for the Defense of Leon Trotsky, 164, 171, 180, 187; criticism of, 167-168, 173
American Federation of Labor (A.F. of L.), 120
American Federation of Teachers, 202, 207
American Labor Party, 207
American League Against War and Fascism, 147
American Mercury, 121, 159
American Writers' Congress, 115
Anarchists, Spanish, 133-136, 141, 142; *see also* Spanish Civil War
Araquistain, Luis, 139

Baker, Newton D., 166
Baldwin, Roger, 69; and Russia, 63-64, 78, 82, 191; and Popular Front, 114; and civil liberties, 122
Bates, Ernest Sutherland, 112
Bates, Ralph, and Spanish Civil War, 133, 136, 137, 140; and Russia, 198
Beals, Carleton, 168, 173, 174

Beard, Charles, 4, 8; and Communism, 13, 14; and capitalism, 36; and New Deal, 41, 219; and planning, 50-62 *passim*, 218; and Russia, 123, 182, 188, 218; and Spanish Civil War, 130; and collective security, 150-151, 152, 153, 154, 155, 160, 161; and World War II, 209
Becker, Carl, and Communism, 13, 14, 218; and planning, 33; and Russia, 66-67; and Moscow trials, 182, 185, 188
Bellamy, Edward, 7
Bingham, Alfred, 4; and liberalism, 7, 15, 21, 29; and Communism, 13, 31-32, 124, 191-192, 219; and capitalism, 14, 35, 37; and social change, 29-30, 31-32; and planning, 32, 50-62 *passim*, 106, 218; attitude toward New Deal, 42-47 *passim;* and Russia, 66, 69, 76, 80, 84, 123-124, 125, 156-157, 219; and Fascism, 91, 92-95, 97, 98, 99, 157-158, 191-192, 218; and Popular Front, 114, 123, 219; and Spanish Civil War, 127-128, 129, 130-131, 138, 141, 219; opposition to collective security, 150, 151, 153-154, 155, 160, 161; and World War I, 152, 156; and Moscow

267